PERSPECTIVES ON SILENCE

edited by

Deborah Tannen
Georgetown University

and

Muriel Saville-Troike
University of Illinois

ABLEX PUBLISHING CORPORATION
NORWOOD, NEW JERSEY 07648

Copyright © 1985 by Ablex Publishing Corporation

Printed in the United States of America.

Library of Congress Cataloging in Publication Data

Main entry under title:

Perspectives on silence.

    Bibliography: p.
    Includes index.
    1. Silence. 2. Communication. 3. Social interaction.
I. Tannen, Deborah. II. Saville-Troike, Muriel.
P95.53.P47 1984   001.56   84-18465
ISBN 0-89391-255-7
ISBN 0-89391-310-3 (pbk.)

Ablex Publishing Corporation
355 Chestnut Street
Norwood, New Jersey 07648

To those who suffer in silence
and those who revel in it

The stupendous reality that is language cannot be understood unless we begin by observing that speech consists above all in silences. A being who could not renounce saying many things would be incapable of speaking. Each language represents a different equation between manifestations and silences. Each people leaves some things unsaid in order to be able to say others.

Jose Ortega y Gasset, *Man and People*

Contents

Foreword

This book began to take shape several years ago when we asked our students in anthropology and sociolinguistics at Georgetown University to consider silence as part of the communicative code in their analyses of 'speech' events. The variety and richness of their responses from the perspective(s) of many different speech communities contributed significantly to the general theoretical and descriptive framework proposed in the opening chapter. The framework for the book developed further as colleagues extended the theme in relation to their own research. For early input and direction, we are particularly grateful to Susan Philips and Ron Scollon. We are grateful as well to Keith Basso for encouragement and advice, and to Rudolph Troike, David Gordon, Shirley Brice Heath, Marianne Mithun, Joel Sherzer, and an anonymous reviewer for critical readings of parts or all of the manuscript. We also thank Glen Merzer for the dedication.

M. S.-T.
D. T.

Introduction

This book focuses attention on a relatively neglected component of human communication—silence—in hopes of both presenting current research from a variety of disciplines and also stimulating further research and thought on the topic. Silence is most often an out-of-awareness phenomenon—the ground against which the figure of talk is perceived. By reversing polarities and treating silence as the figure to be examined against the ground of talk (as well as other actions or events), we aim to heighten awareness of this universal aspect of human behavior while at the same time emphasizing its complex nature as a cultural phenomenon and its richness as a research site.

It is neither surprising nor reproving to note that the study of communication has focused on talk to the relative exclusion of silence. As Saville-Troike observes in the opening chapter:

> Within linguistics, silence has traditionally been ignored except for its boundary-marking function, delimiting the beginning and ending of utterances. The tradition has been to define it negatively—as merely the absence of speech.

Anthropologists and psychologists, however—less centrally concerned with language per se—have been somewhat less likely to ignore silence. Psychologists have the longer history of interest in the subject, including the seminal lifetime work of Frieda Goldman-Eisler (for example, Goldman-Eisler 1951) investigating the relation of pauses to cognitive activity, Maclay and Osgood's (1959) research on hesitation phenomena in speech, or Cook's (1964) analysis of the role of silence in psychotherapy, to more recent interest in the rhythmic and synchronic patterns of silences in interpersonal interaction (Jaffe and Feldstein 1970). Not surprisingly, most of the psychological research has focused on the English language and American (or other European) culture.

A major concern of anthropology is the identification of cultural similarities and differences, and this has included some pioneering work on silence. Hall's (1959) *The Silent Language* focused on the significance of nonverbal behavior, including silence, and Samarin (1965) called attention to cross-cultural differences in the meaning of silence. Bauman (1970) considered silence in Quaker worship, and Basso (1970), showing its importance among the Apache, called for more cross-cultural documentation of silence behavior.

The present volume, more than a decade later, begins to answer that call. At the same time, it explores theoretical issues related to and occasioned by the study of silence, its nature, its meanings, and its uses, in cross-cultural and cross-disciplinary perspective.

PLAN OF THE BOOK

The general plan of the book, with the exception of the opening essay which provides an overall orientation to the topic, is to move from the smaller (micro) level to the larger (macro) level, and (with the exception of the concluding section) to move concentrically from the familiar and close at hand (at least to an American audience) to the less familiar and more distinctively different.

Part II presents 'Psychological and Ethnographic Views of Pausing', primarily in English discourse. Part III, 'Some Meanings and Uses of Silence', takes a more explicitly ethnographic approach, looking at silence among particular groups and in particular settings. Part IV focuses on 'Silence in Cross-Cultural Perspective', examining silence in three different societies and treating it at a more general level of analysis. Part V, 'Silence and Nonverbal Communication', considers silence in relation to nonverbal behavior in particular and the scheme of behavior in general. The Appendix provides 'A Sampling of Sources on Silence'. All the chapters share a fundamental concern for the meaning and use of silence in human communication.

OVERVIEW: THE NATURE AND STUDY OF SILENCE

In the first section, Saville-Troike (Chapter 1, 'The Place of Silence in an Integrated Theory of Communication'), presents an overview of the complex nature of silence, including its varied types and functions. She makes a key distinction between the nonverbal and nonvocal in communication, taking into account both sign language and writing, which are nonvocal but verbal. She points out that silence used for structuring communication is to be distinguished from communicative silence, and that silences which convey meaning but not propositional content are to be distinguished from those which carry illocutionary force. She shows that silence can be used to fulfill the functions of most speech acts, as well as larger discourse functions, such as prayers.

Saville-Troike notes that the symbolic significance of silence makes it inherently ambiguous and thus subject to serious communicative misapprehensions, both interpersonal and intercultural—an observation which is demonstrated by many of the chapters that follow. Finally, she proposes an etic framework for description and analysis which can contribute to further ethnographic research on the topic.

PSYCHOLOGICAL AND ETHNOGRAPHIC VIEWS OF PAUSING

Part II examines the meaning of silence at the micro level of hesitations, or pauses, during verbal interaction. Psychological researchers in this area have distinguished inturn pauses, which occur within the conversational turn of a speaker, from switching pauses, which occur at the boundaries of speaking turns. A further distinction is made between silent and filled pauses.

Scollon (Chapter 2, 'The Machine Stops: Silence in the Metaphor of Malfunction') begins this section with a review of psychological research on pauses, including the work of Feldstein and his colleagues, which is reported and reviewed in the chapter by Crown and Feldstein. Scollon then notes the similarity between findings of this research and that of his own ethnographic research and observations of misunderstandings among Athabaskan Indians in western Canada in communication with non-Indians. In doing so, he reveals as problematic what superficially appeared to be a sociolinguistic universal, and suggests that profound differences in cultural metaphors affect interpretations of silence in interaction, and even our research agendas.

In Chapter 3, Crown and Feldstein ('Psychological Correlates of Silence and Sound in Conversational Interaction') present findings of a large body of psychological research, much of it their own, based on instrumental measurement of chronographic patterning of silence and sound in conversation. They find that silences in English conversations taped in a laboratory setting have a more stable relationship to personality differences as measured on standard psychological instruments (for example, extravert/introvert) than do vocalizations. They find as well that the amount of vocalization by a speaker is determined less by the speaker than by the relative silence of the listener. Their comparisons of patterns among black and white subjects, among the first to be reported, show significant intra- and cross-ethnic differences. In an interesting cross-cultural study, they report that Chinese bilinguals in Canada use more silence when speaking Chinese than when speaking English. Finally, they discuss the possible value of applying a statistical technique used in economics and sociology, time series analysis, to the study of conversation.

Like Crown and Feldstein, Walker (Chapter 4, 'The Two Faces of Silence: The Effect of Witness Hesitancy on Lawyers' Impressions') is interested in the effect of pausing on impression formation. However, whereas they base their study on experimental evidence, Walker bases hers on analysis of transcripts of depositions and attorneys' reactions both at the time of the deposition and in subsequent comments about how they perceived the witnesses. Thus she too draws on and speaks to the psychological literature on pausing, but her own approach is an ethnographically oriented discourse analysis.

Walker draws attention to the crucial duality—what she aptly calls the Janus-like nature—of silence (in particular, unfilled pauses). Lawyers advise their own witnesses to think before they speak—hence, pause—and yet they tend to distrust opposing witnesses who pause, concluding that if they have to think before they speak they must be making something up.

The final chapter in this section (Chapter 5, 'Some Reasons for Hesitating'), by Chafe, demonstrates the need to take content into account in research on hesitation during speech production. Following in the tradition of research on inturn silence as an indication of cognitive activity, he examines hesitations in 'the pear stories', narratives told about what happened in a short film. Chafe shows that hesitations may reflect mental search processes, codability of objects/events, and discourse-organizational considerations in the course of a speaker's attempt to construct a description of an event from memory.

SOME MEANINGS AND USES OF SILENCE

Part III moves to a more global treatment of silence within specific types of situations and events, and among particular subgroups: New York Jewish dinner table conversation; Quaker and Pentecostal worship; and teachers and black students in an inner-city school. This range of contexts and perspectives demonstrates some of the variations—and opportunities for cross-cultural misunderstanding—in the interpretation and evaluation of silence. Moreover, we are reminded by Maltz that noise, like silence, can be ambiguous.

Tannen (Chapter 6, 'Silence: Anything But') continues the treatment of silence at the level of conversational encounter, focusing on features which characterize speakers of New York Jewish background in contrast with Californians of non-Jewish background. Beginning with a theoretical discussion of potential negative and positive meanings of silence in the framework of universals of politeness phenomena, she then describes the features that make up what she calls New York Jewish conversational style and suggests that features of this style may be understood as motivated by the desire to avoid silence which is seen as evidence of lack of rapport. Tannen concludes that silence in interaction is not definable as an absolute but is perceived when expected talk is absent.

Maltz (Chapter 7, 'Joyful Noise and Reverent Silence: The Significance of Noise in Pentecostal Worship') is concerned with silence as symbol and as purposeful means to an end. Maltz develops some of the points in Saville-Troike's discussion of silence as a mechanism of intensification in religious practices. He discusses attitudes toward silence and noise in worship among Pentecostals and uses this 'as an occasion to investigate the variations possible in the interpretation of noise and silence, and some of the similarities that underlie these variations'.

Maltz demonstrates that the rise of the Pentecostal movement paralleled, in some respects, the rise of Quakerism, which is characterized by strikingly different attitudes toward these phenomena. Both were reactions to the Puritan movement, which the Quakers found too noisy and the Pentecostals found too quiet. The silence of the Quakers and the noisiness of the Pentecostals serve similar religious functions. In both cases, an extreme manifestation is the marked departure from the unmarked norm of speaking, and thus is available for symbolic exploitation.

Gilmore (Chapter 8, 'Silence and Sulking: Emotional Displays in the Classroom') likewise describes the use of silence as a symbol and as a purposeful means to an end, but in a very different setting, an inner-city classroom. Here silence takes on very concrete communicative functions and meanings, which are sometimes misunderstood between teacher and student. Teachers (black and white) employ silence as a tool of classroom control. Students (predominantly black) adopt 'silent sulks'—often dramatically stylized—as a defense against teacher authority and as a display of anger. This use of 'silence displays' is closely related to the use of silence described by Saunders in the next chapter.

SILENCE IN CROSS-CULTURAL PERSPECTIVE

Saunders (Chapter 9, 'Silence and Noise as Emotion Management Styles: An Italian Case') in Part IV presents analyses of silence in specific cultural settings. Saunders begins with an ethnographic sketch of the Italian village Valbella, and a theoretical overview of the study of emotion management in anthropological research, as background to his study of silence as emotion management. He concludes that whereas Valbellans employ noisy confrontation in expression of emotion in relatively small matters, they prefer the strategy of silence if the emotion-laden issue is serious enough to threaten family solidarity.

Nwoye (Chapter 10, 'Eloquent Silence Among the Igbo of Nigeria') describes the uses of silence in the range of behaviors and levels of interaction among the 'typically extraverted'—that is, talkative—Igbo. Following the schema outlined by Saville-Troike, he considers institutionally determined silence, as in rituals associated with birth and death; group-determined silence, as in the ostracism of social deviants; and individually negotiated silence, as in the omission of an expected greeting.

Whereas Tannen (Chapter 6) suggests that New York Jews have been negatively stereotyped in part because of their avoidance of silence, Lehtonen and Sajavaara (Chapter 11, 'The Silent Finn') present research and discussion about a group that have been negatively stereotyped because of their frequent use of silence: the Finns. The authors consider popular maxims and other evidence for the silence-favoring attitude of Finns, as well as silence-related features of Finnish conversation. In a section which relates closely to the papers in Part II, they present findings of experiments measuring pauses and rate of speech in the discourse of Finns, Swedes, and English speakers, as well as of speakers from a part of Finland in which inhabitants are believed by other Finns to be particularly slow speakers. The authors discuss these findings in light of the more general phenomena of individual interactive style, cultural differences, and stereotyping.

SILENCE AND NONVERBAL COMMUNICATION

The papers in the final section are concerned with the broader relationship of silence to the range of communicative behaviors, especially nonverbal communication. Philips (Chapter 12, 'Interaction Structured Through Talk and Interaction Structured Through "Silence"') calls attention to the fact that research has focused almost exclusively on interactions structured through talk—where attention is focused on verbal utterances—rather than on interactions structured through silence—where attention is focused on nonverbal physical activity perceived in the visual channel. She proposes these constructs as ends of a continuum along which behavior ranges, and suggests that societies differ in their distribution of these types. Philips reports that Warm Springs Indians engage in proportionately more interaction structured through silence, a finding related to Scollon's that Athakaskan Indians evaluate silence positively. Philips concludes with a call for more research addressed to such interaction.

In the concluding chapter, Kendon (Chapter 13, 'Some Uses of Gesture') also is concerned with communication perceived in the visual channel: deliberate and deliberately silent utterances in the form of gesture. He presents first an overview of studies of gesture and then the results of observations of use of gesture in face-to-face interaction. Kendon shows that the usefulness of gesture in conversation derives from its silent (as well as visual) nature. Finally, he points out implications of his observations for theories of human communication, thus coming full circle to our starting point in Saville-Troike's chapter.

The range of disciplines and definitions of silence represented in the chapters are reflected as well in the sources annotated in the Appendix compiled by Muñoz-Duston and Kaplan.

CONCLUSION: FORMS AND FUNCTIONS OF SILENCE

Silence, as discussed in these chapters, takes various forms. The smallest unit of silence, mentioned by Lehtonen and Sajavaara in Chapter 11, is the normally unnoticed cessation of sound in the production of consonants, which creates the pattern of consonants and vowels that makes 'speech' of a vocal stream. The next level of silence is the pausing, sometimes perceived as hesitation and sometimes not perceived at all, within the stream of speech making up a speaker's turn, and between speaker turns, as discussed in Part II (Chapters 3, 4, and 5) as well as parts of Chapters 2, 6, and 11.

The next level of silence includes pauses that are perceived in interaction, such as those Goffman (1967) calls 'lulls' in conversation. Longer than this is the complete silence of one party to a conversation, seen in Nwoye's example of a young Igbo woman who indicates her rejection of a marriage proposal by standing her ground yet not speaking. The broadest level of silence discussed is that which provides the structure and background against which talk is marked and meaningful merely by virtue of its occurrence. An example of this is the Igbo ritual described by Nwoye in which a sacrifice is carried through the village. If this silent ritual is interrupted by talk, the entire sacrifice is profaned and, indeed, canceled.

The chapters in this collection demonstrate and discuss a range of functions of silence, on varying levels. At one pole are the functions of pausing in cognitive processes (Chapter 5), impression formation (Chapters 2, 3, and 4), and as part of communicative style partly responsible for cultural stereotyping (Chapters 2, 6, and 11). At the other pole are the functions of silence as the background against which talk has meaning, or as the nonverbal activity which structures interaction (Chapter 12). Furthermore, we see that silence can itself be a communicative device in interaction (Chapters 1, 6, and 10); either obstructor or facilitator of divine inspiration (Chapter 7); and a means of emotion management (Chapter 9) and display (Chapter 8). A number of chapters call attention to the function of silence as a marker of juncture, or interruption, on all the levels at which it has been described.

In sum, we present a collection of papers written by scholars in different disciplines, combined to present as comprehensive a view as possible of the nature, meaning, and functions of silence across contexts, cultures, and academic disciplines.

M.S.-T.

D.T.

REFERENCES

Basso, Keith. 1970. To give up on words: Silence in Western Apache culture. Language and social context, ed. by Pier Paolo Giglioli, 67–86. New York: Penguin.

Bauman, Richard. 1970. Aspects of Quaker rhetoric. Quarterly Journal of Speech 56. 67–74.

Cook, John J. 1964. Silence in psychotherapy. Journal of Counseling Psychology 11. 42–46.

Goffman, Erving. 1967. Interaction ritual. Garden City, NY: Doubleday.

Goldman-Eisler, Frieda. 1951. The measurement of time sequences in conversational behavior. British Journal of Psychology 42. 355–362.

Hall, Edward. 1959. The silent language. New York: Doubleday.

Jaffe, Joseph and Stanley Feldstein. 1970. Rhythms of dialogue. New York: Academic Press.

Maclay, Howard and Charles E. Osgood. 1959. Hesitation phenomena in spontaneous English speech. Word 15. 19–44.

Samarin, William John. 1965. Language of silence. Practical Anthropology 12:3. 115–119.

PART I

OVERVIEW: THE NATURE AND STUDY OF SILENCE

Chapter 1

The Place of Silence in an Integrated Theory of Communication

Muriel Saville-Troike
University of Illinois

> To talk little is natural. (Lao Tsu)

The role of silence has long been accorded central importance within such disciplines as philosophy and religion, figuring both in their undergirding framework of belief and value, and in their practices. Performances of silence are not merely passive acts, as can be seen in Catholic and Quaker worship, where silence creates space within which God may work (cf. Bauman 1974), and in Eastern thought, where silence is intimately related to action and desire. In Taoism, for instance, 'at the apex of human performances, authentic speech is one with authentic silence and, in their oneness, they are the most efficacious of human experiences' (Dauenhauer 1980:138).

The significance of silence can usually be interpreted only in relation to sound, but the reverse is also the case, with the significance of sound depending on the interpretation of silence. The importance of noise to Pentecostal Protestant worship, for instance (Chapter 7), is derived in large part from contrasts in Christian belief about who should speak and who should remain silent. And although Hindu scriptures accord silence more basic importance than sound, 'God is both silence and sound. . . Sound must be used as a means to silence, for self-realization' (Subrahamanian 1976:2). The interdependence is further illustrated by Nwoye (Chapter 10) as he describes the ritual and social functions of silence in the Igbo culture; the importance of silence depends in large part on the importance Igbo accords to speech.

Within linguistics, silence has traditionally been ignored except for its boundary-marking function, delimiting the beginning and end of utterances. The tradition has been to define it negatively—as merely the absence of speech. From a different perspective, however, that of a total theory of communication, we can view silence as itself a valid object of investigation, bounded by stretches of verbal material which provide boundary marking for its identification.

The pervasive theme of this volume is that communicative behavior consists of both sounds and silences, and that adequate description and interpretation of the process of communication requires that we understand the structure, meaning, and functions of silence as well as of sound. A total theory of communication should further be concerned with the ways these two modes of behavior pattern in relation to the culture and social organization of a speech community on the one hand, and in relation to the personal emotions and attributions of its members on the other.

DIMENSIONS OF SILENCE

Just as with speech, silence is not a simple unit of communication, but is composed of complex dimensions and structures.

First, a distinction should be made between the absence of sound when no communication is going on, and silence which is part of communication. Just as not all noise is part of 'communication', neither is all silence.

Next, we should distinguish the silence which serves to structure communication, but is neither a communicative act in its own right nor an intervening phenomenon within or between communicative acts. Such silence not only structures communication but—as an integral part of the cultural framework of a speech community—also serves to organize and regulate its social relationships. This silence may be a necessary precondition and accompaniment of ritual acts, for example, or may be required between certain individuals, such as between a man and his wife's mother among certain American Indian tribes. In public encounters between strangers, such as seatmates on a train or airplane, silence may be used to prevent the initiation of verbal interaction, and to maintain social space.

Within a single speech community, social values and norms are closely tied to the amount of talk vs. silence that is prescribed—according to social distinctions such as rank in the social hierarchy, to role (sacred or secular), or to age. The relative value of talk or silence in a society may be partly inferred from whether one or the other is ascribed to its rulers, priests, and sages. It is this dimension being called upon by the Apostle Paul when he enjoined: 'Let a woman learn silence with all submissiveness. I will permit no woman to teach or to have authority over man; she is to keep silent' (1 Timothy 2:11,12). Silence may thus be performed as part of the enactment of a subordinate status (cf. the husband and wife episode below, p. 11).

FIGURE 1.1

		CHANNEL	
		Vocal	Nonvocal
	Verbal	Spoken language	Written language (Deaf) Sign language Whistle/drum languages Morse code
CODE	Nonverbal	Paralinguistic and prosodic fea- tures	Kinesics Proxemics Eye behavior Pictures and cartoons

Within communicative events, not all nonvocal communication is nonverbal, so that a further distinction should be made between verbal silence and nonverbal silence. This requires differentiating the dimensions of code and channel, as in Figure 1.1 (cf. Saville-Troike 1982:143).

Even though sign language may not be accompanied by any vocalization, for instance, it shares all other features of verbal communication with speech. In signing, a range of visual behaviors which would be considered 'nonverbal' in speech operate on the 'verbal' dimension, including some facial expression, which may even operate at a syntactic level in American Sign Language (ASL). The nonverbal dimension of silence in sign language includes the silence deliberately induced by closing the eyes or averting eye gaze.

Written language is obviously also verbal and nonvocal (though it may be 'performed' by reading aloud), but its nonverbal dimension—signaled by spacing and punctuation—has received inadequate consideration. Writing, too, has silences. This is perhaps most highly developed in Japanese literature with the use of the silence marker '. . . . .' Hokari (1980) calculates that in *Kazetachinu* by Tatsuo Hori, '. . . .' is used 173 times in 103 pages; in *Kigadomei* by Kobo Abe, it is used as frequently as fifteen times per page. Hokari's illustrations include the following passages by Hori (translation by Hokari):

1. Ima kosite ano yama no fumoto ni koremade kigatsukazu ni omae to kurasite itanante. . . .

   To think that I have been living with you like this under that mountain without knowing it till now. . . . (isn't it strange).

2. '. . . .' Yoko mo sonna otto no kuse o sirinagara aite ga jibun o miteyoga imai ga kamawanai to iuyoni damatte unazuita dakedatta.

'. . , .'. Yoko, too, knowing that habit of her husband's, just nodded silently, as if she did not care if he was looking at her or not.

The same silence marker also occurs in European writing, as illustrated in this passage by a Greek author:

I didn't speak. . . I just smiled fearfully. . . 'Oh, Kostas, Kostas,' I said to myself, 'if you had any idea how much I love you. . .' Surely I must have the soul of a dog. . . Otherwise there's no explanation. . . Yes, no matter how much you scorn it and beat it, it keeps coming back and looks into your eyes. . . (Nakos 1935: 326; cited and analyzed in Tannen 1983: 73, her translation).

Another basic distinction must be made between silences which carry meaning, but not propositional content, and silent communicative acts which are entirely dependent on adjacent vocalizations for interpretation, and which carry their own illocutionary force.

The former include the pauses and hesitations that occur within and between turns of talking—the prosodic dimension of silence. Such nonpropositional silences may be volitional or nonvolitional, and may convey a wide variety of meanings. The meanings carried by pauses and hesitations are generally affective in nature, and connotative rather than denotative. Their meanings are nonetheless symbolic and conventional, as is seen in the various patterns of use and norms of interpretation in different speech communities (cf. Chapters 2, 6, and 11).

Silent communicative acts conveying propositional content may include gestures, but may also consist of silence unaccompanied by any visual clues. Even in a telephone conversation where no visual signals are possible, silence in response to a greeting, query, or request which anticipates verbal response is fraught with propositional meaning in its own right. Just as 'one can utter words without saying anything' (Searle 1969), one can say something without uttering words. Silence as part of communicative interaction can be one of the forms a 'speech' act may take—filling many of the same functions and discourse slots—and should be considered along with the production of sentence tokens as a basic formational unit of linguistic communication. Silence may be used to question, promise, deny, warn, threaten, insult, request, or command, as well as to carry out various kinds of ritual interaction.

As with speech, silent communicative acts may be analyzed as having both illocutionary force and perlocutionary effect (cf. Austin 1962), although here we clearly cannot use 'locution' in its usual sense. The analogy carries further, since similar inferencing processes are employed to interpret the meaning of what is *not* spoken as in interpreting the meaning of what *is* said. Silence has even been entered in court evidence, with the interpretation of its meaning playing an important role in determining the defendent's guilt or innocence (Shuy 1980). Silence further can have similar truth value to speech, and thus can intentionally be used to deceive and to mislead.

The recognition of silence as an entity in itself is clearly demonstrated by the legal status accorded it in some places. In the United States, for example, a person has the 'right to remain silent', and the U.S. Supreme Court once overturned a conviction in a lower court because the presiding judge had refused to instruct the jury not to interpret silence as guilt. Basing his decision on a different part of the Constitution, another federal judge recently ruled that a state law requiring a moment of silence at the beginning of school was unconstitutional.

STRUCTURES OF SILENCE

My intent in this chapter is to suggest an etic grid or taxonomy of types of silences which will be descriptively applicable across languages and speech communities. From an emic perspective, however, even what is considered 'sound' vs. 'silence' is a relative concept, so that there can be no absolute distinction. To illustrate this relativity, what in American society is considered 'silence' is seldom in fact free of noise from electrical appliances, traffic, barking dogs, chirping birds, and other 'background' sounds which are ordinarily pushed out of consciousness as nonsignificant unless for some reason they become salient. Conversely, one major branch of Hinduism recognizes four distinct forms and stages of sound (said to originate in different parts of the body), only one of which has the auditory realization that we would perceive as 'sound'.[1]

Silence which carries grammatical and indexical meaning may replace different elements within sentences. One form of the WH- question typically used by teachers, for instance, is a fill-in-the-blank structure, e.g., 'This is a———?' (often said with lengthened or tensed *a* and nonterminal intonation), meaning 'What is this?' This form may also occur in conversational contexts when one speaker asks someone he or she has just met, 'And your name is———?' Utterances are also commonly completed in silence when the topic is a particularly delicate one or the word which would be used is taboo, or when the situation is emotionally loaded and the speaker is 'at a loss' for words. The Japanese term *haragei* 'wordless communication' captures the essence of this latter type of silence.

---

[1] In addition to audible sound uttered through the mouth, the *Tantra* recognizes sound that remains in the heart, in the navel, and in the lower abdomen (Subrahamanian 1976).

There is a belief that as soon as an experience is expressed in words (oral or written), the real essence disappears:

> When parents die, when the son passes the entrance examination to a university, and when we see something extremely beautiful, there should be silence. There is a well-known poem which starts 'Oh, Matsushima (name of an island in Japan). . .', but because the poet was so impressed by its beauty he could not continue; this poem is considered one of his masterpieces. (Williams 1979)

The interaction of sound, silence, and movement is of considerable interest in describing performance events, where who is silent versus who generates sound, and who is still versus who is mobile, are both salient dimensions of expression (Abrahams 1979). Sound, silence, and movement are also related in musical events, as described by Bahm for Hindu sacred music:

> Deceleration of rhythm and decreasing loudness of sounds at the end of a performance may not merely fade into silence but be projected into a profounder silence by continued plucking motions for visual appearance after actual plucking has ceased. Western anxiety cannot restrain itself from breaking (rudely) into applause; but the longer the pause before applause, the greater the quiescent effect, the achievement of the artist, and the appreciation by the audience (1965:110).

Complete 'utterances' may also be composed of silence, as illustrated in the following conversational exchanges:

1) A: We've received word that four Tanzanian acquaintances from out of town will be arriving tomorrow. But, with our large family, we have no room to accommodate them. (Implied request: 'Would you help us out?')
   B: [Silence; not accompanied by any distinctive gesture or facial expression] (Denial: 'I don't want to' or 'I don't have any room either')
   A: What do you think?
   B: Yes, that is a problem. Were you able to finish that report we were working on this morning?

The negative response in the cultural milieu in which this took place violated A's expectation that guests would be welcomed, and frustrated his goal in initiating the conversation (Jalbert 1980).

2) A: Please marry me.
   B: [Silence; head and eyes lowered] (Acceptance)

The exchange occurred between Japanese speakers. For the girl (B) to say anything would have been considered very inappropriate in this very emotional situation (Williams 1979). If it had occurred between Igbo speakers, silence would be interpreted as denial if she continued to stand there and as acceptance if she ran away (Nwoye 1978).

3) A: Are you still mad at me?
   B: [Silence] (Affirmative)

It is noteworthy that the silence here conveys a message precisely because it forms part of an interactional communicative structure. It does not deny or terminate the interaction (which would require some other act), and so cooperatively invites interpretation. In each of these exchanges, Speaker B selected silence from the possible repertoire of response forms available to convey his or her intended meaning. Thus, in considering the place of silence in relation to other communicative structures:

> The noematic element in silence is the set of all the things, all the expressions—verbal, gestural, or musical—which it is motivatedly possible for the author of an utterance to employ or refrain from employing. Abstaining from employing any or all of these expressions is on the face of it a positive performance and thus an act which could be taken to be the noetic correlate of the phenomenon of silence. Silence then would be the positive abstinence from employing some determinate expression (Dauenhauer 1980:55).

Silence is often used over longer segments of communication to convey a more generalized meaning, such as in the silences Gilmore (Chapter 8) observed in classrooms which called attention to the 'speaker', and expressed disapproval with others' behavior. Entire communicative events without sound are also common. Expecially in ritual contexts (such as several described in Chapter 10), silence may be conventionally mandated as the only form which could achieve the event's communicative goals. Thus also the invocation in Christian ritual: "The Lord is in His holy temple; let all the earth keep silence before Him."

SEMANTICS AND SEMIOTICS OF SILENCE

Many, perhaps most, languages have a metalinguistic term or terms for silence, though the ethnosemantics will vary from one language or culture to another. The English term *silence* is polysemous. According to the Oxford English Dictionary, its meanings include: (1) abstaining from speech or utterance, sometimes with reference to a particular matter; (2)

the state or condition when nothing is audible; (3) omission of mention or notice; and (4) 'Want of flavour in distilled spirit'. In each of these entries, silence is defined as the absence of something else.

Additional meanings may be inferred from parallel texts in English and other languages. For instance, a Biblical concordance will show that *silence* in the English text corresponds to several unrelated Hebrew roots. Those same roots in different verses correspond in turn to a variety of other English expressions which carry quite divergent meanings, including 'hold peace', 'be unable to speak', 'wait quietly', 'be cut off', 'muzzle' or 'gag', and 'perish'.

Clues to culturally defined connotative meanings of silence may be found in proverbs such as 'Silence is consent', and in metaphorical use (cf. Scollon's discussion [Chapter 2] of the 'metaphor of malfunction', or the equation of silence with death in English culture, epitomized as 'the silence of the tomb').

The relative value of speech versus silence in different speech communities may also be found in their proverbs: 'Silence is golden' (English); 'Because of the mouth the fish dies' (Spanish); 'The way your eyes look can say more than your mouth' (Japanese); and 'Man becomes wise through the ear' (Farsi). Countersentiments are expressed in '(Who) asks does not wander' (Serbo-Croatian) and 'The squeaky wheel gets the grease' (English).

Additionally, attributive meanings are apparent in the adjectives that are used in describing various kinds of silence (e.g. 'threatening silence', 'forbidding silence', 'eerie silence', 'smug silence', 'thoughtful silence', 'worshipful silence') or in describing people who are felt to exhibit relatively silent behavior (e.g. 'taciturn', 'reserved', 'reticent', 'secretive'). The latter also convey some information on cultural norms for, and attitudes toward, loquacity.

Quite apart from dictionary definitions, silence 'means' what it conveys. While that meaning (or in silent speech acts, the perlocutionary effect) can usually be achieved only in contrast with the meaning of sound, the time-spaces occupied by silence constitute an active presence (not absence) in communication. In a summary of his presentation on 'Silence up against the noise', Abrahams (1979) wrote: 'The greater the level of sound or noise, the more profound will the silence be interpreted *to be, to mean.* . . silence is employed as one of the most important devices in the vocabulary of intensification' [emphasis his].

Both speech sounds and speech silences are symbolic in nature, and the meaning of silence is thus also derived by convention within particular speech communities. This accounts for some of the cross-cultural misunderstandings which can result. A very serious instance occurred a few years ago during a period of military tension between Egypt and

Greece. Egyptian pilots radioed their intention to land at an airbase on Cyprus and the Greek traffic controllers reportedly responded with silence. The Greeks intended thereby to indicate *refusal* of permission to land, but the Egyptians interpreted silence as *assent*. The result of the misunderstanding in this case was the loss of a number of lives when Greeks fired on the planes as they approached the runway.

Except for such situations, which must rely entirely on an audible mode of communication, visual or contextual cues are usually available when silence is ambiguous. In general, silence (like all nonverbal communication) is more context-embedded than speech, that is, more dependent on context for its interpretation.

Quantity of speech versus silence may also be interpreted differently across cultural boundaries, as when 'friendliness' is equated differentially with one or the other in a conversation, or 'sincerity' and 'honesty' in a business or political encounter. Differing norms of appropriateness as to when to talk and when to remain silent can give rise to cross-cultural misunderstanding, for example, as occurred in the experience of a German woman who was married to a Japanese man. The husband on one occasion became very angry when she had offered an explanation in response to his question 'Why did you do that?', which he had presumably intended as a rhetorical question. The appropriate response from his perspective should have been an apology, or, preferably, silence to demonstrate her subordinate status.

ACQUISITION OF SILENCE

Almost all research on child language development has focused on how children learn to speak. But also of interest as an essential part of the acquisition of communicative competence, is how children learn when *not* to talk, and what silence means in their speech community.

The relative amount of silence versus talk expected of children in different cultures is related in part to different child-rearing practices, and in part to different values accorded individual achievement and initiative. In general, it appears that children talk more when they are being enculturated into societies which place a high value on individual achievement (e.g. Britain and America), and less when family and group achievement is more valued (e.g. Chinese and Japanese). Wang (1977) illustrates how the latter perspective relates to teaching children appropriate silence:

> In order to keep the children from saying or doing something disapproved of by the authorities, Asian parents teach them to be obedient and to honor their families. Everything is arranged and decided for

them. They are not given any choices; therefore, they do not have to
make choices and justify their actions verbally. Silence is praised, and
talkativeness is scolded. They are taught not to express their feelings.

Additionally, the cultural experience of children who will be less verbal about their wants and needs usually includes closer physical contact
with their early caregivers, and relates to expectations and attitudes that
people (adults as well as children) need not, and should not, have to ask
directly for what they want (cf. Heeschen et al. 1980). Other cultural
beliefs and practices may also be involved, as when Ashanti children
learn to observe silence at meals from an early age under threat that
speaking would cause their father to die (Hogan 1967); this relates to the
prescription which that society has for silence during some of its rituals,
including when the spirits eat.

Socializing young children to silence may thus be considered part of
the transmission of world view, as further illustrated by Locke (1980):

> A Colville Indian child from the Northwest Coast is trained to perceive
> with all of his senses before he learns to speak so that he may become
> sensitive to the world around him. A grandparent will say 'Wighst' and
> slap his hand on a solid surface. The child who is crawling on the floor
> will stop playing or daydreaming or whatever he is doing and become
> alert at the sound of that word and will try to feel through his body and
> his feet the vibrations of the stream or animals walking or people walking
> about him. The child sharpens his peripheral vision. He listens to all the
> sounds about him, he focuses all his senses, including that other sense,
> that is sensitive to the vibrations of the earth. The training is con-
> stant. . . Thus he is prepared to relate to other two-leggeds, four-leggeds,
> the winged creatures, the crawling ones, the finned ones, the rooted
> ones, and all of life, all of our relations.

Children learning to be silent are not necessarily learning adult norms
for sociolinguistic behavior, since rules may be quite different for adults
and children. In some speech communities, for instance, children are
expected to be 'seen but not heard' in contexts which require a formal
register of speech from adults; in other communities, children are expected to talk freely with other children but not in the presence of adults;
in still others, children speak freely, and taciturnity is expected with
maturity.[2]

Learning appropriate rules for silence is also part of the acculturation
process for adults attempting to develop communicative competence in a

---

[2]For example, Gardner (1966) reports the Paliyans of south India become almost silent by
age 40 (cited in Hymes 1972:40).

second language and culture. Perhaps because it functions at a lower level of consciousness than speech, many (perhaps most) otherwise fluent bilinguals retain a foreign 'accent' in their use of silence in the second language, retaining native silence patterns even as they use the new verbal structures.

Navajo speakers functioning in an English language context, for instance, sometimes transfer the Navajo temporal pattern of silence in turn-taking between questions and answers, which occupies a significantly longer time-space than that generally used by monolingual English speakers. I have observed non-Navajo participants in group discussions answer questions which had been addressed to Navajos, because the period of silence following the question had gone beyond their own limit of tolerence; non-Navajo questioners talking with Navajos often repeat or rephrase their questions for the same reason. It is also possible that this kind of 'interference' is so persistent because of the affective meaning carried by this prosodic dimension; many Navajo speakers consider the non-Navajo paralinguistic behavior quite impolite, and would not wish to add it to their bilingual repertory.

SILENCE AND THE ETHNOGRAPHY OF COMMUNICATION

The contributors to this volume do not all share the same theoretical perspective, even as they develop the same basic theme that describing and interpreting communicative processes requires consideration of silence as well as of sound. Some identify themselves primarily with the discipline of the ethnography of communication, and it is this model that I believe is most productive for formulating an integrated theory of communication.[3] Basic to this approach is not merely accounting for what can be said, but *what* can be said *when, where, by whom, to whom,* in *what manner,* and in *what* particular *circumstances.* It follows naturally that this line of inquiry must consider also who may *not* speak about what and in what situations, as well.

A principal concern in the ethnography of communication is the discovery of the regular patterns and constraints (i.e. 'rules') that operate at different levels of communication. At a societal level, this patterning generally occurs along dimensions of social organization, community attitudes, and such macrofunctions as social control, ritual interaction with

---

[3]The discussion of the ethnography of communication is based on the model first suggested by Dell Hymes in 1962. His publication of 'The Ethnography of Speaking' in that year launched a synthesizing discipline which requires holistic treatment of communication within its social, cultural, and affective milieu. General descriptions of the field may be found in Bauman and Sherzer (1975) and Saville-Troike (1982).

the supernatural, and establishment or reinforcement of group identity. At the level of individuals and small interacting groups within a society, this patterning occurs in expression and interpretation of personality, and in microfunctions related to participants' purposes and needs.

Societal level functions are illustrated by the use of silence to differentiate groups within a society according to rank, role, or age; by the description of silence used in ritual by Nwoye and Maltz (Chapters 7 and 10); and by discussions of silence employed to mark or reinforce social identity (Chapters 2, 6, 9, and 11). As an example of social control, silence is one of the strongest forms of punishment which may be invoked (e.g. 'shunning' among the Eskimo, the Igbo, or the Amish in the United States). The use of silence for social control at a microfunctional level is illustrated by Gilmore (Chapter 8) is a classroom setting. Other microfunctions of silence are illustrated in my discussion above of silence as a 'speech' act, and in the affective states and personality traits ascribed to prosodic uses of silence (such as those described in Chapters 3 and 4).

One important reason for incorporating the analysis of microfunctions within a holistic model of communication is to make clear that the interpretation of patterns of sound and silence is dependent on their interrelationship with other patterns of culture. Stereotyping and misunderstanding occur when the patterned use of sounds and silence by members of one speech community are interpreted according to the norms and rules held by members of another.

The analysis of a communicative *event* (a basic unit of the ethnography of communication) begins with a description of components which are likely to be salient to members of the speech community within which the event occurs, and which may affect the choice of linguistic form that is used as well as its meaning. Each component that can call for a different form of speech can also permit or prescribe silence.[4] The *genre,* or type of event, may require silence, for instance, as in many rituals, or different prosodic patterning of sound and silence, as in narrative prose vs. poetry; the *topic* may be too 'delicate' to put into words, or involve a religious taboo requiring silence; the *function* may involve silence at both macro and micro levels, as discussed above; and the *setting* (time and place) may be designated as inappropriate for vocal interaction. These four components comprise the *scene,* or extrapersonal context, of the event.

Another component is that of the *participants,* or who is taking part in the event. Their identity, which includes such factors as their social

---

[4]There is some variation in lists of components and their labels. Those given here are from Saville-Troike (1982); see also Hymes (1967, 1972) and Friedrich (1972).

status and their role-relationships, affects appropriate patterns of speech and silence. The *act sequence,* or ordering of communicative/speech acts, includes turn-taking and overlap phenomena, and thus particularly involves the patterning of silence on the prosodic dimension. Finally, the *rules for interaction* include the properties relating to silence which should be observed, and the *norms of interpretation* include the common knowledge and cultural presuppositions which allow inferences to be drawn about the unsaid as well as the said.

Rules for 'polite' conversational turn-taking in English require an addressee to respond on the next turn if the speaker utters a compliment, request, or invitation, but Philips (1976) reports speakers on the Warm Springs Indian reservation may keep silent with no violation of a politeness constraint, or may give their response at a later time. Norms of interpretation are involved when a speaker infers whether silence in response to a claim or request means agreement, denial, avoidance, or a violation of norms.

Methodologically, in the description of an unfamiliar (or even a familiar) culture, silence is often not documented because it does not attract attention in the same way that audible or visible behavior does. With the Oxford English Dictionary defining silence negatively as the *absence* of other features, Whorf's ghost stalks the pages of field notes and tape transcripts which omit potentially meaningful occurrences of silence. As an example, after videotaping and transcribing data on children's behavior over a period of several months, I found—only after using a timed check-off of interaction by different participants—that some of the children in the group had not spoken in weeks. A special meta-awareness is needed to attend to the range of possible silences, and particular care is required in seeking their proper interpretation.

SILENCE AND AN INTEGRATED THEORY OF HUMAN COMMUNICATION

Perhaps because silence in communicative settings is often taken simply for inaction, or because perceptual bias has led researchers to attend to more readily noticeable behaviors while treating silence as merely background, or because much of the focus of research to date has been on small group and dyadic conversational interaction, the important position of silence in the total framework of human communication has been largely overlooked. Most of the existing research literature on silence is devoted to short silences (pauses) within discourses or at turn-taking boundaries in conversation, while only a marginal amount of data is available on longer silences and their communicative significance.

Two programmatic papers on silence, which appeared almost simultaneously, have discussed certain types and functions of silence: Bruneau

(1973) has dealt with 'interactive silences', which include a broad array of functions, from defining the role of auditor in a communicative exchange, to providing social control, to demonstrating deference, to indicating emotional closeness, to managing personal interaction; Jensen (1973) has presented a similar variety of functions, categorizing them as linkage, affecting, revelational, judgmental, and activating.

A broad classification, more germane to the whole of human communication, is needed both to include and distinguish functions or events that are relevant to different levels of social action. It must also be one which can be applied cross-culturally. What follows is a tentative effort at such a classification, which will unquestionably need to be amplified and refined. It attempts to provide a number of *etic* categories which, taken together with the framework for the ethnography of communication, can provide a grid for treating silences of a broad range of types within a number of pertinent levels and domains.

A. Institutionally-determined silence
    1.   Locational: temples, libraries
    2.   Ritual (except for duly authorized speakers and occasions): religious services, legal proceedings, funerals, classes in school, public performances (operas, movies)
    3.   Membership: religious groups (nuns, monks) with a vow of silence
    4.   Hierarchical/structural: lower-status (less powerful) members of a society or organization versus higher-status persons
    5.   Taboo: persons in certain statuses (e.g., chief) or defined relationships (e.g., wife's mother) with whom communication is proscribed
B. Group-determined silence
    1.   Situational: access to speaking privilege is allocated by group decision, which may be delegated (legislative bodies, committees)
    2.   Normative: differential speaking privileges allocated to individuals or classes of individuals (shunning as punishment, children, audience members)
    3.   Symbolic: communicative actions
C. Individually-determined/negotiated silence
    1.   Interactive
        a.   Socio-contextual
            1) role-indicative (e.g., auditor in conversation)
            2) status-indicative (e.g., deference, superiority)
            3) situation-indicative (e.g., context-structuring, tension-management, social control)

           4) tactical-symbolic/attitudinal (nonparticipation, anger, sorrow, respect, disapproval, dislike, indifference, alienation, avoidance, mitigation, concealment, mystification, dissimulation, image manipulation)

           5) phatic (emotional sharing)

    b.   Linguistic

           1) discursive (prayer, fantasizing, rehearsing)

           2) propositional (negation, affirmation, consent, agreement, refusal, acknowledgement)

           3) didactic ('fill in the blank')

    c.   Psychological (timidity, embarrassment, fear, neurosis)

2.   Noninteractive

    a.   Contemplative/meditative

    b.   Inactive

The preceding is far from exhaustive and is intended to be suggestive rather than a definitive proposal. Elaborating and testing such a taxonomy of settings, relations, functions, context, and determining factors should lead not only to a more complete description and understanding of the uses of silence in a particular society or a given setting, but also to a fuller apprehension of the complexities and universal characteristics of the whole human communication system, within which silence serves variously as prime, substitute, and surrogate, as well as frame, cue, and background.

REFERENCES

Abe, Kobo. 1972. Kigadomei. Tokyo: Shinchosha.

Abrahams, Roger D. 1979. Unpublished manuscript, Claremont College.

Austin, John L. 1962. How to do things with words. New York: Oxford University Press.

Bahm, A. J. 1965. Comparative aesthetics. Journal of Aesthetics and Criticism (Fall), 110.

Bauman, Richard. 1974. Speaking in the light: The role of the Quaker minister. Explorations in the ethnography of speaking, ed. by Richard Bauman and Joel Sherzer. New York: Cambridge University Press.

Bauman, Richard and Joel Sherzer. 1975. The ethnography of speaking. Annual Review of Anthropology 4:95–119.

Bruneau, Thomas J. 1973. Communicative silences: Forms and functions. Journal of Communication 23. 17–46.

Dauenhauer, Bernard P. 1980. Silence: The phenomenon and its ontological significance. Bloomington: Indiana University Press.

Friedrich, Paul. 1972. Social context and semantic feature: The Russian pronominal usage. Directions in sociolinguistics: The ethnography of communication, ed. by John J. Gumperz & Dell Hymes. pp. 270–300. New York: Holt, Rinehart & Winston.

Gardner, Peter M. 1966. Symmetric respect and memorate knowledge: The structure and ecology of individualistic culture. Southwestern Journal of Anthropology 22. 389–415.

Heeschen, Volker, Wulf Schiefenhövel and I. Eibl-Eibesfeldt. 1980. Requesting, giving, and taking: The relationship between verbal and nonverbal behavior in the speech community of the Eipo, Irian Jaya (West New Guinea), The relationship of verbal and nonverbal communication, ed. by Mary Ritchie Key. The Hague: Mouton.

Hogan, Sister Peter Marie. 1967. An ethnography of communication among the Ashanti. Austin, TX: Texas-Penn Working Papers in Sociolinguistics.

Hokari, Keiko. 1980. Unpublished manuscript, Georgetown University.

Hori, Tatsuo. 1967. Kazetachinu. Tokyo: Kaiseisha.

Hymes, Dell. 1962. The ethnography of speaking, Anthropology and human behavior, ed. by T. Gladwin & W. C. Sturtevant. pp. 13–53. Washington, DC: Anthropological Society of Washington.

Hymes, Dell. 1967. Models of interaction of language and social settings. Journal of Social Issues 33(2). 8–28.

Hymes, Dell. 1972. Models of the interaction of language and social life, Directions in sociolinguistics: The ethnography of communication, ed. by John J. Gumperz and Dell Hymes. pp. 35–71. New York: Holt, Rinehart & Winston.

Jalbert, Robert. 1980. Unpublished manuscript, Georgetown University.

Jensen, J. Vernon. 1973. Communicative functions of silence. ETC 30. 249–257.

Locke, Patricia. 1980. The nature of the socio-cultural aspects of American Indian language uses. Paper presented at the Conference on Research in American Indian Education, National Institute of Education, Washington, DC.

Nakos, Lilika. 1935. Oi Parastratimenoi (The Lost). Athens: Nea Estia.

Nwoye, Gregory. 1978. Unpublished manuscript. Georgetown University.

Philips, Susan U. 1976. Some sources of cultural variability in the regulation of talk. Language in Society 5(1). 81–95.

Saville-Troike, Muriel. 1982. The ethnography of communication: An introduction. Oxford, England: Basil Blackwell.

Searle, John. 1969. Speech acts. London: Cambridge University Press.

Shuy, Roger, W. 1980. The role of the linguist as expert witness. Paper presented at the American Association for Applied Linguistics meeting, San Antonio, Texas.

Subrahamanian, K. 1976. Some concepts of silence and sound in Sanskrit. Prabuddha Bharata.

Tannen, Deborah. 1983. Lilika Nakos. Boston: G. K. Hall.

Wang, Peter Chin-tang. 1977. The effect of East/West cultural differences on oral language development. Paper presented at the Chinese Language Teacher's Association, San Francisco.

Williams, Harumi. 1979. Unpublished manuscript, Georgetown University.

PART II

PSYCHOLOGICAL AND ETHNOGRAPHIC VIEWS OF PAUSING

Chapter 2

The Machine Stops: Silence in the Metaphor of Malfunction

Ron Scollon
The Gutenberg Dump, Ltd.
Haines, Alaska

SILENT NIGHT

There is a story that says, because a church organ was broken, 'Silent Night' was composed on and sung with a guitar. As one of the Western world's earliest significant machines, the cathedral organ can be seen somewhat cynically as an instrument of noise designed to dispel the silence. The silence on Christmas Eve signals the malfunction of the machine.

While the idea has been with us for some time (Whorf 1941), recently there has been a renewed interest in the importance of metaphor in generating ways of thinking as well as courses of action (Schon 1979, Reddy, 1979). Bolinger (1979) has said, 'The world we carry in our heads is a vast elaborated metaphor' (p. 260). My purpose in this paper is to argue that research on pausing in conversational interaction has been built on the metaphor of the machine. Researchers still favor Descartes in taking the machine as the model of both human cognition and interpersonal interaction. This, in turn, has consequences both for the ways in which we do research and in our interpersonal interactions with people who do not build their understanding of communication in the metaphor of the machine.

SILENCES IN FACE-TO-FACE INTERACTION: PAUSING

Studies of communication have tended to look at silence as absence—as absence of sound and therefore as absence of communication. In the past decade and a half there have been a number of studies in more than one research tradition which have raised silence to the theoretical level of a problem. I think in particular of work in the ethnomethodological tradi-

21

tion such as that which was given impetus by Schegloff's (1972) study of conversational turn taking. In this tradition, which is now a considerable body of work, pauses are central in raising the problematicity of the negotiated copresence of the participants to an interaction.

In the present context I intend to say very little about this body of research on the assumption that it is reasonably well known. Instead I want to look at another body of work which may be less well known. Psycholinguistic studies of pausing phenomena, as for example those represented in a recent symposium organized by Siegman and Feldstein (1979), seem to polarize about two basic views. Pauses are seen as a coupling mechanism, the rhythmic hitch which holds an interaction together, or they are seen as a form of disfluency. This polarization relates to two types of pauses, switching pauses or, in another vocabulary, turn exchange pauses, and inturn pauses. Beebe, Stern, and Jaffe (1979), for example, look at coaction between a mother and a four-month-old infant. In their view, the rhythm of the pauses between sequences was the critical factor in synchronizing the coaction of mother and infant. They see these pauses as more important than the modality in which the interaction took place, whether verbal or nonverbal. In other studies it has been suggested that the mating of manic-depressives is governed by pause rhythms established in the prepsychosis period of the relationship (Dunner, Fleiss, Addonizio, and Fieve 1976). Natale, Dahlberg, and Jaffe (1979) have looked at the effect of drugs on the rhythm of the patient-therapist interaction. Welkowitz, Cariffe, and Feldstein (1976) have noted a progressive pause matching with maturity up to five to seven years of age. In these studies the length of pauses has been seen to correlate with other features of the interaction, giving to pause length the status of a reasonably reliable predictor of the coupling of the interaction. It should be mentioned that what is meant by pause length for these psycholinguists is a value which has been statistically summarized over a period of interaction.

Researchers in this tradition have assumed that speech will be fluent except where slowed or interrupted by various intervening factors. Among those factors are the cognitive complexity of the utterance as shown by Goldman-Eisler (1968). Siegman and Pope (1967) have shown that alcohol in the bloodstream and anxiety (Siegman and Pope 1972) tend to reduce fluency. That is, these factors tend to increase the length of pauses. Moreover, Welkowitz, Cariffe, and Feldstein (1976) as well as Sabin, Clemmer, O'Connell, and Kowal (1979) have shown that the presumed increase in cognitive ability that comes with maturity results in a decrease in the length of pauses.

These psychologists and psycholinguists have given us some rather extensive experimental evidence that pausing is a factor of considerable significance in human communication. Within psycholinguists' discussions there is some argument about whether pauses are at their root cognitive, affective, or some other kind of phenomenon. While Goldman-Eisler (1968) argues for a cognitive basis, Siegman (1979b) argues that there is not a necessary contradiction in saying the basis is affective since affective states such as anxiety would require one to think over more carefully what one says, and thus an affective issue would be transmuted into a cognitive one. Beattie (1979) sounds a different theme entirely and argues that longer or shorter pauses are used by people because they have been reinforced for speaking in those ways. Beattie, in taking this position, puts some distance between himself and many other psycholinguists and, in doing so, comes closer to my own view which is that pauses may in fact come to have symbolic value in themselves.

My concern here is with one general finding that emerges from this psycholinguistic discussion. This is that in turn pauses and switching pauses are apparently quite different in respect to their variability. Inturn pausing is variable depending on the task. One group has found that pauses are shortest in prose reading, longer in poetry reading, still longer in spontaneous narratives, and longest in story retellings (Sabin, Clemmer, O'Connell, and Kowal 1979). Beattie (1979) was able to significantly reduce inturn pauses with either positive or negative reinforcement delivered in the form of a flashing green light. Siegman (1979a) was able as well to significantly reduce inturn pausing in the speech of interviewees by manipulating interviewer 'warmth'. Switching pauses on the other hand were not affected by task of reinforcement in these same studies. While Matarazzo and Wiens (1972) have been able to vary switching pauses to some extent, very few studies have indicated variability of switching pauses. For instance, Marcus, Welkowitz, Feldstein and Jaffe (1970) found that field dependent women were more influenced by the pausing of their conversational partners than field independent women were. Witkin, Dyk, Faterson, Goodenough, and Karp (1974) have reported that women are more field dependent than men.

The outcome of this body of work then is the suggestion that there are two general classes of pauses. One group—switching pauses—appears to be much less susceptible to change by task or under conditions of reinforcement and is therefore more characteristic of an individual's 'style'. This 'style' may reflect very early infant-caregiver interactions. The other group—inturn pauses—is much more susceptible to task or reinforcement changes. These pauses, because they are more susceptible to situational conditions, may be expected to reflect those conditions more than individual histories.

'SILENT INDIANS' AND NEGATIVE ATTRIBUTIONS

In our own research we have been trying to deal with problems of negative ethnic stereotypes. We are centrally concerned with the negative stereotyping of the 'Silent Indian' in education, legal affairs, politics, and social services, and with the ways in which this stereotyping leads to more overtly discriminatory practices (Scollon and Scollon 1979a, 1979b, 1981, 1983). We have outlined one mechanism by which this stereotyping develops as an interaction between two phenomena, topic control in the initiation of conversations and difference in pausing. We have argued that the reserve with which Athabaskans approach an interaction with a stranger may lead to choosing not to speak immediately. This view compares favorably with that of Basso (1970, 1979). If the non-Athabaskan chooses to speak, this choice is very apt to lead to that same speaker's choice of topic as well (Schegloff 1972). Where this is coupled with an overall tendency to use somewhat longer switching pauses, the Athabaskan finds himself or herself in a situation in which it is very difficult to get a word in edgewise. From Tannen's work (Tannen 1984; see also Chapter 6 in this volume) it should be clear that I am not speaking of any necessarily ethnic difference in rate of turning over participants' turns. What is critical is the difference. Where one is faster and the other is slower relative to each other, the two tend to polarize into a voluble one and a taciturn one. We have argued that it is the coupling of topic control and turn exchange that is largely responsible for the negative stereotypes held by non-Indians of Athabaskans. We hear people say that Athabaskans are 'passive', 'sullen', 'withdrawn', 'unresponsive', 'lazy', 'backward', 'destructive', 'hostile', 'uncooperative', 'antisocial', and 'stupid'. And these are not just the attributions of ignorant bigots. Hippler, Boyer, and Boyer (1978) make these same attributions in a professional article on ethnopsychiatry. The wording is different, perhaps, but the attributions are substantially the same. We find them saying about the Tanaina for example that 'cognitive capacities have been substantially hampered' (p. 119) and that they have a 'distrustful explosive personality' (p. 119). We also see further mention of 'absence of affect', 'frozen rigid responses', and, not surprisingly, that 'response times are slow' (p. 120). My point is that these attributions are made on the basis of inferences drawn by non-Athabaskans based on conversational interaction with Athabaskans. What the 'Silent Indian' sees on the other side of the interaction I cannot say from my own experience, but what we hear on our tapes is an almost breathless rush of talking at them.

In this light, the research of a group of psycholinguists at Maryland is extremely interesting. Feldstein, Alberti, and BenDebba (1979) have studied a group of (presumably) culturally homogeneous college women in conversation with each other. The researchers have looked at two phenomena; the pauses typical of each woman's conversation and personality characteristics each women attributes to herself. What they have found is that women who typically take shorter pauses than their conversational partners attribute to themselves characteristics of being 'warm-hearted', 'easygoing', 'cooperative', 'attentive to people', 'outgoing', 'talkative', 'cheerful', 'adventurous', and 'socially bold'. These women also hold the floor longer by taking longer speaking turns.

On the other hand, women who took longer pauses than their conversational partners felt they themselves were 'reserved', 'detached', 'critical', 'distrustful', 'skeptical', 'taciturn', 'sober', 'shy', 'restrained', 'rigid', 'prone to sulk', 'changeable', 'self-indulgent', 'indolent', 'undependable', 'easily upset', 'apprehensive', 'self-reproaching', 'tense', and 'frustrated'. These women also took shorter speaking turns.

I notice two things here. First is the similarity of these self-attributions to the negative stereotypes I often hear attributed to Indians. The second that there are virtually no positive qualities associated with the second group and virtually no negative qualities associated with the first group. It appears that at least for our society, a slower pace in exchanging turns is a highly negative quality.

I might make one aside here and raise a question that in another context might well be a major issue. To a considerable extent these attributions appear to be made on the basis of switching pauses, not inturn pauses. That is, if the reinforcement literature is to be believed, we may expect that all sorts of situational effects can be brought to bear on inturn pausing without touching switching pauses. That is, such things as interviewer warmth (Pope and Siegman 1968) or, say, teacher warmth (Kleinfeld 1973) could produce highly significant increases in fluency, in verbal output, and even in expressed positive affection for the counterpart (Siegman 1979a) without in any way altering the processes of negative self- and other-attribution. Such a situation could in fact become double-binding (Bateson 1972) for the parties discriminated against if increase in positive affect were coupled with continued negative attribution, and if that were itself treated as something not to be discussed.

SILENCE AND MALFUNCTION

I have noted above that the attributions associated with slower turn exchange are virtually all negative. Conversational silence appears to be a very negative quality. Stokoe (1979:222) writes of the deaf experience:

> Those who profess expertise in pathology or 'disorders'—whether of hearing, speech, language, physiology, or psychology—still regard deaf people negatively.

Thus Feldstein, Alberti, and BenDebba (1979:85) find the results of their research 'intuitively reasonable'. They write:

> It does not seem unduly strange that speakers take longer turns when talking with persons who are reserved, detached, and taciturn than with persons who are talkative, cheerful, and cooperative. Nor is it difficult to believe that persons who are reserved, cold, suspicious, insecure, and tense tend to produce longer pauses. (p. 85)

Notice the implied direction of causation here. The researchers have taken the personality characteristics as given and then assumed that they have caused the pausing phenomena. In their view, it is a suspicious person who pauses longer. It is not that one attributes suspicion when a longer pause is taken. That is, the researchers have made just the same attributions their subjects have made and, of course, find them 'intuitively reasonable'. In my view, these researchers have chosen to suggest this direction of causation on the basis of a generative metaphor. This generative metaphor is the foundation of this research and, in fact, of modern industrial society. It is the metaphor of the machine. If one assumes the engine should be running, the silences will indicate failures. Smooth talk is taken as the natural state of the smoothly running cognitive and interactional machine. Notice the absolute confidence in the following statement:

> The natural tendency of human beings to engage in conversation at the slightest provocation—if only a discussion of the weather—is apparent in all cultures and in people of all ages. (Hayes and Cobb 1979:57)

Since the 1960s Hymes has been reminding us that statements of this sort are simply not true (Hymes 1974, Gardner 1966) but it seems difficult for either individuals or researchers to give up the idea of the humming conversational machine.

Another phrasing of the metaphor is given by Siegman (1979b) who believes that 'silent pauses and other hesitation indices in speech provide us with a window to the brain' (p. 177). The industrial metaphor is further advanced by such technical terms as 'productivity' for a reduction in intra-turn pausing in interviews (Siegman 1979a). The normal state of the machine is thought of as a steady hum or buzz, with hesitation or silences indicating trouble, difficulty, missing cogs, and so forth. We see the quality control engineer sitting at a window on the production line overlooking the production of the gross cognitive product as reflected in verbal outputs.

Overall there seem to be two problems here. The first is whether or not the attributions of personality characteristics are correct. The answer to this is both yes and no. One finds it hard to argue with, for example, the self-attributions in the Maryland study, and it is clear that they are intuitively reasonable to the researchers, perhaps to most readers of this volume as well. On the other hand, they are definitely not correct in the case of the so-called 'Silent Indian'. As we have argued elsewhere (Scollon and Scollon 1979a, 1981, Scollon 1980) Athabaskans, at least, are building on a different metaphor. At Fort Chipewyan, Alberta, for instance, 'quiet' is a term for knowledge, control, cooperation, attention to others, and a socially productive attitude. Basso (1979) has passed on to us the views expressed by some Apaches in their portraits of 'Whitemen' of the 'warmhearted', 'talkative', and 'outgoing' qualities as negative values in most contexts.

If we want to continue to believe, as I do, that there are still universal human characteristics that can be spoken of in studies of communication, then what do we do with the apparent fact that differences in pausing lead to one set of attributions in one society and perhaps to a very different or conflicting set of attributions in another? That is, how can silence in conversation be so regular and predictable a phenomenon in terms of turn-exchange or topic control and yet be so differently used and interpreted?

I think the problem here is with the process of attribution itself. Selby (1975) has argued that a fundamental problem with attribution theory in American psychology is that it takes as universal what is essentially a culture-specific phenomenon. Selby suggests that the making of attributions is characteristic of our society and so is reflected ethnocentrically in attribution theory. On another front, Argyris and Schon (1974) have suggested that the behavior model so typical of modern bureaucratic life, which they call Model I, is learned through a process of attribution and social evaluation. This model of behavior seeks to 'define goals and try to achieve them', 'maximize winning and minimize losing', 'minimize generating or experiencing negative feelings', and to be 'rational' (Argyris and Schon 1978:61). These goals lead to designing and managing the environment unilaterally, owning and controlling tasks, unilaterally protecting the self and unilaterally protecting others from being hurt. Argyris and Schon argue that this win/lose mode of behaving is based on a socialization process that emphasizes attributing attitudes, goals, motives, and feelings to others but not making reality checks of those attributions. The self-attributions found by Feldstein, Alberti, and BenDebba (1979) are certainly consistent with this model of behavior which Argyris and Schon (1974, 1978) argue is typical of modern industrial society. I might also suggest that the double-binding of controlling the situation through interpersonal warmth while maintaining unilateral control through the manipulation of switching pauses is a consistent example of this 'Model I' behavior. In any case, this theoretical framework corroborates Selby's suggestion (1975) that attribution itself is a significant aspect of modern industrial society.

On the other side of the coin, Suzanne Scollon (1982) has found that Athabaskan children are socialized not to make attributions as an aspect of a general cognitive and interactive strategy of nonintervention (Scollon and Scollon 1979a). It is generally inappropriate to attribute qualities to Athabaskans and, in this context, it is especially inappropriate having said what I have just said. How can we say then what Athabaskans make of silence? It does seem clear that if Athabaskans regard silence in conversation as significant, it is not because it is heard as the malfunctioning of a machine. Changing the metaphor changes the meaning of silence. Even the process of attribution itself seems to reflect the machine as we imagine both conversationalists and researchers to be tireless engineers drawing inferences from the sounds and silences of the conversational machine. I believe that if we are going to get any further in our understanding of the meaning of silence in conversation, we must first examine the metaphors generating our research and our conversational stance.

REFERENCES

Argyris, Chris and Donald A. Schon. 1974. Theory in practice: Increasing professional effectiveness. San Francisco: Jossey-Bass Publishers.

Argyris, Chris and Donald A. Schon. 1978. Organizational learning: A theory of action perspective. Reading, MA: Addison-Wesley Publishing Company.

Basso, Keith. 1970. To give up on words: Silence in the Western Apache culture. Southwestern Journal of Anthropology 26(3). 213–230.

Basso, Keith. 1979. Portraits of 'The Whiteman'. New York: Cambridge University Press.

Bateson, Gregory. 1972. Steps to an ecology of mind. New York: Ballantine Books.

Beattie, Geoffrey W. 1979. The modifiability of the temporal structure of spontaneous speech, Of speech and time, ed. by Aron W. Siegman & Stanley Feldstein. Hillsdale, NJ: Lawrence Erlbaum Associates.

Beebe, Beatrice, Daniel Stern, and Joseph Jaffe. 1979. The kinesic rhythm of mother-infant interactions, Of speech and time, ed. by Aron W. Siegman & Stanley Feldstein. Hillsdale, NJ: Lawrence Erlbaum Associates.

Bolinger, Dwight. 1979. Metaphorical aggression: Bluenoses and coffin nails, Georgetown University round table on languages and linguistics 1979, ed. by James E. Alatis. Washington DC: Georgetown University Press.

Dunner, D. L., J. L. Fleiss, G. Addonizio, and R. R. Fieve. 1976. Assortative mating in primary affective disorders. Biological Psychiatry, 11.43.

Feldstein, Stanley, Luciano Alberti, and Mohammed BenDebba. 1979. Self-attributed personality chararteristics and the pacing of conversational interaction, Of speech and time, ed. by Aron W. Siegman & Stanley Feldstein. Hillsdale, NJ: Lawrence Erlbaum Associates.

Gardner, Peter. 1966. Symmetric respect and memorate knowledge: The structure and ecology of individualistic culture. Southwestern Journal of Anthropology 22. 389–415.

Goldman-Eisler, Frieda. 1968. Psycholinguistics: Experiments in spontaneous speech. New York: Academic Press.

Hayes, Donald P. and Loren Cobb. 1979. Ultradian biorhythms in social interaction, Of speech and time, ed. by Aron W. Siegman & Stanley Feldstein. Hillsdale, NJ: Lawrence Erlbaum Associates.

Hippler, Arthur, E., L. Bryce Boyer, and Ruth M. Boyer. 1978. Tanaina ethnopsychiatry, past and present: A reflection of cultural personality dynamics. Internord, No. 15. 117–123.

Hymes, Dell. 1974. Foundations in sociolinguistics. Philadelphia: University of Pennsylvania Press.

Kleinfeld, Judith. 1973. Using nonverbal warmth to increase learning: A cross-cultural experiment. Fairbanks, AL: Institute of Social, Economic and Government Research.

Marcus, E. S., J. Welkowitz, S. Feldstein, and J. Jaffe. 1970. Psychological differentiation and the congruence of temporal speech patterns. Paper presented at the meeting of the Eastern Psychological Association, Atlantic City, NJ, April 1970.

Matarazzo, Joseph D. and Arthur N. Wiens. 1972. The interview: Research on its anatomy and structure. Chicago: Aldine-Atherton.

Natale, M., C. Dahlberg, and J. Jaffe. 1979. The effect of psychotomimetics on therapist-patient matching of speech 'rhythms'. Journal of Communication Disorders 12 (1). 45–52.

Pope, B. and Aron W. Siegman. 1968. Interviewer warmth in relation to interviewee verbal behavior. Journal of Consulting and Clinical Psychology, 32(5). 588–595.

Reddy, Michael J. 1979. The conduit metaphor—A case of frame conflict in our language about language. Metaphor and thought, ed. by Andrew Ortony. New York: Cambridge University Press.

Sabin, Edward J., Edward J. Clemmer, Daniel C. O'Connell, and Sabine Kowal. 1979. A pausological approach to speech development. Of speech and time, ed. by Aron W. Siegman & Stanley Feldstein. Hillsdale, NJ: Lawrence Erlbaum Associates.

Sacks, Harvey, Emanuel A. Schegloff, and Gail Jefferson. 1974. A simplest systematics for the organization of turn taking for conversation. Language 50 (4). 696–735.

Schegloff, Emanuel. 1972. Sequencing in conversational openings, Directions in sociolinguistics, ed. by John Gumperz & Dell Hymes. New York: Holt, Rinehart & Winston.

Schon, Donald A. 1979. Generative metaphor: A perspective on problem-setting in social policy, Metaphor and thought, ed. by Andrew Ortony. New York: Cambridge University Press.

Scollon, Ron. 1980. Communicative style and research style: A problem in discovery, application, and reportage. Paper presented at the 40th Annual Meeting of the Society for Applied Anthropology, March 19–22, Denver, Colorado.

Scollon, Ron and Suzanne B. K. Scollon. 1979a. Linguistic convergence: An ethnography of speaking at Fort Chipewyan, Alberta. New York: Academic Press.

Scollon, Ron and Suzanne B. K. Scollon. 1979b. Literacy as interethnic communication: An Athabaskan case. Working Papers in Sociolinguistics, No. 59. Austin: Southwest Educational Development Laboratory.

Scollon, Ron and Suzanne B. K. Scollon. 1981. Narrative, literacy and face in interethnic communication. Norwood, NJ: Ablex.

Scollon, Ron and Suzanne B. K. Scollon. 1983. Face in interethnic communication, Language and Communication, ed. by Jack Richards & Richard Schmidt. London: Longman.

Scollon, Suzanne B. K. 1982. Socialization to non-intervention and its relation to linguistic structure. Doctoral dissertation, Department of Linguistics, University of Hawaii.

Selby, Henry A. 1975. Semantics and casuality in the study of deviance, Sociocultural dimensions of language use, ed. by Mary Sanches & Ben C. Blount. New York, Academic Press.

Siegman, Aron W. 1979a. The voice of attraction: Vocal correlates of interpersonal attraction in the interview, Of speech and time, ed. by Aron W. Siegman & Stanley Feldstein. Hillsdale, NJ: Lawrence Erlbaum Associates.

Siegman, Aron W. 1979b. Cognition and hesitation in speech, Of speech and time, ed. by Aron W. Siegman & Stanley Feldstein. Hillsdale, NJ: Lawrence Erlbaum Associates.

Siegman, Aron W. and Stanley Feldstein. 1979. Of speech and time. Hillsdale, NJ: Lawrence Erlbaum Associates.

Siegman, Aron W. and B. Pope. 1967. The effects of alcohol on verbal productivity and fluency. Paper presented at the annual meeting of the Eastern Psychological Association, Boston, April 1967.

Siegman, Aron W. and B. Pope. 1972. The effects of ambiguity and anxiety on interviewee verbal behavior, Studies in dyadic communication, ed. by A. W. Siegman & B. Pope. New York: Pergamon Press.

Stokoe, William C. 1979. Language and the deaf experience, Georgetown University round table on languages and linguistics 1979, ed. by James L. Alatis. Washington, DC: Georgetown University Press.

Tannen, Deborah. 1984. Conversational style: Analyzing talk among friends. Norwood, NJ: Ablex.

Welkowitz, J., C. Cariffe, and S. Feldstein. 1976. Conversational congruence as a criterion of socialization in children. Child Development, 47. 269–272.

Whorf, Benjamin. 1941. The relation of habitual thought and behavior to language, Language, culture, and personality: Essays in memory of Edward Sapir, ed. by Leslie Spier. Menasha, WI: Sapir Memorial Publication Fund.

Witkin, H. A., R. B. Dyk. H. F. Faterson, D. R. Goodenough, and S. A. Karp. 1974. Psychological differentiation. Hillsdale, NJ: Lawrence Erlbaum Associates.

Chapter 3

Psychological Correlates of Silence and Sound in Conversational Interaction

Cynthia L. Crown
University of Delaware
Stanley Feldstein
University of Maryland Baltimore County

This is an odd chapter in a book concerned primarily with anthropological and linguistic approaches to the meaning of silence. In this chapter, the silences and sounds of conversational interactions are considered psychological variables. Anthropological and psychological approaches are differentiated by the types of questions they raise and by the methods they use to address the questions. Here, the questions asked about the silences and sounds of conversation and the methods used to answer those questions reflect, in great part, the traditions and assumptions of psychology.

In its broadest sense, psychology may be considered a science of individual behavior. In their attempts to account for the variability of behavior, psychologists have usually focused on issues of development, learning, cognition, personality, social interaction, and psychopathology. These and other issues have become major 'areas' of psychological inquiry, and questions appropriate to them are typically explored within laboratory settings on the assumption that confident decisions of causality depend upon careful control of 'extraneous' variables. The research reviewed in this chapter has its roots in this psychological tradition. However, much of it is exploratory and thus has not incorporated all the controls that ultimately may prove necessary. Moreover, the research has not stayed within the boundaries of a particular area of psychology, but has examined the functioning of a specific behavioral structure from the perspective of several areas. It should also be noted that the studies reviewed here are limited primarily to those conducted by the authors and their colleagues and students. Within the past decade or so, other investigators have begun to ask similar questions about the same and similar behavioral structures, and much of their work is reviewed by Feldstein and Welkowitz (1978), Matarazzo and Wiens (1972), and Rosenfeld (1978).

The behavioral structure to which we refer is the chronographic patterning of conversation, or the pacing of speech sounds and silences in dialogues. It was the anthropologist Eliot Chapple (1939) who initiated the study of what he called 'interaction chronography', or the timing of 'actions' and 'inactions' (speech silences as well as kinesic 'silences') in an interpersonal encounter. Conversation chronography, on the other hand, is limited to speech sounds and silences. An underlying expectation of research in conversation chronography is that the impressions interactants form of one another are influenced, at least in part, by the flow, or pattern, of the sounds and silences in which the lexical message is embedded. It is also expected that the timing of these sounds and silences communicates somthing about the personalities of the interacting speakers as well as something about their relationship. For the purpose of testing these expectations, Jaffe and Feldstein (1970), Feldstein and Welkowitz (1978), and Feldstein, BenDebba, and Alberti (1974) developed a model designed to describe conversational pacing objectively. The model segments the conversational speech stream into five empirically defined categories or parameters: *speaking turns, vocalizations, pauses, switching pauses,* and *simultaneous speech* (Table 3.1).

Conversations are analyzed by the Automatic Vocal Transaction Analyzer, or AVTA (Jaffe & Feldstein, 1970). AVTA does not require the use of a human observer. It is essentially a threshold device that considers any sound above the threshold (set by the investigator on the basis of voice and situational factors) to be speech and any sound below it to be silence. It includes a component that thus 'perceives' the verbal behavior of each participant in an autiotaped or ongoing dialogue simply as a sequence of sounds and silences. The component is an analog-to-digital converter but includes a cancellation network that electronically cancels the spill of each speaker's voice into the other speaker's microphone. The component functions by 'inquiring', at a rate of from 100 to 1000 msec., about whether each of the speakers is talking or silent. The inquiry rates that have been used most often in the past have been 100 and 300 msec . The information about the speakers is transmitted to a computer component of the system that provides a record of the digitized sound-silence sequence and descriptive statistics summarizing the parameter values derived from them (see Jaffe and Feldstein 1970, and Feldstein and Welkowitz 1978 for details of parameter reliabilities and interrelationships).

TABLE 3.1
DEFINITIONS OF THE PARAMETERS OF CONVERSATION CHRONOGRAPHY

1. A *speaking turn* begins the instant one of the speakers in an interaction begins talking alone and ends immediately prior to the instant the other speaker starts talking alone. Thus, a *turn* is the interval between two successive speaker switches.

2. A *vocalization* is a segment of sound (speech) uninterrupted by any discernible silence and uttered by the speaker who has the turn (or floor), and it is credited to him/her.

3. A *pause* is an interval of joint silence bounded by the vocalizations of the speaker who has the turn, and is therefore credited to him/her.

4. A *switching pause* is an interval of joint silence that is initiated by the speaker who has the turn, or floor, and terminated by the other speaker, who thereby obtains the floor. Thus, it marks a change of speakers and, inasmuch as it occurs within the turn of the speaker by whom it is initiated, it is credited to him/her.

5. *Simultaneous speech* is speech uttered by a speaker who does not have the floor during a vocalization by the speaker who does have the floor.
    a. *Interruptive simultaneous speech* is part of a speech segment that begins while the speaker who has the floor is talking and ends after he has stopped. Only that portion uttered while the other speaker is talking is considered simultaneous speech.
    b. *Noninterruptive simultaneous speech* begins and ends while the speaker who has the floor is talking.

Feldstein and Welkowitz 1978

SOUND-SILENCE CORRELATES OF PERSONALITY

Many studies have focused on the relation between personality traits and the voice (e.g. Kramer 1963; Siegman 1978), although most of the earlier ones were marred by such methodological problems as the use of poorly validated external criteria and inadequate observer preparation. During the 1960s, the focus of such research shifted from the early holistic approach of relating the voice per se to personality to that of determining whether there are objective characteristics of speech that are related to personality attributes. It is from this latter perspective that we conducted two studies that examined the relation between the sound-silence patterns of speech and the personality variable, *extraversion*. The variable is usually discussed in terms of its poles, introversion and extraversion.

People frequently characterize others and even themselves as introverts or extraverts on the basis of their notions about how the variable translates into behavior. It is, in fact, one of the few personality variables that much research has shown to have specific vocal correlates. It has been suggested, however, that the relation between extraversion and vocal behavior is a function of the stereotypes people have about extraversion. The possibility that the relationship is a function of stereotypes made it important that further research concerned with associations between extraversion and features of the voice must distinguish those based upon stereotyped expectations from actual associations. This distinction was investigated in the following experiment.

Speech Tempo and Extraversion

Feldstein and Sloan (1984) designed an experiment to examine speech tempo as determined by stereotyped notions of extraversion as well as the actual speech tempo of extraverts and introverts. This distinction between the actual vocal behavior of extraverts and introverts and stereotyped notions of their vocal behavior was obtained by the use of role playing. That is, individuals were asked to talk as if they were extraverts and introverts and it was expected—on the basis of prior research with and popular images of extraverts and introverts—that they speak faster when role-playing extraverts than when role-playing introverts. It was also expected, on the basis of theory, that people who can be characterized as extraverts speak faster than those who can be considered introverts.

The participants of the study were 46 American-born, white, female, college undergraduates who were selected on the basis of their scores on the Extraversion Scale of the Eysenck Personality Inventory (Eysenck and Eysenck 1963). Each participant took part in five conditions. In each condition, she was asked to tell a story about one or more of three cards from the Thematic Apperception Test, or TAT (Murray 1938). In the first condition, she simply told a story. In each of the second and third conditions, she listened to a recorded description of an introvert or an extravert. The descriptions were taken from the manual of the Eysenck Personality Inventory and were modified to exclude how introverts and extraverts talked. Following each description, the participant was asked to tell a story as a person who fit the description might tell it. (The order of the two conditions was counterbalanced.) The last two conditions tested whether the participant was, in fact, capable of changing her speech tempo deliberately; in one she was asked to speak slowly, in the other to speak rapidly.

Speech tempo was indexed by the ratio of the probability of continuing to talk (while talking) to the probability of continuing to pause (while silent). The two probabilities are easily derived from the pause and vocalization parameters yielded by the AVTA system, and their ratio has been shown to be highly correlated with words per minute (Feldstein 1976), the usual measure of speech rate. The results clearly supported the hypothesis that extraverts talk faster than introverts. They also supported the expectation that both extraverts and introverts talk faster when they play the role of extraverts than when they play the role of introverts. What is especially interesting, however, is that when the extraverts role-played extraverts, they talked faster than the introverts when the latter role-played extraverts, and when the extraverts role-played introverts, they talked faster than the introverts when the latter role-played introverts. Thus, the study quite nicely distinguished between the actual speech tempo of extraverts and introverts and the tempo associated with the stereotypes of extraverts and introverts.

On the other hand, this study, as all previous studies of extraversion, involved only monologues. Most natural speech, however, occurs within dialogues. What needed to be examined, therefore, was the influence of extraversion upon the sound-silence patterns of conversation. This was the issue addressed in the second study of extraversion (Feldstein and Crown 1978).

Extraversion and Conversational Time Patterns

The participants of the study were both white and black college students. Interestingly, no previous study of extraversion had ever used, or reported using, black participants. Moreover, no previous study appeared to have examined systematically the possibility of gender differences in the expression of extraversion. Of our white participants, 43 were men and 53 were women; of the black participants, 24 were men and 50 were women.

The participants were asked to come to the laboratory in prearranged pairs, or dyads, that represented all possible combinations of race and gender. In most of the dyads, the members did not know each other and in the rest, they were not more than passing acquaintances. As in the previous study, each person was asked to complete the Eysenck Personality Inventory, after which the members of each pair were asked to engage in a 20-minute conversation that would help them get to know each other better. When their conversation was finished, they were each asked to describe themselves and each other in terms of a set of 20 adjective scales, the purpose of which we will explain presently. The recorded conversations were processed by the AVTA system.

The results of the study were surprising. Contrary to the prior study, no simple relationships were found between extraversion and the conversational time patterns of the participants. The ways in which the introverts and extraverts paced their sounds and silences depended upon their race and, to a lesser extent, their gender. It was only among the blacks, for example, that the expected relation between extraversion and speech was obtained: black extraverts used faster speech tempos than did black introverts. It is not clear why the white participants did not behave vocally in the ways in which white introverts and extraverts have in previous studies of extraversion involving the use of monologues. It is not clear whether the differences that occurred are a function of the whites having engaged in dialogues, per se, or of having engaged in dialogues with persons of another gender and race. These questions could not be answered by the data of the study because not enough participants could be obtained to provide the number of dyads of each race and gender combination that would be needed to make the implied comparisons. What is clear is this: Extraversion as a personality attribute has sparked a very large amount of psychological research and is thought to be one of the few personality characteristics predictably related to various expressive behaviors. It is important, therefore, to further investigate whether or not the behavioral expression of extraversion is dependent upon race and gender.

We have been talking about speech tempo and the two components of tempo are speech sounds and silences (Feldstein 1976). It is the silences, however—particularly the pauses—that form the more important component. The analysis of pauses in the first study (Feldstein and Sloan, 1984) found them almost mirroring the tempo results whereas the analysis of the vocalizations showed them to be much less sensitive. The same is true in the second study described above. Indeed, estimates of the stability of pauses and vocalizations (Jaffe and Feldstein 1970; Feldstein and Welkowitz 1978) suggest that the durations of pauses are much more likely to be susceptible to the influences of situational, personal, and interpersonal attributes than are vocalizations.

Psychological Differentiation and the Matching of Silences

Another study (Marcus, Welkowitz, Feldstein, and Jaffe 1970) examined changes in silence in the interactions of individuals who varied in degrees of *psychological differentiation* (Witkin, Dyk, Faterson, Goodenough, and Karp 1962) and in the personality characteristics indexed by the Cattell Sixteen Personality Factor questionnaire (Cattell, Eber, and Tatsuoka 1970). Psychological differentiation essentially refers to the tendency of individuals to respond differentially to internal and external cues. Those persons who are more psychologically differentiated have been found to be more responsive to internal and less responsive to external cues than are less differentiated individuals. The latter are more responsive to, interested in, and aware of other persons in interpersonal contacts, and are more likely to be influenced by other persons. The characteristics associated with the Cattell Sixteen Personality Factor Questionnaire are rather complex and will be discussed in context with the pertinent findings.

The study examined the verbal exchanges of 24 female college students who have been divided into six equally sized groups. The design of the study required that each participant in a group meet with each of the other three participants in the group on eight consecutive occasions. On each occasion, the two participants spent 30 minutes talking together, the purpose of which was to help them get to know one another. Thus, each woman engaged in three conversations on each of the eight occasions.

The first hypothesis of the study was that women characterized by a greater degree of psychological differentiation (i.e. more sensitive to internal cues) are less likely to achieve conversational congruence. Congruence is defined as the occurrence of similar intensity, frequency, or durational values for the two participants in a conversation on one or more of the parameters that index temporal patterning. Conversational congruence, then, implies a susceptibility to interpersonal influence in terms primarily of the temporal and vocal dimensions of speech. It may be considered an aspect of the more inclusive notion of interpersonal accommodation (e.g., Crown and Feldstein 1981; Thakerar, Giles, and Cheshire 1982). Interpersonal accommodation is concerned with not only the convergence and divergence of temporal patterns but also of such other aspects of speech as pitch, accent, and even linguistic constructions. In any case, the rationale for the hypothesis was that psychologically more differentiated individuals tend to be more aloof and less gregarious than less differentiated persons and are, therefore, less likely to be susceptible to interpersonal influence and achieve congruence in their conversations with others.

The analyses provided no evidence of any relationship between degree of psychological differentiation and changes in the vocalization durations used by the participants in the 36 dyads on each occasion. However, support for the hypothesis came from changes in the two types of silence used in the conversations. It was found that the more highly differentiated women tended not to match the pause durations of their partners. There was, in other words, an inverse relation between pauses, congruence, and degree of differentiation. The analysis of the switching pauses yielded results that were somewhat more complex. The relation between switching-pause congruence and psychological differentiation was such that although the degree of congruence achieved by the more differentiated participants was not markedly influenced by the degree of differentiation of their conversational partners, the less differentiated participants achieved a greater degree of switching-pause congruence, or accommodation, with partners who were less differentiated than with partners who were more differentiated. The results make good sense, given the other interpersonal characteristics associated with psychological differentiation. The results also demonstrate that it is the silence in the temporal structure of conversation that reflects the participants' degrees of psychological differentiation.

Self-Attributed Personality Characteristics

Apart from psychological differentiation, the study was also concerned with the relations between the speakers' pacing of the conversational interactions and the personality characteristics they attribute to themselves (Feldstein, Alberti, and BenDebba 1979). The characteristics investigated were those dimensions measured by Cattell's Sixteen Personality Factor Questionnaire (Cattell, Eber, and Tatsuoka 1970), or the 16 PFQ. The 16 PFQ was first published in 1949 and since that time has undergone extensive investigation with regard to the reliabilities and validities of its scales and their applicability in different types of contexts. The Questionnaire consists of 16 factor-analyzed scales considered by Cattell and his associates to index what they call 'personality source traits', which have been found to be dimensions of personality that operate across all age ranges and, to a great extent, cross-culturally. The *Handbook* of the 16 PFQ stresses the importance of using the entire Questionnaire rather than a selection of its scales. The importance of the 16 PFQ for the study we are describing is that it provided a reliable method for obtaining the participants' self-attributions.

Rather than report the results in terms of the formal dimensions delineated by Cattell and his associates, we describe them in terms of those adjectives that have been used to characterize the dimensions. Perhaps the major and most intriguing finding of the study was the revelation that: (1) the average duration of turns, vocalizations, pauses, and switching pauses, and the frequencies of simultaneous speech are a function not only of the self-attributed personality traits of the speakers who produced them but also of the traits of the persons with whom they are speaking; and (2) the extent to which the traits of each interactant are responsible for his or her parameter durations and frequencies and those of the other interactant appears to depend, at least in part, upon the topography of the parameters. For example, the duration of a vocalization is dependent solely upon the traits of the speaker who uttered it. Persons who might be considered easygoing, assertive, talkative, enthusiastic, unsentimental, and group dependent tend to produce the longer vocalizations. The duration of a pause seems also to be determined primarily by the characteristics of the person who produces the pause—primarily but not completely. The longer pauses tend to be produced by individuals who can be described as distrustful, easily upset, worrying, shy, suspicious, troubled, fussy, and driven, but also self-sufficient and resourceful. However, the duration is also somewhat determined by the listener such that those who are precise, skeptical, self-reliant, unsentimental, and practical, but also somewhat careless about social rules, tend to elicit the longer pauses.

Pauses and vocalizations, at least topographically, depend only upon the person who produces them in the sense that they are the two temporal events that occur in a monologue. It might be expected that they are less susceptible to the influences of the listener than are switching pauses and speaking turns. The later two parameters are clearly dyadic events; they do not exist in a monologue. Recall that the switching pause is terminated by the person who does not have the floor, that is, by the person who was considered the listener until he or she terminated the switching pause and acquired the floor. It should not, then, be surprising to discover that the durations of switching pauses are affected at least as much by the traits of the listener as by those of the speaker. Speakers who tend to have the longer switching pauses are described by the *Handbook* (Cattell, Eber, and Tatsuoka 1970) as aloof, rigid, and prone to sulk, but also as indolent, self-indulgent, and undependable. Their partners also tend to be aloof, critical, and rigid, as well as changeable, insecure, troubled, tense, frustrated, and fretful.

Most surprising, perhaps, is that the average durations of speaking turns are influenced wholly by the personality attributes of the listener and not at all by those of the speaker. That is, speakers seem to use longer turns when their conversational partners are reserved, detached, taciturn, sober, timid, and restrained than when they are warm-hearted, participating, talkative, cheerful, adventurous, and socially bold. Partners who are, in addition, forthright and unpretentious also elicit longer turns than partners who are astute and worldly.

The shift in responsibility for the parameter durations from the speaker him- or herself, in the case of vocalizations, to the conversational partner in great part, in the case of switching pauses, is reflected in a different way in previous research concerned with the type of interpersonal influence we have called temporal congruence, or accommodation. The prior studies (Feldstein and Welkowitz 1978) have demonstrated that conversational participants tend to match the average durations of each other's pauses and switching pauses, but not of each other's vocalizations. However, they also suggest that the matching of switching-pause durations occurs more readily than that of pause durations and occurs earlier developmentally (Welkowitz, Cariffe, and Feldstein 1976). The interpersonal matching of speaking turns has not yet been investigated.

Like vocalizations, simultaneous speech does not involve any silence. However, the analysis of simultaneous speech in this study yielded results that are worth noting. Unlike the durations of vocalizations, the frequencies with which simultaneous speech were initiated were influenced by the attributes of the speakers who initiated them as well as by the attributes of their conversational partners. Women who saw themselves as relaxed, complacent, secure, and not overly dependent upon the approval of others tended to initiate more simultaneous speech than women who considered themselves to be generally apprehensive, self-reproaching, tense, and frustrated. But apart from their own characteristics, women tended to initiate more simultaneous speech when they spoke with others who viewed themselves as cooperative, attentive, emotionally mature, and talkative than with those who saw themselves as aloof, critical, emotionally labile, introspective, silent, and self-sufficient.

The most surprising aspect of the results was that none of the self-attributed personality characteristics, or traits, were related to the *outcome* of simultaneous speech, that is, to whether the simultaneous speech was interruptive or noninterruptive. It would seem more likely that the outcome, rather than just the initiation of simultaneous speech, is influenced by personality attributes. Perhaps such attributes become important to the outcome in conversations that are task-oriented or argumentative rather than informal and casual.

INTERPERSONAL PERCEPTION

Concern with interpersonal perception dates from the beginnings of social psychology and continues to generate abundant research (Schneider, Hastorf, and Ellsworth 1979). Indeed, for those interested in the person within the social context, interpersonal perception is a central process that seems to touch all aspects of psychological functioning. Early research in person perception was much concerned with accuracy of perception, that is, the accuracy with which judges were able to assess various aspects of a stimulus person. This research essentially failed, but did shift the direction of research in the area. Specifically, it became increasingly apparent that accuracy of perception was not expecially relevant to the functions and consequences of interpersonal perception. Perceivers tend to act in terms of their judgments whether or not the latter are accurate. Theory and research shifted to the process of person perception and the factors that meaningfully impinge upon that process.

As was mentioned earlier, an assumption of conversation chronography is that the pacing of the silences and sounds in the conversational stream influences the perceptions that the interactants form about one another. Moreover, such influence may be so much a part of the human experience that it goes undetected, that is, it may operate outside the awareness of the perceiver. Thus, we have conducted a series of studies that has examined the role of temporal patterning in interpersonal perception.

Induced Impressions
The earliest study (Welkowitz and Feldstein 1969) in the series was an experiment designed to explore the effect of induced interpersonal per-

ception on temporal congruence, or accommodation. Both intuitively, and on the basis of data (Marcus, Welkowitz, Feldstein, and Jaffe 1970) that revealed a relationship between interpersonal attraction and accommodation, it seemed reasonable that the interpersonal perceptions of dyad members would influence the degree to which the matched each other's time patterns. Thus, the experiment attempted to manipulate the extent to which the participants in a conversation perceived each other's 'personality' as similar.

The persons who volunteered to participate in the experiment were asked to complete a battery of personality inventories. They were then randomly assembled into 40 dyads and divided into three groups. In one group of 15 dyads, the members of each dyad were told that they had been paired with each other because the results of their personality tests indicated that they were very much alike. In a second group of 15 dyads, the members of each dyad were told that their test performance had shown that they were different from each other. The participants in each of the remaining 10 dyads were told that they had been randomly paired. In addition, the participants in each group were informed that the purpose of the study was to determine 'how people who are similar (dissimilar, or randomly paired) get to know each other'.

The members of a dyad were seated in separate soundproof rooms between which only verbal communication was possible. They were then instructed to engage in a 60-minute conversation for the purpose of getting to know one another. They then met for two subsequent conversations at weekly intervals.

Averaged over the three conversations, the results showed that the randomly paired dyads did not match the average durations of their pauses or switching pauses. The conversations of the other two groups, however, exhibited some evidence of such matching although only in the case of the switching pauses of the 'similar' group was the coefficient that indexes accommodation statistically significant. The lack of significant pause accommodation for the similar group, and pause and switching-pause accommodation for the dissimilar group may have been a function of inadequate statistical power (given the relatively small number of dyads) or an actual lack of accommodation. The results were sufficiently interesting to warrant replication. A subsequent study (Welkowitz and Feldstein 1970), that provided both a replication and extension, used 20 dyads in each group and found significant accommodation to have occurred in the cases of pauses and switching pauses for the similar and dissimilar groups but not for the random group. The point of the experiment, however, was to compare the influence upon accommodation of actual differences in degree of psychological differentiation of the dyad members with the influence of induced differences in their perceptions of each other's personality. The results of the experiment suggested that conversationalists' *perceptions* of each other's personality are more important to achieving accommodation than are those characteristics of their *actual* personalities that are represented by the construct, psychological differentiation.

Positive and Negative Impressions

The next study of interpersonal perception (Feldstein and Crown 1979) that we conducted used data from the investigation of extraversion and conversational time patterns described earlier. The purpose of the study was to explore the relations between the conversational time patterns and interpersonal perception. However, the study incorporated an unusual feature. The perceptions were truly interpersonal; they were the perceptions of two individuals about one another after actually speaking together and they were, therefore, quite likely to be different from one pair to another. Most previous studies of person perception had used the judgments of one or more groups of observers who had never been involved with, nor had even known, the stimulus person or persons. We were not certain that the strategy of using the perceptions of dyad members about each other could yield, over many dyads, stable relationships.

Recall that the participants of the dyads were asked to describe themselves and their conversational partners in terms of a set of 20 seven-point, bipolar adjective scales. Our concern in this first study was only with the participants' perceptions of each other. Each of the 20 scales was scored in terms of the degree to which it was positive or negative, with the score of 1 being the most positive, the score of 7 being the most negative, and the score of 4 being neutral. The total score used to describe an individual was the sum of the 20 scales scores. Thus, a score of 20 was the most positive obtainable and a score of 140 was the most negative obtainable.

The findings of the study indicated that the perceptions of the conversationalists were complexly related to the temporal patterns of their verbal exchanges primarily as a function of their race and gender. White men and black women were described more negatively when the likelihood of their pausing was high rather than low. White women, on the other hand, were described in more positive ways the more likely they were to continue pausing. The perception of black men did not seem to be affected by the probability of their pauses. Again, white men and black women were viewed more negatively the more probable it was that their switching pauses would continue while, for the same behavior, black men and white women were viewed more positively. Still another finding was that white men and black women were perceived in more positive ways when they spoke faster rather than slower. However, when black men spoke faster they were described in more negative ways, and the description of the white women was not influenced by their speech rate.

The results are important for two reasons. First, they indicate that conversational silences did influence interpersonal perception, although whether the attributes they elicited were positive or negative seemed to depend upon the race and gender of the person being perceived. A relevant finding, which had to do with the self-perceptions of the participants, was that, regardless of race or gender, speakers who were more likely to continue pausing evaluated *themselves* in a more negative direction than did speakers who were less likely to do so. Speech rate also affected interpersonal perception and in equally complex ways. An especially interesting aspect of the findings is that the participants' impressions seemed to link white men with black women and, to a lesser degree, black men with white women. That is, the direction of the impressions elicited by silences and speech rate was the same for white men and black women, but only that elicited by speech rate was the same for black men and white women. However, the direction of their impressions of white men and black women differed from that of their impressions of black men and white women! It is not clear why such linking emerged but it is certainly an issue worth pursuing in further studies.

The second reason for the importance of the results is that they demonstrate the possibility of obtaining reliable information about the relations between conversational time patterns and interpersonal impressions from a laboratory context—conversational interaction—that is very similar to the actual context in which such impressions are usually formed. It can, of course, be argued that the context involved many other vocal and verbal cues that may have served as mediators of the relationships found in the study. The problem is discussed further elsewhere (Feldstein 1982) and the results of at least one important study by Hayes and his associates (1977) suggest that the obtained relationships are primary. The study showed that the characteristics attributed by observers to a pair of flashing lights that depicted the time patterns of two persons in a conversation were very similar to those they attributed to the actual conversation.

Impressions within Interviews

Still another study (Crown, 1982) involved the use of interviews rather than unconstrained conversations. It also utilized a somewhat complicated paradigm because it was intended to serve several purposes. One purpose, of course, was to further examine the role of speech sounds and silences in impression formation, this time within the context of interviews. Another was to investigate the effects of an interviewer's demeanor on the vocal behavior of an interviewee as well as on his or her impressions. A third purpose was to examine the influence of topic intimacy on impressions and speech patterns.

The interviewees were 63 females undergraduates and the interviewers were five women in their second year of graduate study in a community-clinical psychology program. Thus, each of the interviewers conducted either 12 or 13 interviews, each with a different interviewee. Although the interviews were structured, they were only moderately constrained in that they included not only predetermined questions but also spontaneous questions based upon specific remarks of the interviewees. Part of the structure of the interview was the type of demeanor it required of the interviewer. Another part was the type of questions that had to be asked. Specifically, an interviewer behaved towards an interviewee in a manner that was (1) warm, or (2) cold, or (3) warm followed by cold within the same interview, or (4) cold followed by warm within the same interview. Different interviewees were assigned to these four conditions. Moreover, in each interview, half of the questions were intimate and half were not intimate.

Because the interactions were interviews rather than conversations, the parameter, *switching pauses,* was not used in the study. Instead, the measure called *latencies* was used. A latency is topographically identical to a switching pause but its value is assigned to the person by whom it is terminated. The reason for the change is that it is assumed that in an interview (and particularly in the interviews in this study) it is clear when the interviewer has finished his or her remarks.

The results were complex and are difficult to report simply, but they may be summarized by describing the ways in which interviewers with specific sound-silence patterns were likely to be perceived. The interviewers seen as self-assured, persevering, purposeful, and reflective were those who, in the 'cold' interviews, tended to have short vocalizations and to ask nonintimate questions. They were perceived in the same ways in the 'warm' interviews when they had longer vocalizations regardless of whether they asked intimate or nonintimate questions. Those interviewers who were viewed as responsible, exact, mature, articulate, and scholarly, asked nonintimate questions in the 'cold-to-warm' interviews and had long latencies, or asked nonintimate questions in the 'warm-to-cold' interviews and had short latencies. The interviewers were perceived to be conscientious when they behaved warmly and had long vocalizations or when they asked intimate questions and had brief vocalizations.

There are at least two important conclusions to be drawn from the experiment. First, the results confirm the finding of the prior study that the sound-silence patterns of verbal interactions influence interpersonal perception. Note, however, that in this study pauses do not appear to have played an important role and vocalizations were considerably more influential than in the prior study.

A second implication is that contextual factors modify the influence of interactional sounds and silences. The characteristics attributed to the interviewers, for example, depended not simply on their sound-silence patterns, but also on the type of questions they asked and on whether their behavior was warm or cold. Combined, the two studies suggest that both contextual and demographic variables need to be considered in studies that further explore the relations between temporal speech patterns and impression formation.

Similarity of Interpersonal Impressions

As part of a larger study comparing the conversational time patterns of Chinese and Canadian speakers (Feldstein, Hennessy, and Bond 1981) an effort was made to explore the relation between the extent to which the participants in a conversation match the time patterns of their speech and the degree to which they perceive each other in similar ways.

The 22 Canadian undergraduate men who participated in the study were randomly assembled into dyads and asked to engage in two 12-minute conversations for the purpose of getting acquainted with each other. After the conversations, each member of the dyads was asked to describe his partner in terms of a set of 25 bipolar, 6-point adjective scales drawn from a larger set of scales developed by Goldberg (1977).

The analyses of the data first established that the dyad members matched their pause and switching-pause durations. Then three sets of absolute differences were obtained and compared. The first set consisted of the absolute differences between the average pause durations of the conversational partners; the second, between their average switching-pause durations; and the third, between the partners' ratings of each other on each of the 25 adjective scales, summed over the 25 scales. Note that the smaller the absolute differences, the more similar were the partners' pauses and switching pauses and the ways in which they perceived each other. Comparisons of the pause and switching-pause differences with the differences between the partners' ratings of each other yielded quite significant correlation coefficients.

The most general implication of the results is that participants in a conversation who have or achieve similar durations of silences tend to also perceive each other in similar ways. It should be noted, at least in passing, that the obtained relations are between actual behavior (pauses and switching pauses) and paper-and-pencil behavior (adjective ratings).

Impressions of Interruptive and Noninterruptive Behavior

A subsequent analysis of data from a study described earlier (Feldstein and Crown 1979) was concerned with the effects of simultaneous speech on interpersonal behavior (Crown, Feldstein, and Bond 1982). It may be recalled (Table 3.1) that there are two types of simultaneous speech that are distinguished by their outcome, that is, interruptive and noninterruptive simultaneous speech. Our expectation was that interruptive speech may be experienced as a violation of polite interaction and elicit negative impressions while noninterruptive speech may be perceived as support and reinforcement and thereby lead to the formation of positive impressions.

Again, the findings indicated that the impressions elicited by a speaker's temporal patterns depended also upon the speaker's gender and race. Positive impressions were found to be related to the tendency for white men to engage in noninterruptive simultaneous speech, for white women to engage in interruptive simultaneous speech, and for blacks to engage in neither type of simultaneous speech.

That noninterruptive speech of the white men and interruptive speech of the white women were viewed as positive seems somewhat counterintuitive. It may be that the white women who engaged in such interruptive speech were thought to be assertive rather than impolite, and that the assertiveness of white females may be a quality of which college students approve. For white men, however, noninterruptive simultaneous speech may be viewed as supportive and as expressing interest and, therefore, worthy of approbation. That the blacks, whether male or female, only tended to be viewed positively by other blacks and whites when the former refrained from interruptions of any kind is open to several imaginable interpretations.

CURRENT AND FUTURE DIRECTIONS

We have thus far reviewed those studies that address some of the basic expectations underlying the investigation of conversational time patterns. It is clear that many more experimental tests need to be conducted before we can unequivocally describe the role of such patterns in personality and interpersonal perception. Not surprisingly, independent manipulation of the temporal parameters is exceedingly difficult and expensive. However, an experiment by Furr and Feldstein that is in progress has manipulated the frequencies of interruptive and noninterruptive simultaneous speech in four dialogues and is investigating the effects of the manipulation upon observers' perceptions of the dialogue participants. Nevertheless, our own work and that of other investigators (Feldstein and Welkowitz 1978) do seem to indicate that the temporal structure of a conversation embodies a set of important psychological parameters. Of late, investigations of this behavioral structure have taken a number of directions that represent not only a concern for generalizability, but also for measurement adequacy and practical application.

Measurement of Accommodation

The measurement of accommodation, or congruence, or convergence—all refer to the same process—has usually involved many dyads. Specifically, it was measured by comparing an average parameter value of one member of each of a group of dyads with that of the other member of each of those dyads. The procedure has at least two important limitations. The first is that although it allows for the measurement of convergence or the lack of it, it is unable to measure divergence. The second limitation is that it is unable to provide a measure of the degree of convergence or divergence within a single dialogue. These limitations make it impossible to discover whether there are individuals whose temporal patterns diverge during the course of conversations and/or to investigate issues that are best examined within the context of single dyads.

A solution to this measurement problem was recently proposed by Cappella (1979), who recommended the use of a time series regression (TSR), a technique more commonly used by econometricians.

It may be helpful for us to provide a very brief notion of how TSR can be used to measure accommodation within a dialogue. The dialogue is divided into a sequence of time units, for example, one-minute units. The parameters' values within each of the time units are averaged for each participant in the dialogue. Thus, for each parameter, the operation yields two distributions of time units, one for each of the participants. Each distribution represents an aspect of one participant's temporal behavior as it varied during the course of the dialogue. At least two sources of influence presumably account for the shape of each distribution. One source is the past temporal behavior of the participant represented by the distribution. TSR, when used to examine accommodation, 'removes' the influence of the participant's past behavior upon his or her present behavior and indexes the extent to which the participant is influenced by his or her partner's temporal behavior or, to put it another way, the degree to which the participant has accommodated to (diverged from, or remained independent of) the temporal behavior of his or her partner. Concretely, then, the TSR analysis provides a numerical estimate of accommodation or nonaccommodation for each participant. This description of the use of TSR for estimating interspeaker influence is simplistic, but it may, we hope, provide some sense of how the procedure functions and what it yields.

Cappella and Planalp (1981) examined the usefulness of the TSR procedures for assessing interspeaker influence in a study of 12 unconstrained conversations. They found that their conversational participants tended to match the durations of their switching pauses, their probabilities of simultaneous speech, and their probabilities of ending their silences. Moreover, these types of influence appeared to operate on a moment-to-moment basis. A constructive replication and extension of the study was conducted by Crown and Feldstein (1981). Its primary purposes were (1) to determine whether the parameters obtained from the Jaffe and Feldstein (1970) model would reflect interspeaker influence in a dialogue-by-dialogue TSR analysis as well as they do when the data-analytic procedure requires a group of dialogues, and (2) to determine whether the regression coefficient yielded by the TSR procedure provides an adequate individual index of interspeaker influence.

The results of the study were encouraging but not sufficiently conclusive. The average durations of pauses and switching pauses showed significant convergence for 11 of the participants while the probabilities of continuing a pause and a switching pause showed significant convergence for three of the participants and significant divergence for four others. The 14 significant coefficients that characterized the average durations of vocalizations and the probabilities of continuing a vocalization reflected divergence, a direction that remains difficult to explain. Moreover, inspection indicated that the magnitudes of the significant coefficients were lower than many of the nonsignificant coefficients. We are now exploring the possibility that the standardized regression coefficients offer a better estimate of degree of influence than the raw coefficients used in the study.

Some Cross-Language Findings

Until very recently, the study of conversation chronography was limited to the English language and, for the most part, it still is. Then the second author was provided with the opportunity of obtaining, in a controlled setting, recordings of conversations conducted in another language (Feldstein, Hennessy, and Bond 1981). The basic questions that suggest themselves are, of course, the same for any language. Every language must have a temporal structure and if, as Miller (1963) suggested, the speaking turn can be considered a language universal, it seems likely that the temporal structure of every language can be described by the same model, namely, the one proposed by Jaffe and Feldstein (1970). If such is the case, are the parameters of the model as stable within and across conversations in other languages as they are in English? How do their average durations compare?

The conversations recorded by Feldstein were in Chinese and English and part of the study has been described earlier in this chapter. The conversations were recorded in Canada and involved bilingual Asian and monolingual Canadian undergraduates at the University of Toronto. One of the reasons that Chinese was chosen as the language of comparison was that its sounds are produced not only on the expiration of breath (as are the sounds of spoken English), but also on the inspiration of breath.

Parameter reliabilities were obtained by comparing the first half of the 12-minute conversations with the second half. The reliabilities for the 11 Chinese conversations in which the 11 Chinese dyads engaged ranged from .55 to .88 whereas those for their 11 English conversations ranged from .52 to .73. The reliabilities for the English conversations of the Canadians ranged from .68 to .73.

Comparisons were made between the Chinese and English conversations of the Chinese speakers and between those conversations and the English conversations of the Canadian speakers. The comparisons indicated that the Chinese speakers used longer pauses and switching pauses in both their Chinese and English conversations than did the Canadians. Moreover, not only did they use shorter vocalizations, in general, than the Canadians, but they used even shorter vocalizations when they spoke English than when they spoke Chinese.

The design of the study did not allow for estimates of the parameter reliabilities from conversation to conversation, but the stability of the parameters within conversations appear to be invariant for the Chinese speakers across both their Chinese and English conversations. Their parameter durations were certainly not less stable than those of the Canadian speakers. These findings suggest that the parameter durations reliably characterize the ways in which Chinese speakers pace their conversational interactions, whether in Chinese or English, that is, that they characterize an individual's style of interacting with others. It might, then, be expected that the durations relate—as they do for American speakers—to personality attributes and interpersonal perception. However, other findings of the study question the possibility. Recall the three sets of absolute differences described earlier that were obtained for the Canadian dyads. The same differences were obtained for the Chinese dyads. When the scale differences that represented the similarity with which the dyad members perceived each other were correlated with the pause and switching-pause differences obtained from their English dialogues, the magnitudes of the resulting coefficients were statistically significant and high. When the same comparisons were made using the pause and switching-pause differences obtained from their Chinese dialogue, the magnitudes of the resulting coefficient were very low! Might it be that, although the pause and switching-pause durations of the Chinese dialogues were quite stable, they were primarily a function of some aspect of the language structure?

The results of the study also suggest that the longer silences and shorter vocalizations of the Chinese speakers are a function of the speakers rather than of the language, but further clarification is obviously needed. Indeed, it seems to us that many more cross-language comparisons are worth making to both clarify and extend the results of the study described here and to provide some test of Chapple's (1940) original notion that the timing of interpersonal interactions may offer a 'culture-free' method of describing personality.

Clinical Applications

A host of investigators have begun exploring clinical applications of conversation chronography.[1] Interestingly, the first clinical study employing the use of interaction chronography was conducted by Chapple and Lindemann in 1942 and examined the vocal behavior of psychiatric patients. Clinical studies using similar measures have been done by Matarazzo and others (e.g., Matarazzo and Wiens 1972; Rutter 1977). A study that is now in progress in Canada has been examining the possibility that the parameters of conversation chronography can be used to monitor changes in depth of schizophrenic psychopathology; a preliminary report of the study was published recently (Glaister, Feldstein, and Pollack 1980). Another Canadian study still in progress (Feldstein, Konstantareas, Oxman, and Webster 1982) is investigating the chronographic patterns of interactions involving autistic youths and their parents. A very recent exploration by Howland and Siegman (1982) represents a first step in an onging effort to use the temporal parameters to automate the prediction of coronary risk. Jaffe and Anderson (personal communication) are using the temporal parameters to predict favorable and unfavorable outcomes of the administration of imipramine in the treatment of depression.

One assumption underlying the application of conversation chronography to clinical concerns is that if there are illnesses thought to be, or to involve disturbances of communication, then those disturbances are likely to be reflected by the most basic dimension of interpersonal verbal communication, that is, its temporal structure. If so, then the detection of such disturbances and perhaps even of their development ought to be easier, quicker, and possibly less expensive than it is by our current methods. The clinical applications mentioned above may ultimately tell us whether the assumption is viable.

The Channel Issue

The temporal structure of a conversation may be considered a single communication channel. Our intent, in studying the temporal structure, has been to learn as much as possible about the information it conveys before integrating it with other channels about which much is known. An initial attempt to compare the information of two channels was made in

---

[1]Reports of many of these studies will appear in a book edited by Feldstein, Crown, and Welkowitz (in preparation).

1967 (Gerstman, Feldstein, & Jaffe). The study assessed the relative importance of pauses and syntax as determinants of speaker switching in spontaneous dialogues. The data were obtained from four 15-minute spontaneous dialogues. The pause frequencies and durations were provided by the AVTA system. The syntactic information was provided by two linguists who independently determined the boundary markings (points of linguistically permissible phrase endings) for 10,642 words of text transcribed from the dialogues. The comparisons revealed that switching occurred nine times more often after pauses than after non-pauses and 21 times more often after boundaries than after nonboundaries. Moreover, the effects were not additive, since the co-occurrence of both cues made switching 42 times more likely than the co-occurrence of neither cue. Finally, switching occurred 2.6 times more often after a nonpause boundary than after a nonboundary followed by a pause, suggesting that in the case of speaker switching, the syntactic cue was more powerful than the temporal cue.

Two other cross-channel experiments are in progress. One is concerned with the effects of gaze direction during a conversational exchange upon the time patterns of the exchange and the body movements of its participants. The other is concerned with whether the mutual attraction of conversational partners influences the extent to which the gaze and time patterns of their interaction show evidence of interpersonal accommodation.

The strategy of studying a single channel at a time represents a classical approach to the development of knowledge although it is clearly not the only one possible. The temporal structure is, after all, part of what can be considered a complex stimulus array and other investigators (e.g., Duncan and Fiske 1977) have ignored channel boundaries in their efforts to understand the transmission of information. Quite recently, Ekman and Oster (1979) have suggested that 'the whole question of how much information is conveyed by "separate" channels may inevitably be misleading. There is no evidence that individuals in actual social interaction selectively attend to another person's face, body, voice, or speech or that the information conveyed by these channels is simply additive' (p. 545). At the same time, there is no good evidence to the contrary. It seems entirely conceivable that different individuals pay special attention to different channels of communication. Hall (1979), for example, concludes from her review of the pertinent literature, that women are more sensitive than men to certain types of nonverbal communication. It also seems quite likely that some persons are especially concerned with what is said in a verbal message while others are more concerned with how it is said. Given the paucity of our present knowledge, it does not seem reasonable to conclude that the separate channel approach is not useful.

REFERENCES

Cappella, Joseph. July, 1979. Turn-by-turn matching and compensation in talk and silence: New methods and new explanations. Paper read at the International Conference on Social Psychology and Language, Bristol, England.

Cappella, Joseph N. and Planalp, Sally. 1981. Talk and silence sequences in informal conversations: III. Interspeaker influence. Human Communications 7. 117–132.

Cattell, Raymond B., Eber, H. W., & Tatsuoka, M. M. 1970. Handbook for the sixteen personality factor questionnaire. Champaign, IL: Institute for Personality Ability and Testing.

Chapple, Eliot D. 1939. Quantitative analysis of the interaction of individuals. Proceedings of the National Academy of Sciences 25. 58–67.

Chapple, Eliot D. 1940. 'Personality' differences as described by invariant properties of individuals in interaction. Proceedings of the National Academy of Sciences 26. 10–16.

Chapple, Eliot D., and Lindemann, E. 1942. Clinical implications of measurements of interaction rates in psychiatric interviews. Applied Anthropology 1. 1–11.

Crown, Cynthia L. 1982. Impression formation and the chronography of dyadic interactions. Interaction rhythms: Periodicity in communicative behavior, ed. by M. Davis. New York: Human Sciences Press.

Crown, Cynthia L., and Feldstein, Stanley. April 1981. Conversational congruence: Measurement and meaning. Paper read at the Eastern Psychological Association, New York.

Crown, Cynthia L., Feldstein, Stanley, and Bond, Ronald N. 1982. Effects of simultaneous speech on interpersonal perception. Paper read at the Eastern Psychological Association, Baltimore.

Duncan, Starkey, Jr., & Fiske, Donald W. 1977. Face to face interaction. Hillsdale, NJ: Lawrence Erlbaum.

Ekman, Paul, Friesen, W. V., O'Sullivan, M., and Scherer, Klaus. 1980. Relative importance of face, body, and speech in judgments of personality and affect. Journal of Personality and Social Psychology 38. 270–277.

Ekman, Paul, and Oster, Harriet, 1979. Facial expressions of emotion. In Annual Review of Psychology, ed. by Mark R. Rosenzweig and Lyman W. Porter, Palo Alto, California: Annual Reviews Inc. 30. 527–554.

Eysenck, Hans J., and Eysenck, Sybil B. G. 1963. Manual for the Eysenck Personality Inventory. San Diego, CA: Educational and Industrial Testing Service.

Feldstein, Stanley, 1976. Rate estimates of sound-silence sequences in speech. Journal of the Acoustical Society of America, 60 (Supplement No. 1) S46. (Abstract)

Feldstein, Stanley, 1982. Impression formation in dyads: The temporal dimension. In Interaction rhythms: Periodicity in communicative behavior, ed. by Martha Davis. New York: Human Sciences Press.

Feldstein, Stanley, BenDebba, Mohammad, and Alberti, Luciano. April 1974. Distributional characteristics of simultaneous speech in conversation. Paper presented at the Acoustical Society of America, New York.

Feldstein, Stanley, and Crown, Cynthia L. March 1978. Conversational time patterns as a function of introversion and extraversion. Paper read at the Eastern Psychological Association, Washington, DC.

Feldstein, Stanley, and Sloan, Barbara. 1984. Actual and stereotyped speech tempos of extraverts and introverts. Journal of Personality, 52, 188–204.

Feldstein, Stanley, and Welkowitz, Joan. 1978. A chronography of conversation: In defense of an objective approach. Nonverbal behavior and communication, ed. by Aron W. Siegman & Stanley Feldstein. Hillsdale, NJ: Lawrence Erlbaum.

Feldstein, Stanley, and Crown, Cynthia L. April 1979. Interpersonal perception in dyads as a function of race, gender, and conversational time patterns. Paper read at Eastern Psychological Association, Philadelphia.

Feldstein, Stanley, Alberti, Luciano, & BenDebba, Mohammad. 1979. Self-attributed personality characteristics and the pacing of conversational interaction. Of speech and time: Temporal speech patterns in interpersonal contexts, ed. by Aron W. Siegman & Stanley Feldstein. Hillsdale, NJ: Lawrence Erlbaum.

Feldstein, Stanley, Hennessy, Brian, and Bond, Ronald N. August 1981. Conversation chronography and interpersonal perception in Chinese and English dyads. Paper read at American Psychological Association, Los Angeles.

Feldstein, Stanley, Konstantareas, Mary, Oxman, Joel, and Webster, Christopher. 1982. The chronography of interactions with autistic speakers: An initial report. Journal of Communication Disorders. 15. 451–460.

Gerstman, Louis J., Feldstein, Stanley, and Jaffe, Joseph. Syntactic versus temporal cues of speaker switching in natural dialogue. Journal of the Acoustical Society of America 42. 1183. (Abstract)

Glaister, Joseph, Feldstein, Stanley, and Pollack, Herbert. 1980. Chronographic speech patterns of acutely psychotic patients: A preliminary note. Journal of Nervous and Mental Disease 168. 219–223.

Goldberg, Lewis. August 1977. Language and personality: Developing a taxonomy of trait-descriptive terms. Invited address to the American Psychological Association, San Francisco.

Hall, Judith A. 1979. Gender, gender roles, and nonverbal communication skills. Skill in nonverbal communication. Individual differences, ed. by Robert Rosenthal. Cambridge, MA: Oelgeschlager, Gunn & Hain Publishers, Inc.

Hayes, Donald, and Bouma, G. D. 1977. Patterns of vocalization and impression formation. Semiotica 13(2). 113–129.

Howland, Eric, and Siegman, Aron W. 1982. Toward the automated measurement of the Type A behavior pattern. Behavioral Medicine. 5. 37–54.

Jaffe, Joseph, and Anderson, Samuel W. In preparation. Speech rate studies in major depressive disorders: Prediction of early response to medication. In Speech sounds and silences: A social-psychophysical approach to clinical concerns, ed. by Stanley Feldstein, Cynthia L. Crown, and Joan Welkowitz. Hillsdale, NJ: Lawrence Erlbaum.

Jaffe, Joseph, and Feldstein, Stanley. 1970. Rhythms of dialogue. New York: Academic Press.

Kramer, Ernest. 1963. Judgment of personal characteristics and emotions from nonverbal properties of speech. Psychological Bulletin 60. 408–420.

Marcus, Esther S., Welkowitz, Joan, Feldstein, Stanley, and Jaffe, Joseph. April 1970. Psychological differentiation and the congruence of temporal speech patterns. Paper presented at the meeting of the Eastern Psychological Association, Atlantic City.

Matarazzo, Joseph D., and Wiens, A. N. 1972. The interview: Research on its anatomy and structure. Chicago: Aldine-Atherton.

Miller, George A. 1965. Speaking in general. 1963. Review of J. H. Greenberg (Ed.), Universals of language. Contemporary Psychology 8. 417–418.

Murray, Henry. 1938. Explorations in personality. New York: Oxford.

Rosenfeld, Howard M. 1978. Conversational control functions of nonverbal behavior. Nonverbal behavior and communication, ed. by Aron W. Siegman & Stanley Feldstein. Hillsdale, NJ: Lawrence Erlbaum.

Rutter, Derek R. 1977. Visual interaction and speech patterning in remitted and acute schizophrenic patients. British Journal of Social and Clinical Psychology 16. 357–361.

Schneider, David J., Hastorf, Albert H., and Ellsworth, Phoebe C. 1979. Person perception. California: Addison-Wesley.

Siegman, Aron W. 1978. The telltale voice: Nonverbal messages of verbal communication. Nonverbal behavior and communication, ed. by Aron W. Siegman & Stanley Feldstein. Hillsdale, NJ: Erlbaum Associates.

Thakerar, J. N., Giles, Howard, and Cheshire, J. 1982. Psycholgical and linguistic parameters of speech accommodation theory. Social and psychological dimensions of language behavior, ed. by C. Fraser & K. Scherer. Cambridge: Cambridge University Press.

Welkowitz, Joan, and Feldstein, Stanley. 1969. Dyadic interaction and induced differences in perceived similarity. Proceedings of the 77th Annual Convention of the American Psychological Association 4. 343–344.

Welkowitz, Joan, and Feldstein, Stanley. 1970. Relation of experimentally manipulated interpersonal perception and psychological differentiation to the temporal patterning of conversation. Proceedings of the 78th Annual Convention of the American Psychological Association 5. 387–388.

Welkowitz, Joan, Cariffe, Gerald, and Feldstein, Stanley. 1976. Conversational congruence as a criterion of socialization in children. Child Development 47. 269–272.

Witkin, Herman A., Dyk, R. B., Faterson, H. F., Goodenough, Donald R., and Karp, S. S. 1972. Psychological differentiation. New York: Wiley.

Chapter 4

The Two Faces of Silence: The Effect of Witness Hesitancy on Lawyers' Impressions*

Anne Graffam Walker

Georgetown University

Depending on who is doing the observing, silences which occur as part of speech carry different weights. Scientists who are interested in the mysteries of speech production regard unfilled pauses as clues to the relationship between cognition and language. Scholars interested in motivational aspects of speech consider silent pauses as markers of disturbance in the speaker's affective state. Still other investigators view silence from a social perspective, observing how speakers use and perceive silence during the construction of dialogue.

It is on this last interactional aspect of speech silence that I will concentrate in this chapter. It will be my argument that in situations where issues of truth are important, silence is two-faced in nature, one face representing the speaker's cognitive need to organize thought, the other the hearer's need to attribute motives to a break in an established flow of speech. I will develop this hypothesis by studying the impressions of witnesses that lawyers form during the first five minutes of a pretrial legal proceeding known as the deposition.

Among the most significant findings to emerge from this study are the facts that (1) hesitation takes different forms which have different effects on the hearer; (2) hesitation behavior is an important but misunderstood feature in assessment of witnesses by attorneys; and (3) the witness who pauses before answering questions put to him or her is subject to negative inference about his or her veracity. The irony of this inference, its origins, its accuracy or inaccuracy all are examined, and I will suggest at the

---

*This chapter is an expansion of a paper entitled The First Five Minutes: A study in forensic linguistics. A look at pauses, which was presented at the 79th Annual Meeting of the American Anthropological Association, December 1980.

conclusion that the Janus-like nature of silence carries interesting implications for the oral practice of law.

THE FACE OF COGNITION

The practice of law can be fairly characterized as both a function of intellect and a quest for information gathered for a purpose; language, in law, is seen primarily as a vehicle for transmission of that information. While the subject matter dealt with may be dry or dramatic, the language traditionally used, and the rules governing that language, are structured in such a way as to reflect, optimally, 'just the facts, ma'am'. This cognitive approach to language is clearly demonstrated by the type of instructions which conscientious lawyers give to their clients who are to testify before opposing counsel. Some examples of these instructions, taken from a manual for lawyers (Barist 1978), follow:

1. Do not answer a question you do not understand.
2. Talk in full, complete sentences.
3. Do not answer a compound question unless you are certain that you have all parts of it in your mind.
4. Never express anger or argue with the examiner.

And most salient to this discussion,

5. Think before you speak.

This last instruction is expanded upon by Summit (1978:110) who adds that the witness 'should not begin to talk until he knows the last word he is going to say'. This admonition expresses the common notion that thinking and speaking are mutually exclusive, that a person who can 'think on his feet' is both admirable and rare. Such a view, in fact, has been buttressed by some thirty years of scientific research. This research, begun by Goldman-Eisler (1951), established the tradition of a cognitive approach to speech production, by investigating pauses—their existence, distribution and patterning—as indices of steps in the language encoding process. In a summary of her work, Goldman-Eisler (1968:51) suggests that pauses are 'synchronous with and indicative of encoding processes responsible for generation of information'. Further, she says, speech must come to a full stop in order for planning to occur, except in cases of well-used utterances. In other words, planning requires pausing.

Operating under this belief means, then, that a witness could be expected to need time, silent time, to consider a question (as in instructions

1 and 3 above) and more time to plan what is to be said (instructions 2 and 5), all the while, of course, filtering out any emotional, or affective response (instruction 4). Cognition is not expected to be confounded by affect.

THE FACE OF ATTRIBUTION

The affective aspect of speech is, however, not to be ignored, and lawyers, like everybody else, not only know that it is there, but in fact regularly search *in witnesses not their own,* for affective clues which might indicate areas of vulnerability. Although neither the lawyers I have interviewed personally, nor the legal texts and casebooks I have researched (e.g., Morrill 1976; Kelner and McGovern 1981) are able to pinpoint exactly what all those clues they look for are, a few have mentioned pausing behavior as one. For example, in a textbook on trial tactics, Morrill (1976:36) makes the following observation:

> The "Thinker."—Some persons allow considerable time to elapse between the time a question is asked and the time the answer is given. This characteristic is often interpreted as indicating either that the witness is not too sure of himself or perhaps that he is thinking up a lie. Extreme slowness is unconvincing and lacks spontaneity.

This negative attribution of 'unconvincing' is the best thing lawyers can hope for in unfriendly (opposing) witnesses, but the last thing they want for their own. And if pausing and lying are sometimes equated, then the following expansion of instruction 5 to witnesses by Barist (1978:13) seems curious.

> *Think before you speak.* Allow five full seconds to elapse before the witness begins to answer each question. This allows counsel to formulate objections; it further allows the witness to think through his answer.

Summit (1978:110) writing to the same purpose, offers the same advice:

> No less than five seconds should elapse between the last word of the question and the first word of the answer. The witness should be drilled to know what five seconds are, and to stay perfectly quiet for at least that long.

He advances a quite different reason, however:

> The witness must be taught that this long pause before answering is *invariable*—once he has given his name and address, that must be his

pattern. If he answers some questions quickly, he will be unable to sustain the pattern, and may warn the examiner of areas of concern.

Barist's instruction would seem to stem from the cognitive approach: time to think is needed before speaking, while Summit implicitly takes into account the attributive nature of breaks in normal patterns, in this case, of pausing. Barist speaks for the speaker, Summit for the hearer. These speaker/hearer, cognitive/attributive approaches reflect the two-sided nature of silence.

THE DEPOSITION

Closely connected to these two faces of silence are the positive/negative valuations attributed to them, and it is in adversary proceedings that the negative face of silence shows most clearly. In cross-examination, the adversary nature of trial law reaches its peak, and this kind of confrontation can occur either before or during trial. Pretrial cross-examination takes place during a legal process known as the deposition, a device provided by law to litigants who wish to obtain information before trial about the other side's case.

The setting for oral depositions[1] is typically the office of the attorney who calls the deposition on behalf of his or her client, and there are usually four people present: the attorney who is asking the questions, the deponent (witness) who is answering them, the deponent's own lawyer, and a court reporter, who, by swearing in the witness and by making a verbatim record of the proceeding, serves as a visible symbol of the formality of the event.

Since the deposition is oral in nature and consists of sustained questioning and answering, it is classifiable as an interview and as such can be examined in light of the rules which Sacks, Schegloff & Jefferson (1978) found to operate within turn-organized speech systems. In the interview, turn order is generally fixed, relative distribution of turns is fixed, and the number of turns is determined by the questioner. The two most salient features of the Sacks model for talk are unchanged: one party speaks at a time, and speaker change recurs. What I call cospeech (Walker 1982), or simultaneous talk, and self-selection of turns do occur, but are variables of accident, power plays, and conversational style. The basic linguistic fact of the deposition, typical of all interview events, is that question (Q) is followed by answer (A), and upon completion of A, Q recurs.

---

[1]Depositions are occasionally taken in writing, but such a practice is rare and will be of no concern here.

It is the centrality of the Q–A pairing, a form of adjacency pair (Sacks, Schegloff & Jefferson 1978:28) which gives the deposition procedure its peculiar power. As Goody (1978:23) puts it:

> A basic rule of adjacency pairing is that when the first member of a pair is spoken, another person *must* complete the pair by speaking the second member as soon as possible. . . [This provides] a way in which one person can *compel* another to speak, to him, and on a topic of his own choosing.

Indeed, in the legal framework of the deposition, the question—whatever its surface form—assumes the force of a command (Walker, in press). The first 'question' asked in any taking of testimony always concerns the witness's name. The form, however, varies widely. For example:

> Mr. G., for the record, will you please state your full name for the court reporter?

> State your full name please.

The illocutionary force of both question and order above is the same: the intention of the speaker may or may not be to seek information (a question); it is always to compel an answer (a command). This ability of the question to function as a command is of particular importance in law, and serves as the foundation of the legal discovery process. Refusal to answer questions in a legal proceeding leaves the witness vulnerable to severe sanctions, including the loss of freedom.

In this setting of a highly conventionalized and relatively formal legal procedure, designed not just to gather facts but to give the questioner an opportunity to 'size up' the witness (as discussed in detail in Walker 1980), deponent speech patterns assume a significance beyond that of normal conversation. Pauses—and hesitation behavior in general—take on added interest as the questioning attorney seeks clues toward accurate assessment of the witness.

DATA: PROCEDURE

It was interest in how attorneys go about the business of making assessments of witnesses that led me to the original study upon which this chapter is based (Walker 1980). My years of being present as the court reporter during deposition procedures had led me to formulate the notion that the first five minutes of the interview somehow structured the remaining time, and that the crucial impressions made of the witness were formed for the most part during those opening minutes. To test this hypothesis, I selected 10 transcripts representing 10 depositions taken by 10 different questioning attorneys (all male). The transcripts of those proceedings, typed by me from my stenotype (machine shorthand) tapes, were shown to the appropriate attorneys who were asked to refresh their recollections as to the first five minute section only. I then asked each lawyer a series of questions designed to ascertain how clearly he recalled the setting, participants, and event; what he had known about the witness beforehand, if anything; his purpose for choice of questions; his impression of the witness; and whether or not he knew how and when he had formed that impression.

The results of these interviews gave me inner-world data on impression formation. Real-world, or objective data, were gathered by checking the Sony audiotapes I routinely made of every deposition for elapsed-time data that my stenotype tapes cannot provide, and by searching each transcript for a large number of linguistic variables. Using as a guide observation, intuition, and the studies of a long line of social scientists who precede me in studying impression formation (Labov 1966; Gumperz 1977; Conley, O'Barr, and Lind 1978; Tannen 1984; and others), I then identified three factor configurations which I believe are significant in the work attorneys do in making judgments about deponents: congruence, deference, and flow.

Congruence is a configuration which expresses a relationship of similarity between the backgrounds and speech styles of questioner and answerer. *Deference* deals with issues of cooperation, politeness, and power. *Flow,* the feature of concern here, treats such factors as the number of sentences per turn, number of words per sentence, speech rate per speaker (number of syllables per second), and pause phenomena. Of the features in the constellation of flow, the only one to receive comment from attorneys during my postdeposition interviews was the hesitation or lack of it observed in a deponent; pauses, filled and unfilled (silent) accounted for the highest percentage of the hesitation variables. It is with these data, particularly with aspects of silent pauses, that this study will be concerned.

DATA: TERMS

Pauses

But when is it that silence becomes a pause? How are pauses identified in the stream of speech? The literature shows no agreement at all as to the definition of a pause, except to agree generally that it is the absence of speaker sound. In one review of pause studies up through 1973, this lack of phonation was considered meaningful if it lasted anywhere from 10 milliseconds (a precise if exceedingly short period of time) to 'silence of unusual length' (Rochester 1973). In work done since 1973 in the field of sociolinguistics, a pause generally is considered significant at .5 second and in increments thereof (Labov and Fanshel 1977, Schenkein 1978, and others) although Chafe (1980) counts speech lapses of .1 second on up.

What is generally referred to as simply 'pause' has at least the universal definition of some unit of time in which phonation is absent, but filled pauses have no agreed-upon definition at all. Mahl (1956), one of the first scholars to investigate filled pauses, talked in terms of 'ah's', but as 'pause' began to be associated more and more closely with 'hesitation' in general, the category of filled pause became correspondingly more broad, widening to include, in one study, 'pause fillers such as uh, um, ah, and meaningless particles such as oh, well, let's see, now, so, you see, etc.' (Conley, O'Barr, and Lind 1978:1838). Other studies refer to filled pauses without ever specifying their nature, and many simply do not address filled pauses at all.

Researchers in psychology who study dyadic interaction, however, are quite consistent in defining pauses by distribution, dividing them into the two main classes of *switching* and *inturn,* although each operates under a variety of names. Inturn pauses take place during the utterance of a single speaker only; switching pauses occur at margins of speakers' turns.

The typology of pauses which I have formulated follows these same general lines. I consider that there are two classes of pauses: switching and inturn, and two manifestations: silent and filled. *Switching pauses* are broken down into what I call A-pause (for Answerer) and Q-pauses (for Questioner), and they are so named for 'ownership' of the stretch of time in which they occur. As I referred to earlier, critical times and names of pauses are not standardized in the field, but in the interview, at least, responsibility for the silence of what I call the A-pause, variously called 'response time' (Norwine and Murphy 1938), 'reaction time latency' (Matarazzo and Wiens 1972) and 'initial response' (Brotherton 1979), is generally conceded to be that of the person whose speech breaks the silence.[2] In other words, once a question is completed, any silence which follows belongs to the answer.

---

[2]Feldstein and Welkowitz (1978:342) make the interesting observation that the only difference between a pause and a switching pause is its outcome, and apparently on that ground, they, along with Jaffe and Feldstein (1970), assign switching pause silence to the *last,* rather than the next, speaker. In an interview situation, however, this would be counterintuitive, since, as pointed out before, a question is a command for a response to be made, and made without delay. This would involve immediate relinquishment of the turn by the speaker upon conclusion of his or her utterance, which by necessity would assign the switching silence to the answerer.

Brotherton (1979:184) agrees about the responsibility for the A-pause, but questions it for the Q-pause (which she calls 'interface pause') saying, 'These pauses are ambiguous in that the interviewer may be waiting for the subject to say more, or may be searching for the next most appropriate question'. For that matter, however, the same may be said for A-pauses during the deposition procedure. Given the fact that in depositions, examiner eyegaze patterns vary widely, and witnesses cannot rely on normal conversational cues or rules being in effect, it has been my experience that deponents make the error of judging a completed utterance as unfinished far more often than do questioners. Part of the reason for this is the deponent's relative helplessness in determining his or her own utterance length. In the data under discussion here, however, all A-pauses were judged to be unambiguously owned,[3] and it is on them and the inturn pauses of the deponent that this study focuses.

Inturn pauses are those which occur once a turn's speaking has begun and before it ends, and include both silent and filled manifestations. These data show inturn pause patterns for the witnesses from a low of only 4 pauses in 40 verbal turns for one deponent, to a high of 42 inturn pauses during only 16 verbal turns for another. I converted the relationship of pause to turn to an Inturn Pause Ratio (IPR), and those figures form a part of Table 4.1, which gives an overall picture of the hesitation data for each of the deponents studied.

Accompanying inturn pauses as manifestations of hesitation are what I call lexical hesitations: phenomena such as false starts, stammers, word repetitions, repairs and retracings (e.g., 'ind—, indicate'). These lexical hesitations are expressed as a ratio (LHR) of occurrence to number of turns and, together with the IPR and the A-pauses, combine to give an overall hesitation ratio (OHR) for each deponent.

The question posed at the beginning of this section as to how pauses are identified in the stream of speech is answered, then, by the typology outlined above. As to the question of when silence *becomes* a pause, I define a pause in general as a noticeable hiatus in an ongoing speech stream, which implies, of course, that what is a pause in some circumstances is not in others. In any comparative study, however, there must be some standard of measurement, and for that reason—based on both personal experience in the recording of testimony, and the literature in fields touching on chronology of speech—I have established two critical times for pauses for these data. A pause between turns becomes a switching pause when it meets or exceeds 1.5 seconds; inturn pauses are counted when they reach or exceed 1 second.

---

[3]No deponent asked, for example, after a pause by the examiner, 'Is that the end of the question?'

TABLE 4.1

			A. Deponent Hesitation Data					
Speaker	Sex	Judged Hesitant	A-Pause in percent			LHR	OHR	Number Verbal Turns
			S	F	IPR			
A		X	8	0	.10	.13	.30	40
B		X	7	3	.10	.07	.22	58
C			2	19	.19	.00	.40	48
D			2	31	.25	.06	.59	51
E	♀	X	0	21	.23	.12	.44	43
F	♀		12	0	.44	.04	.56	25
G			7	18	.75	.04	1.00	28
H			6	38	2.63	.19	3.06	16
I			14	28	2.23	.59	2.59	22
J	♀	X	27	8	.50	.04	.85	48

S: silent   IPR: inturn pause ratio   OHR: overall hesitation
F: filled   LHR: lexical hesitation ratio   ratio
♀: female

B. Lawyers' Impressions of Deponents

A   'A little hesitant'
B   'Had something to hide'
C   'No hesitation; straightforward and cooperative'
D   'Wanted to answer my questions'
E   'Gave excess consideration to her answers'
F   'Shot from the hip'
G   'Responsive to my questions'
H   [Unremarked]
I   'No hesitation; blurted out answers'
J   'Paused for answers; somewhat slow in responses'

Turns

If the question of the identity and ownership of a pause is difficult to answer, the problem of determining the boundaries of a turn is even harder. As Feldstein and Welkowitz (1978:344) put it, considering that the turn is the 'pivotal unit in conversation' it is 'surprising to find so little agreement about not only what a turn is, but when it occurs and who has it'. The difficulty of making decisions about turn identification in depositions is compounded by the asymmetry in the power relations between examiner and deponent, since in legal proceedings turns can be thought of as either a *right* or an *obligation* to speak. The first turn of the event is properly the *right* of Q. It then becomes A's *obligation* to take the second turn, and the process repeats itself until Q declines to exercise that right any further, as in, 'I have no more questions of this witness'.

If all goes smoothly, turns alternate in that orderly fashion, right and obligation, right and obligation, although self-selected turns (ones occurring out of order or in the midst of another's turn) can occur, as can turns by another participant present.

For this study of pausing behavior, I considered only the data generated by verbal turns, ignoring nonverbal answers such as head nods, or long silences which generated a [No answer] in the transcript text. Most of the depositions in this study proceeded in a fairly regular QAQA fashion, but there were exceptions, usually generated by self-selection, such as answers which anticipated the direction of the question, or those which misjudged the first speaker's turn-end. In these cases, I considered the second speaker to be taking a turn in the middle of the first speaker's utterance, as in the following example. The exchange was about rental of a vehicle.

> Q. Okay. You mean the one you had on the fourteenth was the one you
>   got the first day you had a rental [0.7]—
> A. Right.
> Q. —or took one?[4]

In my system (pauses are shown in the text in brackets), this sample consists of one Q turn and one A turn.

Another more complicated problem in determining what was or was not a pause concerned a self-selected utterance by a third participant, as in the sample below. In this exchange, the deponent's own attorney stepped in with an implicit explanation for his client's silence in response to a question, and his observation touched off a series of broken utterances by both the examiner (Q), and the witness, a woman.

---

[4]Identifying data are altered in all examples presented in this study. The examples of testimony are shown in essentially the same format as they appear in the legal transcripts with a few alterations: pause measurements are added and appear in brackets. Latching and cospeech are shown as follows:

Latching: Well,⌐
                ⌐But

and

Cospeech: Don't tell—
                [Wait a minute.

Lengthened continuant sounds are indicated in this text only by a colon following the sound involved (n:o: = nnnooo). Dashes, when both at the end and the beginning of follow-on lines (e.g., example on this page), generally indicate a continuous utterance. When necessary to accommodate latching and cospeech, the first word of an utterance is moved here to make the correspondence clearer. That practice is not followed in legal transcripts.

Q. How did you find out that [2.2] Mary Jones [1.6] had taken the initiative to look for investment possibilities?
A. [No answer] [7]
WITNESS'S COUNSEL: I think she answered that by saying that she [Mary Jones], had come there.
THE WITNESS: Well,⌐
EXAMINER:(Q)   ∠ But [1]
THE WITNESS: Yeah and she ⌐ had
EXAMINER:(Q)   ⌐ She could have come
there to [1.5] talk about a number of things, I'm sure.

Although the witness's 7-second silence here is very significant as a [No answer], I could not count it for pausing purposes since it was terminated not by her examiner but by her own counsel. Therefore, this sample yields two turns each for Q and A.

Turns, then, were defined essentially as beginning when a speaker began to talk and ending when he or she relinquished the floor, whether or not the utterance was 'complete'. Within the framework which this view on turns provided, I examined my data for pausing behavior in witnesses, and its effects on lawyers. My findings and discussion follow.

FINDINGS

Seven general facts about hesitation behavior are revealed by this study.

1. Hesitancy is the linguistic feature most often commented upon by attorneys who are asked their impressions of witnesses.
2. Hesitancy is relative.
3. Hesitations manifest themselves in several ways.
4. Hesitations cluster.
5. Hesitancy lends itself to generalization.
6. The different aspects of hesitancy show different degrees and types of correlation between behavior and impression formation.
7. Hesitancy behavior, important as it is, counts less as a factor which influences impression formation than does obedience to the social rules which govern behavior for witnesses in giving testimony at a deposition.

Discussion

1. Of all the variables in the flow factor (number of sentences per turn, number of words per sentence, speech rate, pause phenomena), pausing, or hesitancy, was the only feature to be commented on by attorneys in this study when they were asked for their impressions of the witness. A reason for this is suggested by the fact that litigation is an adversary

procedure, with each side fighting either to win or to keep losses to a minimum. To accomplish this, a lawyer must look for chinks in the other side's armor, and comments made by attorneys both in the literature referenced earlier and in this study indicate that pausing is viewed as one of those chinks.

Two of the attorneys whom I interviewed in connection with this study spoke explicitly about looking for clues as to witness trustworthiness by saying, 'I was listening for [the witness's] pauses', and 'I look for the pausing witness'. In speaking of the significance to lawyers of pauses in general, another lawyer said, 'Pauses before an answer may indicate lying', and the same attorney who said he looks for a pausing witness agreed with this point of view when he explained, 'The witness who pauses is less likely to be truthful'.

But perhaps the most telling comment about the attitude toward hesitant witnesses was expressed by the lawyer who said:

> If a person is being honest, the time to respond is going to be shorter than it is if they are going to be dishonest. If you're dishonest, you have a mental construct which does not equate to reality, so if you're being dishonest, you have to refer back to that construct and see where this question fits in.

Note that in this comment, 'the time to respond [to a question]' is the focus of attention. This response time is the switching pause I have been referring to, and the attorney's comment provides good evidence of its importance in forming impressions of a witness.

2. Hesitancy is relative, and here I am speaking of real-time duration of pauses. When the Q-A pace is fast, say 50 or more Q-A pairings in five minutes' times, a pause between question and answer of as little as half a second can become marked. In a more leisurely paced session, A-pauses of up to 2.5 seconds can occur without eliciting any sign of markedness from the attorneys, such as a raised eyebrow, a questioning look, a shifting in the chair, or an overt reference such as, 'Did you not understand my question?' This relativity also is evidenced in depositions (as elsewhere) by the fact that when a deponent suddenly slows his established rhythm of response, a 'pause' occurs. This phenomenon of breaks in patterns becoming noticeable is what Summit (1978) was referring to when he advised 'invariable' patterns of response for his own witnesses.

3. Hesitation manifests itself in many ways, most of which have been touched on before in this discussion. From the form of complete silence, it ranges through lengthened continuant sounds (n:o:) to pauses filled by *er, um, uh, mm,* and the like (hesitation fillers), and includes as well, utterances of a more complicated sort: false starts, stammers, and what I

have called lexical hesitations. These are all manifestations of what Mahl (1956) first investigated as speech disturbances and, for attorneys, they seem to fit as malfunctions into the construct which Scollon (Chapter 2) refers to as the 'metaphor of the machine'. There may be still another type of hesitation which keeps the machine humming, yet buys time for the speaker: hedges of a phrasal kind frequently found in testimony. I refer to those expressions which not only buy time, but avoid certainty: 'to my recollection', 'to my knowledge', 'roughly speaking', and so on. It is not a phenomenon which I have investigated closely, and I mention it here only as a matter of interest, but semantic hesitation of this nature is not only useful to deponents, it is almost required as one of the few linguistic forms of self-protection available to them.

4. Hesitations cluster: silent pauses, filled, lexical and what I have postulated to be semantic hesitations are frequently found in the same environment. In these data, a total of 31 answers began with a silent pause. Of those, 11, or 35 percent, were followed immediately by a filled pause ('uh', 'um', and 'well'). Ten more of the 31 A-pauses were followed by hedges both legal and linguistic, such as 'To my knowledge', 'I think so', and 'Roughly'. Nine more answers which began with hesitation were marked by further, sustained pausing behavior. One typical example:

Q. A:nd what were your duties there.
A. [1.9] Well, let's see. [1] I [1] paid bills, hired personnel [2.3] ummm, [3.6] good lord I don't know [laughs] million things I did.

This answer had five silent pauses and two hesitation fillers ('well', 'umm'), both of which were accounted for as inturn pauses; a laugh, and what Shuy (1979) calls an agenda organizer ('let's see'). The latter two were not considered as pauses but are certainly recognizable as strategies for postponing transfer of information.

5. Hesitancy lends itself to generalization. In the same deposition from which the preceding example was taken, the attorney noted that his witness paused before answers 'she omitted vital information on'. Further investigation by both the attorney and me, however, showed that although this witness was perceived as, and could be characterized fairly as, a pausing witness (15 out of 48 verbal turns, or 31 percent, were marked by initial hesitation alone) only 2 of those 15 answers 'omitted vital information'. That number was apparently enough, however, and the omitted information important enough, for a spread effect to occur, leading to the attorney's generalization about hesitancy as providing a clue to what he saw as a typical pattern of concealment. Hesitancy was linked for him to omitting information, despite the apparent facts.

6. The different manifestations referred to above, and their distribu-

tions, have different effects upon formation of impressions. Silent manifestations which occur between question and answer correlate with an
impression of hesitancy; filled manifestations in any position do not.
That filled, or voiced, pauses lack this correlation may be related to a car-
ryover of a principle of general conversation noted by Mahl and others
that 'the vast majority of the speech disturbances are "unintended" and
escape the awareness of both speakers and listeners in spite of their very
frequent occurrence' (cited in Maclay and Osgood 1959:22).[5] Or it may
also expose what may be an underlying principle of cooperation applicable not only to general conversation but even to so highly structured an
exchange of speech as the deposition: once an answer is begun, indicating
that the summons to respond has been met, pausing behavior fades in
importance, and content becomes the feature most closely attended to.

Whatever the reason, the figures in Table 4.1 show the lack of pattern
between judgments about hesitancy and witness hesitation ratios, both
overall (OHR) and inturn. The spread, for instance, of IPR's (inturn
pauses) for witnesses judged as 'hesitant', was .10 to .50; the spread for
'nonhesitant' witnesses was .19 to .75. And while there was a closer clus-
tering for the OHR's (overall hesitation ratio)—.38 to .85 for hesitant; .40 to 3.06 for nonhesitant—the curious fact is that the highest
OHR's were found in witnesses *not* adjudged hesitant by lawyers.

Deponent H, for instance, was not considered hesitant, yet he had the
highest OHR of these subjects, had also the highest proportion of inturn
pauses, and his speech was characterized by a number of lexical hesitations. But it also turns out that most of his pausing was voiced, and in his
A-pauses, 38 percent were marked by fillers while only 6 percent were
marked by silence. In other words, when this witness did pause between
question and answer, he did so with sound far more often than with
silence. This fact captures the importance of the type and distribution of
pausing in impression formation: switching pauses, and silence, are the
critical variables.

Table 4.2 makes this variable-to-impression relationship easier to see.
When all those speakers about whom no hesitation was either imputed or
implied are grouped together, it can be seen that the percentage of their
filled A-pauses is higher than those of the silent, as with Deponent H. For
the remaining speakers—those who were considered to be hesitant—the
ratio is reversed: silent A-pauses are more frequent than filled. The two
exceptions to the pattern depicted in Table 4.2 are marked by asterisks,

---

[5]My experience as a verbatim court reporter who, as a matter of practice, faithfully recorded
false starts, stammers, 'uh's', and 'um's' bears this out. Both attorneys and deponents who
see their utterances in print for the first time are startled at 'seeing' what they said but
didn't 'hear'.

TABLE 4.2
PATTERNS OF LAWYER IMPRESSIONS OF WITNESS HESITATION

Hesitation Noted			No Hesitation Noted		
	A-Pause in %			A-Pause in %	
Speaker	Silent	Filled	Speaker	Silent	Filled
A	8	0	C	2	19
B	7	3	D	2	31
E*	0	21	F*	12	0
J	27	8	G	7	18
			H	6	38
			I	14	28

and as exceptions, they provide another insight into the nature of hesitancy. But before discussing them, it is instructive to note the polarity of
comments made in connection with these two general pause patterns
depicted in Table 4.2.

About *filled* A-pause speakers, the comments by attorneys were:

C: Straightforward and cooperative
D: Wanted to answer my questions
G: Responsive to my questions
I: Spoke immediately at the end of each question

About those who used more *silent* A-pauses:

A: Nervous and afraid
B: Recalcitrant
F: Not careful in her answers
J: Not spontaneous

These comments suggest that there is an inverse relationship between
attributions of hesitancy and the notions about cooperation alluded to
earlier. Apparently, deponents who begin more of their answers with a
filled pause are viewed as cooperating with the questioner; those whose
silent pauses outweigh the filled are viewed in a more derogatory manner.

7. Impressions about a witness's hesitancy are sensitive to alteration
and falsification by variables of power. In the foregoing discussion I mentioned the fact that for each of the two patterns of distribution of silent
and filled A-pauses, there is one exception in the data. Neither example of
variance from the pattern can be explained by appeal to purely linguistic
facts. The exception in the 'Hesitant' column is Witness E, about whom

her examiner commented that 'she gave excess consideration to her answers'. When I asked how he meant that, he replied it was because of the time she took to answer. Yet none of the flow factor components for this deponent would seem to support this impression. If, for example, her speech rate had been lower than counsel's, it might have lent a feeling of contrastive slowness to her response,[6] but in fact, her speech rate was considerably higher than his (5.3 S/S, or syllables per second, to 4.69 S/S). Inturn data showed a middle-range lexical hesitation ratio of .12—5 false-start-stammer type in 43 verbal turns—and her IPR, inturn pause ratio, was also unremarkable (.23). Further, her silent A-pause rate, the factor to which counsel seemed to be referring, was an astonishing zero percent; in other words, she never once paused silently between question and answer.

However, a breakdown of this witness's answers did show that 11 of them came so quickly that they resulted in cospeech, 23 of them were latched, or instantaneous, and the remaining nine answers (21 percent) began with hesitation fillers. It might be, therefore—in view of the deponent's general rapid-fire response pattern—that it was these nine answers which began with fillers that were the ones the attorney remembered, thus accounting for his impression.

Another, more context-oriented explanation could also be that early in the deposition, and by means to be discussed shortly, the witness had violated the expectations this and other attorneys have about the proper conduct of a deponent. She had thus acquired for herself, one might say, the feature of +[negative]. Once this feature is assigned, it establishes a general construct in which negative attribution with reference to one feature spreads (generalizes) to other characteristics of the witness, both linguistic and personal.

In both cases of deviation from the pattern—E and F—clashes with norms of expectation could account for the aberration. In an earlier study (Walker 1982) I showed that interrupting counsel is something a witness 'doesn't do', and both E and F violated this rule. Deponent E interrupted her questioner twice in the opening seven questions of the deposition, and in F's deposition, on the seventh question she broke in twice, once with an implied command to the attorney to be quiet, thus compounding the violation. The exchange occurred as counsel asked questions about the witness's own curriculum vitae which he had just handed to her:

---

[6]Technically speaking, as soon as contrast is mentioned, the configuration of congruence is now under discussion since that is the factor which deals with interactional comparisons of speakers.

Q. All right. And uh is it complete in the categories that you've listed on
there? [5.85][7] 'N other words, uh—
A. Just a second.
Q. —under education, you have got uh—
A.   ⌈ Yeah, this is complete.

By such behavior (counsel commented to me, 'I saw the interruption
as a sign I needed to reassert control'), Deponent F laid the groundwork
for future misattributions about her testimony. In an effort to understand
some of these misattributions, I did some further investigation of the
observable data, and the findings were mixed.

The first discrepancy was in the data themselves. Reference to Table
4.2 will show that although Deponent F had only 3 A-pauses (12 percent
of her total number of answers) all of them were marked by initial silence;
none began with fillers. According to the pattern identified before, this
should have marked her as a hesitant witness. It did not. A possible
explanation for this puzzling exception to the rule that silence in the A-
pause position leads the hearer to attribute hesitancy to the speaker
might be found, however, in the fact that in two out of those three answers, the first sound uttered (following the initial silence) was a filled
pause: a drawn-out 'We::ll', and the data have shown that filled pauses are
not perceived as hesitation.[8]

A second discrepancy in the data for this witness lay in a difference of
opinion between the attorney and me (and, I contend, the facts) over his
statement that this deponent 'shot from the hip' and was 'not careful in
her answers'. I was present during the same taking of testimony as the
attorney; I heard the same surface features as did the attorney: delivery,
content, speed of talk, and so on. I also experienced the testimony twice:
once during the deposition, and again during the typing of the transcript.
Yet not only did I *not* consider this witness as careless or quick with her
answers, I thought of her as a very thoughtful deponent of superior verbal
skills. Why the difference of opinion?

The answer may lie partly in contrasts.[9] I speak at a fairly rapid rate, in
bursts separated by frequent inturn pausing. The lawyer in question

---

[7]This 5.85-second pause occurred as the witness read over the document which had been
handed to her.
[8]Since these data are concerned with impressions formed during the first five minutes of the
deposition, another possible explanation is, of course, that the remainder of the proceeding
altered the first impression. It has not been my experience that this often occurs; the
possibility, however, is still under investigation.
[9]I acknowledge the fact that the varying tasks of the listeners can affect perception, but that
is a subject for consideration at a later time.

speaks at what in other studies (Walker 1980) I have determined to be a 'Slow' pace—4.16 syllables per second (S/S)—also in bursts separated by frequent pausing. (His IPR was a high 1.39 in this deposition.) The deponent's speech rate fell in between the attorney's and mine: an 'Average' 5.6 S/S; and her utterances, unlike counsel's and mine, were generally smooth, with a very low incidence of inturn filled pauses (one answer of 59 words accounted for over 60 percent of them). So perhaps the answer is that to my ear, the transition from fast to slower made her speech seem measured and thoughtful; to the attorney, the transition from slow to faster made it seem like she was 'shooting from the hip'.

Besides characterizing the deponent as someone who was 'shooting from the hip', the attorney also saw her as 'not careful in her answers'. A check of the content of each of her responses, however, belies that impression. Not only did this deponent, unlike many others both in this study and throughout my experience as a court reporter, answer each question right to the point, but her answers were tightly organized both syntactically and semantically. Further, the questions frequently called upon her to make judgments about the correctness of their propositions, and nothing about the answers given indicated lack of care. The following exchanges are typical examples, and occurred as part of the continuing examination on her qualifications as an expert witness.

> Q. Am I correct that you have not uh authored anything as far as uh, uh, ah academic uh writings of—or, in your profession?
> A. I consider a doctorate dissertation, since it is copyrighted, to be a major academic publication. Apart that, true.

And seconds later:

> Q. 'l right. With regard to the presentations that you've listed on page 3, am I correct that these would be uh, uh speeches or talks uh given uh as indicated on: the subjects that you indicated as opposed to uh a research project?
> [1.85]
> A. Well, yes and no. The uh '79 presentation in the hospital and Area A '79 presentation were both summaries of research work.

These examples, especially the latter, which is marked by (1) a silent A-pause of 1.85 seconds, (2) the opening hesitation filler 'Well', and (3) equivocation in using 'yes and no', do not seem to support a characterization of either 'shooting from the hip' or being careless with answers. As I suggested, however, at the outset of discussion about the two 'exceptions to the rule', E and F, the answer to their existence may lie beyond personal and contrastive linguistic features, and rest in consideration of the spread of a negative attribution acquired by not meeting expected norms of interaction. Pause data, while very significant in impression formation, cannot stand alone. As only one feature in a vast constellation of linguistic phenomena, pausing behavior is subject to a number of influences, among which is asymmetry of power. Like any other variable, it must be understood in reference to the social settings in which it occurs.

CONCLUSION

From the foregoing study of silence as it occurs in patterned forms in the deposition—a social setting of great constraint—three findings have emerged which carry with them implications for the oral practice of law.

First, it is the silent pause that occasions doubt in the hearer.

Second, issues involving asymmetries of power in a confrontation between lawyer and witness form a frame of higher influence within which issues of personal speech are susceptible to misinterpretation. If the witness violates the rules which govern the conduct of a legal proceeding, he or she is at risk, since negative attributions of one feature can lead to misattributions about others. In this case, the negative load assigned to the feature of 'hesitant' contributes to negative notions about the veracity of the deponent.

Third, the face of silence presented by the speaker as a result of lexical, syntactic, semantic, and idea planning, and the face perceived by the hearer as a result of prior cultural and occupational experience, are in diametric opposition. What appears as a pause for thought in the friendly witness is suspect as a pause for concealment in a witness for the other side.

That does not mean, however, that the advice, 'Think before you speak' is bad advice, nor does it suggest that taking the drastic and impractical measures suggested by some to manipulate habits of speech is recommended, even if possible. What it does suggest is a necessity to become more aware of *how* impressions are formed, what their origins may be, the effect they may have upon critical judgment, and their susceptibility to error. This study has shown that the nature of the attributions associated with silence depends on the position of the observer. Recognition of that fact can be a tool to assist attorneys in sorting out possibilities for error as they advise witnesses on the one hand, and assess them on the other.

ACKNOWLEDGMENTS

To the many attorneys who have shared their time so generously with me, I would like to offer my deep appreciation. To Deborah Tannen, for helpful criticism and incisive comments, on this and earlier drafts, I would like to express my sincere thanks.

74   WALKER

REFERENCES

Barist, Jeffrey A. 1978. Preparation of a witness for deposition. The Deposition: A simulation with commentary, 8–23. American Bar Association.
Brotherton, Patricia. 1979. Speaking and not speaking: Processes for translating ideas into speech. Of speech and time, ed. by Aron W. Siegman & Stanley Feldstein, 179–209. Hillsdale, NJ: Lawrence Erlbaum Associates.
Chafe, Wallace, L. 1980. The deployment of consciousness in the production of a narrative. The pear stories: Cognitive, cultural, and linguistic aspects of narrative production, ed. by Wallace Chafe, 9–50. Norwood, NJ: Ablex.
Conley, John M., William M. O'Barr, and E. A. Lind. 1978. The power of language: Presentational style in the courtroom. Duke Law Journal, 78 (6). 1375–1399.
The Deposition: A simulation with commentary. 1978. American Bar Association.
Feldstein, Stanley and Joan Welkowitz. 1978. A chronography of conversation: In defense of an objective approach. Nonverbal behavior and communication, ed. by A. W. Siegman & S. Feldstein, 329–378. Hillsdale, NJ: Lawrence Erlbaum Associates.
Goldman-Eisler, Frieda. 1951. The measurement of time sequences in conversational behaviour. British Journal of Psychology 42. 355–362.
Goldman-Eisler, Frieda. 1968. Psycholinguistics: Experiments in spontaneous speech. London: Academic Press.
Goody, Esther N. 1978. Towards a theory of questions. Questions and politeness, ed. by E. N. Goody, 17–43. New York and Cambridge: Cambridge University Press.
Gumperz, John J. 1977. Sociocultural knowledge in conversational inference. Georgetown University round table on languages and linguistics, 1977, ed. by Muriel Saville-Troike, 191–211. Washington, DC: Georgetown University Press.
Jaffe, Joseph and Stanley Feldstein. 1970. Rhythms of dialogue. New York: Academic Press.
Kelner, Joseph and Francis E. McGovern. 1981. Successful litigation techniques (Student edition). New York: Matthew Bender.
Labov, William. 1966. Social stratification of English in New York City. Washington, DC: Center for Applied Linguistics.
Labov, William and David Fanshel. 1977. Therapeutic discourse: Psychotherapy as conversation. New York: Academic Press.
Maclay, Howard and Charles E. Osgood. 1959. Hesitation phenomena in spontaneous speech. Word 15. 19–44.
Mahl, G. F. 1956. Disturbances and silences in the patient's speech in psychotherapy. Journal of Abnormal Social Psychology 53. 1–15.
Matarazzo, J. D. and A. N. Wiens. 1972. The interview: Research on its anatomy and structure. Chicago: Aldine-Atherton.
Morrill, Alan E. 1976. Trial diplomacy. Chicago. Court Practice Institute, Inc.
Norwine, A. C. and O. J. Murphy. 1938. Characteristic time intervals in telephonic conversation. Bell System Technical Journal 17. 281–291.
Rochester, S. R. 1973. The significance of pauses in spontaneous speech. Journal of Psycholinguistic Research 2 (1). 51–81.
Sacks, Harvey, Emanuel A. Schegloff, and Gail Jefferson. 1978. A simplest systematics for the organization of turn-taking for conversation. Studies in the organization of conversational interaction, ed. by Jim Schenkein, 7–55. New York: Academic Press.
Schenkein, Jim (ed.). 1978. Studies in the organization of conversational interaction. New York: Academic Press.
Shuy, Roger. 1979. Direct testimony in the matter of State of Texas v. Thomas Cullen Davis, Criminal District Court No. 4, Tarrant County, Texas.
Summit, Stewart A. 1978. The witness needs help. The Deposition: A simulation with

commentary. American Bar Association, 110–114. Reprinted from 1977, 3 Litigation No. 2, American Bar Association.

Tannen, Deborah. 1984. Conversational style: Analyzing talk among friends. Norwood, NJ: Ablex.

Walker, Anne Graffam. 1980. The first five minutes: Toward a linguistic understanding of a legal event. Unpublished Masters' paper, Georgetown University.

Walker, Anne Graffam. 1982. Patterns and implications of cospeech in a legal setting. Linguistics and the professions, ed. by Robert J. DiPietro, 101–112. Norwood, NJ: Ablex.

Walker, Anne Graffam. In press. Linguistic manipulation, power, and the legal setting. Power through discourse, ed. by Leah Kedar. Norwood, NJ: Ablex.

Chapter 5

Some Reasons for Hesitating*

Wallace Chafe
University of California, Berkeley

There is a natural tendency, when some interesting phenomenon is being explored, to want to treat it as something which can be studied in and of itself, without regard for its interrelationships with other phenomena. The entire field of linguistics has to some extent suffered from this tendency, in that a great deal of research has attempted to deal with language apart from its psychological, social, and cultural settings. It is a healthy development that fields like psycholinguistics, sociolinguistics, and ethnolinguistics have begun to bring a broader perspective to linguistic studies. On a different level it has seemed to me that there has been the same tendency in research on hesitations, or pausology, or whatever it may be called, to look at the phenomenon in isolation. But in the long run I am sure we are going to find that such a specialization of effort is futile; that hesitational phenomena can be understood only as natural consequences of the processes which occur during the production of speech. Viewed in that way, they can be seen as contributing important clues to the nature of these processes.

Perhaps the only time that hesitations have been thoroughly integrated into a theory of speech production was in Lounsbury's brief discussion (1954). There, the production of speech was seen to be governed by habits associating each linguistic unit in turn with the unit next to be uttered. It was thought that these units were associated by habits having varying degrees of strength, so that there were varying transitional probabilities from one unit to the next. 'Hesitation pauses correspond to the points of highest statistical uncertainty in the sequencing of units of any

*Reprinted with permission from Hans W. Dechert and Manfred Raupach (eds.), Temporal Variables in Speech. The Hague: Mouton, 1980, pp. 169–180. Additional discussion of the points raised in this chapter is now available in Chafe 1980.

77

given order.' Transitional probabilities were making a splash in linguistics at the time (cf. Harris 1955), and it was natural to combine them with the behaviorist notion of habit strength to produce such a model of speech production. Nowadays, for a variety of reasons, few would believe that speech is well explained as the implementation of association habits between linguistic units. But there has never since then been a theory that accounted for hesitations as an aspect of speech production in as straightforward a way.

In fact, the dominant linguistic theory in the meantime has been content to focus most of its attention on an ideal condition of language production, thereby sweeping hesitations under the rug. 'A record of natural speech will show numerous false starts, deviations from rules, changes of plan in mid-course, and so on. The problem for the linguist [. . .] is to determine from the data of performance the underlying system of rules that has been mastered by the speaker-hearer and that he puts to use in actual performance' (Chomsky 1965:4). This view is, I think, misleading to the extent that it suggests that the speaker has some grammatical ideal toward which he is striving, and which he is often prevented from attaining because of various imperfections in the psychological processes involved in 'performance'.

I would like to suggest on the contrary that the speaker's chief goal is to get across what he has in mind, and that he is not likely to be interested in grammaticality unless there is some special reason to think of it, as there usually is not. The speaker is interested in the adequate verbalization of his thoughts. Pauses, false starts, afterthoughts, and repetitions do not hinder that goal, but are steps on the way to achieving it. After someone has said something, it would not be a damaging criticism to tell him, 'You spoke ungrammatically (or disfluently).' I doubt if the average person would care. But it would be damaging to say, 'You didn't get across what you had in mind.' For that, I suggest, the speaker might have genuine regrets. We may even find, when we study comprehension in relation to these phenomena which we are too prone to regard as infelicities, that they not only enable the speaker to express his ideas more effectively, but also enable the hearer to assimilate them more effectively too.

The more specific, if only partially developed suggestions I will put forward here come from a concern with the ongoing, real-time production of speech as a reflection of the ongoing sequencing of the speaker's thoughts. In this kind of investigation 'ungrammatical', 'disfluent' speech constitutes the primary data, and hesitation phenomena are welcome as overt, measurable indications of processing activity which requires a certain amount of time. They provide good evidence that speaking is not a matter of regurgitating material already stored in the mind in linguistic form, but that it is a creative act, relating two media, thought and language, which are not isomorphic but require adjustments and readjustments to each other. A speaker does not follow a clear, well-traveled path, but must find his way through territory not traversed before, where pauses, changes of direction, and retracing of steps are quite to be expected. The fundamental reason for hesitating is that speech production is an act of creation.

I have been particularly interested in how people talk about things they have recalled from memory (cf. Chafe 1977 and 1979, which explain some of the assumptions underlying the present discussion). Let us regard memory as a vast store of information, somehow established by previous experience but also creative in itself, which is potentially ready to be activated by a process which may be called 'bringing into consciousness'. Such activation takes place as a series of brief resting places. William James suggested a similar metaphor when he wrote of the stream of consciousness: 'Like a bird's life, it seems to be made of an alternation of flights and perchings. The rhythm of language expresses this, where every thought is expressed in a sentence, and every sentence closed by a period' (James 1890:243). Introspection, I believe, supports this notion. We recall the past more as a series of salient snapshots than as a continuous movie film. Eye movements lend support to the idea too, by showing that the focusing of consciousness on visual phenomena follows discrete, discontinuous 'centers of interest' (Buswell 1935). The work of Newtson (1976) also shows that we break up continuous experience into a sequence of discrete actions. And as James suggested, language lends support to the perching metaphor. Numerous recent observers of spontaneous speech have noticed that it is produced in well-defined spurts (see, for example, the 'information units' of Halliday 1967). In the data available to me at the moment these spurts are slightly less than two seconds in mean duration, and contain a mean of about five words. They tend to be single clauses syntactically, but under certain conditions may be more or less than a clause. They usually exhibit a 'clause-final' intonation contour. I hypothesize that these spurts of language are expressions of underlying perchings of consciousness. If so, they provide us with excellent evidence of how consciousness successively activates small chunks of information: the kinds of information it lights on, how long and for what purpose it dwells there, and the patterns it follows in moving from one perching to the next. Hesitations are especially useful in showing us where it is easy to move on, and where it is difficult.

In what follows I will refer to each separate perching as a 'focus of consciousness', or simply as a 'focus'. Many hesitations, I will suggest, are attributable to the kind of process just described: the speaker's need to find the next focus. Others, as we will see at the end of this discussion, stem from the need to find the best way to verbalize a focus, once found. In other words, sometimes speakers hesitate while they are deciding *what* to talk about next, and sometimes they hesitate while they are deciding *how* to talk about what they have chosen. Most of the hesitations in the data I will be discussing stem from one or the other of these two main types of reasons.

The data in question come from a situation in which 20 adult female speakers of American English were asked to 'tell what happened' in a movie they had seen shortly before. It was a seven-minute color and sound film produced as a means of eliciting speech about the same subject matter from speakers of various languages at various times. All the subjects were quite willing to tell what they remembered of the film, and most of them probably regarded the exercise as a memory task. Although the situation was an unusual one, the language was in all cases natural and spontaneous. Preliminary comparisons with narratives embedded in more typical conversations suggest that the findings from these film narratives are generalizable to less artificial speech situations, but more systematic comparisons of this sort have yet to be made.

The basic method I will follow here is to note correspondences between hesitational phenomena and other phenomena available in the linguistic record, including the content of what was said. I realize that there is a research tradition which regards the interpretation of content as too subjective or intuitive to allow any reliable conclusions. I would urge on the contrary that it is only by looking in detail at what a speaker is talking about at each point in a discourse that we can come significantly closer to an understanding of speech production processes. What follows is, among other things, an attempt to illustrate this point.

Most of the 20 speakers began their narratives by expressing acquiescence in the interviewer's request that they 'tell what happened in the movie'. Twelve said 'OK', two said 'all right', one each said 'sure', 'certainly', and 'I'll try', and only three plunged in without any acknowledgment of the request. For most speakers there then followed a considerable period of floundering, filled with pauses, pause fillers, lengthened syllables, false starts, and repetitions. The following is an example:

1. OK.
2. (.3) Um—(1.0) let's see.
3. (1.1)Uh—the first part of the . . m (.45) movie,
4. (.4) uh well,
5. the . . . the—. . the basic action,
6. (.5) i—s that there's—(.2) a man (.4) uh . . on a ladder,
7. (.55) uh picking pears from a pear tree.

Clearly this speaker was having trouble getting started. The content of her floundering provides some evidence as to what her mind was doing.

After the initial 'OK', it is evident that she was buying time as she searched for a satisfactory initial focus to verbalize. The phrase 'let's see' in line 2 is a commonly used way of communicating such a state. By line 3 she had apparently gotten no further than to decide she was going to talk about the first part of the movie. She bought more time in lines 4 and 5 with 'well' (another commonly used word in this situation) and the thrice repeated 'the'. At this point she had at least settled on 'the basic action', though still without a clear focus on what that action involved. There is a familiar narrative pattern in which a speaker introduces first a character and then an ongoing background activity in which that character is engaged. Apparently guided finally by that pattern, this speaker got around to introducing the pear picker by the middle of line 6, and his activity in line 7. Everything prior to line 6 is a gradual zeroing in and clarifying of these first substantive foci of her story.

It is interesting to compare another subject who seems to have avoided this need to search and clarify:

8. Sure.
9. There was a man—,
10. picking—,
11. (.9) um—(.1) a Latin looking man,
12. and he was picking pears,

This speaker moved directly from acquiescence in the interviewer's request to the introduction of a character and his activity. In spite of this efficiency, however, she showed signs that she had moved too precipitously, first through her lengthening of the words 'man' and 'picking', then through her significant hesitating at the beginning of line 11, where she evidently felt the need to bring the man into clearer focus and describe his most salient property. In summary, when one begins a narrative, some time-consuming mental processing usually needs to be devoted to the finding and clarification of an initial focus. Even when this processing is accomplished with ease, as in the last example, there is still a need to allow enough time to establish the essentials of this starting point.

The majority of foci of consciousness are expressed in linguistic phrases or clauses which end in a rising pitch contour (marked here with a comma), but approximately one-third of those in our data end instead with the kind of falling pitch contour interpreted as 'sentence-final intonation' (marked here with a period). This conspicuous sentence-final contour, as well as various other criteria including the syntactic properties associated with a 'grammatical sentence', define what I will call a 'focus cluster'. In other words, foci of consciousness appear to cluster together to form larger units which are verbalized as sentences. There are various kinds of coherence that bind the foci within such clusters together. Here I will point out only two patterns which occur with considerable frequency. One involves focusing on various simultaneous facets of a single image, much as the eye scans a scene to acquire various kinds of information from it. In the following excerpt the separate foci achieve an overall coherence through the unity of the scene being described:

13. OK,
14. . . uh—(.3) there's a—. . man,
15. (.45) picking pears,
16. in a pear tree,
17. Out . . somewhere in the country,
18. (1.1) uh—he looks (.95) like your uh (.2) typical . . farmer,
19. or (.3) whatever,
20. kind of plump,
21. and (.7) moustache,
22. and he wears a white apron,
23. (1.3) to . . hold the pears in.

Another common pattern is one in which a series of foci are unified by their contribution towards a single goal, the fulfillment of an intention of one of the characters. In the following excerpt everything is aimed toward the theft of the pears, and coherence is provided by this single aim:

24. (.95) Then um—(1.5) a little boy on a bicycle,
25. (1.15) comes riding past the tree.
26. (.75) a—nd (.2) sort of goes past the pears (.3) the (.2) pears in the baskets
27. and then stops,
28. (1.0) and looks up at the guy in the tree,
29. he's still on the ladder,
30. and he's not . . watching him,
31. so he (1.0) st . . puts his bike (.6) down,
32. (.85) he walks over,
33. a—nd he picks up a (.2) the whole basket of pears,
34. (.9) and puts it on the handle (.2) no, on the (.4) front (.15) fender of his bike.

In general there is more hesitating between focus clusters—that is, between sentences—than there is between foci within a cluster, as Table 5.1 shows. In other words, the breaks in coherence which are found at sentence boundaries—whether they result from a shift to a new image, to

TABLE 5.1
HESITATIONS AT FOCUS BOUNDARIES

	Within Cluster	Across Clusters
No Hesitation	42%	26%
Hesitation	58%	74%
Mean Length of Hesitation when Present	.84 sec.	1.18 sec.

a new goal, or whatever—require more time-consuming mental process-ing than does the moving from focus to focus within a cluster.

However, if we look at all the cases of hesitating between sentences, we find a range all the way from no hesitating at all up to seven seconds or more (including pauses, pause fillers, and false starts). Notice the great variety in hesitation lengths between the sentences in the following excerpt:

35. . . And he pulls the (.8) tsk goat by the guy who's up in the tree,
36. (.9) and disappears.
37. (.9) A—nd (2.9) the next people . . who come by,
38. (.9) and there's a little boy on a bicycle
39. . . who comes by from the other direction,
40. . . he's riding a bike,
41. . . it's a little too big for him.
42. (1.5) A—nd (.4) he rides by.
43. . . and then he stops,
44. (2.2) tries to . . take a pear,
45. . . a—nd then he (.35) he can't reach it.
46. . . So he puts down his bike,
47. (.9) he sort of takes a pear,
48. and then he decides he wants the whole basket.
49. . . So he takes the whole basket,
50. . . and puts it near his bike,
51. . . lifts up the bike,
52. . . puts the basket on . . the front part of his bicycle,
53. (.5) and rides off.
54. And all the time the guy's up in the (.6) tree,
55. . . and he doesn't notice it.
56. (.9) However the sounds are extremely loud.
57. (1.95 including cough) So . . it's kind of funny.

The sentence beginning in line 54 is preceded by no hesitation at all. The sentences beginning in 35, 46, and 49 are preceded by less than 50 milliseconds of pausing. On the other hand, the total hesitating at the beginning of 37 adds up to 4.35 seconds, and at the beginning of 42 to 2.5 seconds. Significant hesitating occurs also at the beginning of 56 and 57. It thus does not go very far to say that the mean length of hesitating between sentences is 1.18 seconds. We would like to be able to explain why the individual lengths vary as much as they do.

Again, observation of the content of what is being said can lead us towards some answers. The simplest hypothesis would be that focus clusters themselves cluster into larger conceptual units—call them 'episodes'—which correspond in written language to paragraphs. Thus we could explain the very brief hesitation at the beginning of line 35 by saying that the sentence in 35–36 expresses a focus cluster that belongs to the same episode as the cluster immediately preceding (not shown here), whereas the long hesitation at the beginning of 37 reflects the beginning of a new episode. This interpretation is supported by the fact that 35 begins with a pronoun, and in fact maintains the same grammatical subject as the preceding focus, whereas 37 begins with a full noun phrase which represents a change of subject. Differences like these can be interpreted as additional evidence for same-episode vs. different-episode transitions.

Closer examination of the variability of hesitations between sentences suggests that the episode explanation, while on the right track, is something of an oversimplification. The factors which lead to such hesitating are in fact several, and while they sometimes coincide to produce what appears to be a clear-cut episode boundary, they may also occur independently and in various combinations to produce hesitations of various lengths at various places in a narrative. Rather than to think of 'episode boundary' as a monolithic notion, therefore, it is preferable to think of several kinds of transitions which are likely to require extra processing time.

Looking again at the long excerpt in lines 35–57 above, we can see some of these factors illustrated. The importance of the factors I will mention is confirmed in other narratives, but there is not space here to present the range of evidence available. The factors which seem to be important in triggering significant hesitations between sentences are the following:

(a) Introduction of a new character or set of characters
(b) Change of location
(c) Change of time period
(d) Change of event schema
(e) Change of world

In other words, speakers seem to require some time to recall or clarify in their minds any changes of these types. When several occur together, as they often do, the processing time required generally increases.

Such a combination is illustrated in lines 37–38. A new character enters the narrative at this point, there is a minor spatial change (he 'comes by from the other direction'), and there is the beginning of a new event schema in that it is here that the events culminating in the theft of the pears begin. It took the speaker more than four seconds to cope with this combination of changes. In fact, line 37 is actually a false start, and the speaker did not really settle on a clear focus until she was one second into line 38.

The foci within the rest of this cluster (37–41) were settled on without much further interruption. It is interesting, however, to observe that 38–39 make use of a highly familiar syntactic pattern, 'there is a . . . who . . . ', which is commonly used for introducing a new character and involving him in some kind of background activity, in this case his 'coming by'. By the end of 39 the speaker had used up this syntactic pattern. She had not, however, said everything she wanted to say about the image she had activated; specifically, she needed two more clauses to communicate the inappropriate size of the bicycle. Hence 40 and 41 were tacked on, syntactically as afterthoughts, to complete the cluster. It is often the case that a syntactic pattern will prove inadequate to what a speaker has in mind, and be supplemented by independent clause increments like 40 and 41.

Once the boy had been introduced in 37–41, the speaker used up again a considerable amount of time getting started on a description of his actions. Although the section beginning with line 42 would probably be regarded as belonging to the same episode or paragraph as the preceding sentence, it nevertheless represents the beginning of a coherent event schema which the speaker evidently needed more time to pull together. Introducing a new character thus does not necessarily bring automatically into focus the actions of that character. Getting the character involved in his actions may be another reason for hesitating.

The 2.2 second hesitation at the beginning of line 44 has a special kind of interest. Lines 44–45 are in a sense false; they describe an event which did not happen in the film. The boy did not try to take a pear while he was still on his bicycle. An interesting possibility is that the construction and verbalization of a nonveridical piece of information is also likely to be a cause for hesitating. Constructive recall takes time.

From here on speech moves fairly fluently through four sentences, up to the end of 55. Lines 42–53 present three basic actions involved in the theft of pears: trying to take one pear while still on the bicycle, taking one while on foot, and taking the whole basket. Three separate sentences are used to express this sequence here. However, six weeks later the same speaker, asked to tell about the film again, coalesced the three into a single sentence, giving evidence of a conceptual unity in 42–53 which helps to account for the easy transitions at the beginnings of 46 and 49.

But why should there be no hesitation at the beginning of 54, where a different character is reintroduced and there is a clear change of both grammatical subject and subject matter? The six-week-later version may shed some light here too. In that version the speaker began to make this comment about the man in the tree just after she had begun the theft sequence, but she then immediately abandoned it, uncompleted, as inappropriate at that point:

58 And he stops,
59 (4.45) bu—t (.25) the man who's in the tree.
60. . . . And he um

It seems that the unwatchfulness of the pear picker in the tree was something the speaker had 'in the back of her mind', or was peripherally conscious of, simultaneously with the events of the theft, so that this idea was ready to be brought forward without hesitation in 54–55. This example suggests both (1) that it may sometimes be instructive, in explaining hesitations, to see how a speaker would verbalize the same material on another occasion, and (2) that it is also of some interest to see where people do *not* hesitate, especially under conditions where a hesitation might normally be expected.

Lines 56 and 57, which end this excerpt, exhibit the effect of change in worlds. The longest hesitation by this speaker, 7.05 seconds long, came at a point earlier in her narrative where she inserted a comment on the sound track:

61. (2.55) Um (4.05 the thing I noticed all the way through is that
. . there's (.5) there's no—. . dialogue in the film,
62. but there . . is (1.0) a lot of sound effects. etc.

Here, at the beginning of 61, there was a clear shift from the world inside the film to the world outside it, where one could take a critical stance and talk about properties of the film as a film. In 61 this shift was a highly time-consuming process. A recurrence of the shift in 56 required only .9 seconds of extra time, suggesting that once a transition between different worlds has been established in the speaker's mind, it subsequently becomes easier to move back and forth between them.

Finally, line 57 provides an evaluative comment (cf. the discussion of evaluative devices in Labov 1972:354–396). Such a comment is in a sense a shift to still another world: the world of the speaker's attitudes. It is clearly another reason for hesitating. Of additional interest is the fact that evaluative material is often accompanied by some audible expression of affect: often a laugh—sometimes, as here, a cough.

My discussion up to this point has dealt with hesitations caused by the speaker's need to decide what to talk about next. Such hesitations typically occur between the phrases and clauses which express the foci of consciousness. But many hesitations occur within these phrases and clauses as well. One may also hesitate *during* the verbalization of a focus. Such hesitations are usually attributable to difficulty the speaker is having in deciding, not what to verbalize, but how to verbalize something he already has in mind. The basic problem for the speaker here is one of categorization, more or less in the sense of Rosch (1973) and others. Some concepts that a speaker may have in mind are easy to categorize, are 'highly codable', while others may be more or less difficult, may be low in codability. In the seminal study of Brown and Lenneberg (1954), 'reaction time' was one of the indices of codability investigated. The implication of that study for the explanation of hesitations is that it takes time to verbalize a referent which has low codability. Put simply, some referents are harder to find words to communicate than others, and the degree of hesitating is correlated with the degree of difficulty.

We deliberately included in our film both objects that we expected to be high in codability and objects with which we expected speakers to have difficulty. In the former class, for example, was the boy's bicycle. Although people called it either a 'bicycle' or a 'bike', no one hesitated even briefly before such a word. No one said anything like:

there's a boy on a . . . uh . . . bicycle,

The object at the other extreme, the one which was most successful in causing difficulty for speakers, was something we have come to call the 'paddleball'. Only one of the sixteen subjects who mentioned this object failed to hesitate in referring to it:

63. (1.6) um one's playing with a paddleball.

Others said things like:

64. one of them has a . . what do you call those little . . um (.85) paddleball?

or:

65. one was (.25) had a little (.55) paddle with a ball—,

but the prize for the best attempt to communicate the idea of this object went to the speaker who said:

66. (.4) I don't remember,
67. I used to play with it when I was a kid,
68. but (.75) it's like a . . wooden paddle
69. (.3) that (.15) there's an elastic string attached to
70. and there's a ball,
71. (.3) you know that that kind of thing that you (.4) you
72. (.15) I . . don't remember the name of them,
73. (.35) but I played with them for hours.

Although this excerpt may seem ungrammatical or 'disfluent', I suggest that the speaker was quite successful in conveying what she had in mind, and that this kind of hesitation-ridden speech should actually be highly valued as an accurate expression of a speaker's thoughts.

In summary, I have tried with a few examples, which are representative of numerous others in our material, to show some of the factors which produce hesitations as the speaker's consciousness moves from focus to focus. Such factors include finding and clarifying an initial focus, moving to the next focus within a cluster, and moving across a cluster boundary. There may be more or less difficulty in the transition, depending on such factors as change of characters, of scene, of time period, of event structure, of world. Evaluative comments function as world changes, but may be accompanied by audible expressions of affect. Other factors may enter the picture sporadically, such as the construction of nonveridical material. Having something in one's peripheral consciousness may inhibit hesitating where it would otherwise occur. Finally, a considerable proportion of hesitating stems from the need to verbalize something that is low in codability. I expect that this procedure of carefully examining the content factors which are present at the points where hesitations occur is going to be an important and necessary aspect of hesitation research.

REFERENCES

Brown, Roger W. and Eric H. Lenneberg. 1954. A study in language and cognition. Journal of Abnormal and Social Psychology 49.454–462.
Buswell, G. T. 1935. How people look at pictures. Chicago: University of Chicago Press.
Chafe, Wallace L. 1977. The recall and verbalization of past experience. Current issues in linguistic theory, ed. by R. W. Cole, 215–246. Bloomington: Indiana University Press.
Chafe, Wallace L. 1979. The flow of thought and the flow of language. Discourse and syntax, ed. by Givon Talmy, 159–181. New York: Academic Press.
Chafe, Wallace L. 1980. The deployment of consciousness in the production of a narrative. The pear stories: cognitive, cultural, and linguistic aspects of narrative production, ed. by W. L. Chafe, 9–50. Norwood, NJ: Ablex Publishing Corporation.
Chomsky, Noam. 1965. Aspects of the theory of syntax. Cambridge, MA: MIT Press.
Halliday, Michael A. K. 1967. Notes on transitivity and theme in English. Part 2. Journal of Linguistics 3.199–244.

Harris, Zelig S. 1955. From phoneme to morpheme. Language 31.190–222.

James, William. 1890. The principles of psychology. New York: Henry Holt. Rpt. Dover Publications.

Labov, William. 1972. The transformation of experience in narrative syntax. Language in the inner city. Philadelphia: University of Pennsylvania Press.

Lounsbury, Floyd G. 1954. Transitional probability, linguistic structure, and systems of habit-family hierarchies, Psycholinguistics: A survey of theory and research problems, ed. by Charles E. Osgood & Thomas A. Sebeok, 93–101. Baltimore: Waverly Press. Supplement to: Journal of Abnormal and Social Psychology 49. Also supplement to: International Journal of American Linguistics 20.

Newtson, Darren. 1976. Foundations of attribution: The perception of ongoing behavior. New directions in attribution research, Vol. 1. ed. by J. H. Harvey, W. J. Ickes, & R. F. Kidd. Hillsdale, NJ: Erlbaum.

Rosch, Eleanor H. 1973. On the internal structure of perceptual and semantic categories. Cognitive development and the acquisition of language, ed. by T. E. Moore, 111–144. New York: Academic Press.

PART III

SOME MEANINGS AND
USES OF SILENCE

Chapter 6

Silence: Anything But

Deborah Tannen

Georgetown University

The research I will be drawing on here is an extensive and ongoing analysis of conversational style, focusing in particular on the style of three New Yorkers of East European Jewish background as evidenced in conversation with three non-New Yorkers at a Thanksgiving dinner.[1] I will suggest that features of this style can be understood as growing out of an effort to avoid silence.

I became aware early on that silence, for speakers of this style, has a negative value in many communicative contexts. This became apparent as I analyzed the transcripts of the Thanksgiving conversation, and also in my observations of New Yorkers. New Yorkers, for example, are much more likely than Americans from most other places to talk to strangers when they find themselves within hearing range—for example, while waiting in lines or waiting rooms, or when overhearing conversations while passing in the street or sitting at a restaurant. With intimates, too, New Yorkers seem more inclined to expect talk to be continuous, as reflected in the complaints of partners of New Yorkers following, for example, a long car drive during which the New Yorker talked the whole time.

It was the work of Ron Scollon (Chapter 2) which prompted me to think about the place of this style on a cross-cultural continuum of values associated with noise and silence. As the chapters for this volume arrived, the existence of such a continuum became increasingly apparent, and with it the significance of New York Jewish style, which shares relatively positive valuation of noise and relatively negative valuation of si-

---

[1]Analysis of conversation presented in this chapter is based on Tannen (1984), wherein may be found numerous extended examples of conversational transcripts demonstrating the features listed.

lence in casual conversation with such communicative styles as Antiguan (Reisman 1974), Italian (Saunders, Chapter 9), Italian-American (Erickson 1982), Igbo (Nwoye, Chapter 10), Afro-American (Kochman 1981, Erickson 1984), Cape Verdean (Gomes 1979), and Armenian-American. The consideration of the uses of silence in a range of cultures suggested, moreover, the underlying question of when a pause is perceived as a silence.

Before addressing the question of silence in New York Jewish conversational style I will consider the general theoretical question of the ambiguity of silence as a communicative sign. In discussing features of New York Jewish conversational style, I will consider how these attitudes toward silence are accommodated and reflected in conversational interaction, and the effects on interaction of differing attitudes toward silence. In conclusion, I will address the larger question of what is silence.

POSITIVE AND NEGATIVE VALUATION OF SILENCE

We have two conflicting yet simultaneous views of silence: one positive, and one negative. Allen (1978), in a literary analysis of the work of three contemporary women writers, notes that silence serves two functions in the literature she surveyed, one negative—a failure of language—and one positive—a chance for personal exploration. She notes that the poetry of Adrienne Rich emphasizes the former aspect of silence, as in, for example, the 'husband who is frustratingly mute'. Cliff (1979), in an article in a 'magazine of woman's culture', suggests that women have not been able to do creative work to their capacity because their fruitful silence is continually interrupted—a hypothesis akin to that of Virginia Woolf in *A Room of One's Own*.

The positive and negative valuation of silence is a facet of the inherent ambiguity of silence as a symbol, which Saville-Troike highlights in Chapter 1. The ambiguous value of silence can be seen to arise either from what is assumed to be evidenced or from what is assumed to be omitted.

Silence is seen as positive when it is taken as evidence of the existence of something positive underlying—for example, proper respect; the silence of the telephone when it represents solitude for creative work; the silence of 'sweet silent thought'; and the silence of perfect rapport between intimates who do not have to exchange words. But silence is also seen as positive if it is assumed to represent the omission of something negative—'If you can't say something nice, don't say anything'; or when Congressman Emanuel Celler is remembered for having said, 'To what the gentleman from Ohio says, I give the thunder of my silence' (*Newsweek* January 26, 1981:63).

Silence becomes a bad thing if it seems to represent the existence of something negative—the silence of seething anger, as described by Gilmore (Chapter 8). But it is also negatively valued if it is assumed to represent the omission of something positive—the silence of the telephone when you are anxiously awaiting a particular telephone call; the omission of a greeting which constitutes being snubbed; inaction because appropriate action is not being taken as reflected in Anita Bryant's statement, 'When the homosexuals burn the Holy Bible in public . . . how can I stand by silently?' (*New York Review of Books*, September 25, 1980:27).

These positive and negative views of silence apply as well to silence in conversation. *Washington Post* columnist Dick Dabney takes silence to be a sign of especially good communication when he writes of his eight-year-old daughter sitting in her grandmother's lap 'engaged in leisurely conversation that had long satisfactory silences in it', and observes that 'these two were enjoying each other's company . . .' The same assumption surfaces in a novel by Colette (1971):

> I suggested that he and I go for a voyage together, a pair of courteously egotistic companions, accommodating, fond of long silences . . .
> (p. 55)

> We had the comfortable habit of leaving a sentence hanging midway as soon as one of us had grasped the point. . . She fell silent. No one can imagine the number of subjects, the amount of words that are left out of the conversation of two women who can talk to each other with absolute freedom. (p. 57)

Given the freedom to say anything, the women come to understand each other so well that they need to say less. In a similar vein, a pop poster showing the usual waterfall and green scene displays the line, 'If you do not understand my silence you will not understand my words.'

In these examples, silence represents something positive which is evidenced—interpersonal rapport so great that people understand each other without putting their thoughts into words. This view, supported by informal research conducted in my classes, reflects the common notion that silence is positive among intimates.

Yet there is also a common view that silence among intimates evidences lack of rapport. In an early scene of the film *Two For The Road,* Audrey Hepburn and Richard Harris, as young, talkative lovers, regard an older couple sitting at a nearby table in a restaurant. 'What kind of people eat without talking to each other?' Hepburn asks. 'Married people', Harris responds—with distaste and disdain.

Similarly, Labov and Fanshel (1977:313), in a study of a psychotherapeutic conversation, describe what they call 'an eloquent silence of
13 seconds' as 'more negative than anything we have seen so far'.

Colette (1972) also gives us a 'silent, menacing lover', 'obstinate silence', someone 'irritated by his silence', someone 'silent, discouraged',
'silence and dissimulation', a silence that separates people, 'an embarrassing silence', and people who 'sadly . . . remained mute'. All of these
seem to reflect the common notion that there should be talk among
intimates who are comfortable, honest, happy.

The assumption that silence in conversation is negative also underlies
a comment by the actress Jane Fonda about her father: 'I can remember
long car rides where not a word would be spoken. I would be so nervous
that my palms would be sweaty from riding in absolute silence with my
own father' (*Newsweek*, August 23, 1982:47). And the same assumption
can be seen reflected in a column by Ellen Goodman (1979:19) portraying 'The Company Man' as unable to communicate with any of his children, but in particular with his daughter who 'lives near her mother and
they are close, but whenever she was alone with her father, in a car
driving somewhere, they had nothing to say to each other'. Goodman
contrasts 'being close' on the one hand with having 'nothing to say to
each other' on the other.

Thus whether or not silence is uncomfortable in interaction hinges on
whether or not participants feel something should be said, in which case
silence is perceived as an omission. This underlies, as well, Goffman's
(1967:36) observation that 'Undue lulls come to be potential signs of
having nothing in common, or of being insufficiently self-possessed to
create something to say, and hence must be avoided.' (Note, however,
that this leaves open the question of how much lull is undue, or, put
another way, how much silence is a lull—a question that will be addressed later).

As Bateson has observed, in the framework of interaction, one cannot
not communicate. The omission of expected behavior or words is as
eloquent as the inclusion of the unexpected, as noted by Sapir (1949:533):

> We often form a judgment of what [a person] is by what he does not
> say, and we may be very wise to refuse to limit the evidence for judgment
> to the overt content of speech.

Perhaps the clearest examples of silence as omission of the required is
seen in the case of situational or politeness formulas. When a formulaic
expression is expected—and some cultures, such as Arabic (Ferguson
1976) and Greek and Turkish (Tannen and Oztek 1981), use more of

these than Americans do, while other, such as Athabaskan Indians (Scollon personal communication) and Eskimos (Sadock 1982) use far fewer[2]—its omission is automatically perceived, as for example when a failure to utter a greeting might be reported as, 'He snubbed me', or the failure to utter a closure might be reported as, 'He hung up on me'. The eloquence of silence as an omission is reflected in Colette's (1972:23) depiction of the point of view of an adolescent boy: 'It's incredible what cheek girls have, putting on that act of saying nothing!'

SILENCE AND NEGATIVE AND POSITIVE POLITENESS

Silence is the extreme manifestation of indirectness. If indirectness is a matter of saying one thing and meaning another, silence can be a matter of saying nothing and meaning something. Like indirectness, silence has two big benefits in rapport and defensiveness. The rapport benefit comes from being understood without putting one's meaning on record, so that understanding is seen not as the result of putting meaning into words— which presumably could be achieved with any two people who speak the same language—but rather as the greater understanding of shared per-spective, experience and intimacy, the deeper sense of 'speaking the same language'. This is the positive value of silence stemming from the existence of something positive underlying.

The defensive value of silence comes from omitting to say something negative—not confronting potentially divisive information (cf Saunders, Chapter 9), or being able later to deny having meant what may not be received well ('Don't look at me; I didn't say anything!').

Thus the meaning of silence in interaction, like other features of dis-course, can be understood to grow out of the two overriding goals of human communication: to be connected to other people, and to be inde-pendent, which correspond to the rapport and defensive benefits of si-lence, respectively. The goals of connection and independence, in turn, correspond to what Goffman (1967) calls presentational rituals and avoidance rituals; what Lakoff (1979) refers to as the needs for deference or distance on the one hand and camaraderie on the other; and what Brown and Levinson (1978) refer to as positive face (the need to be approved of by others) and negative face (the need not to be imposed on by others). Ways of serving these needs, then, are positive and negative politeness.

---

[2]Both Sadock and Scollon claim that speakers in the cultures they have studied use no formulaic language.

Negative and positive politeness result from the paradoxical nature of interpersonal rapport. Closeness is to be sought, because people need to be involved with others. But it is also to be avoided, as a threat to the integrity of the individual. Scollon (1982) points out that politeness is not a matter of serving one or the other of these needs but of finding the right linguistic concoction to serve both at the same time in each utterance.

Silence has a positive value as a way of serving negative politeness—not imposing on others. This can occur in any culture but seems to be the unmarked case in cultures which may be characterized as relatively 'silent'—among Finns (Lehtonen and Sajavaara, Chapter 11), Athabaskan and Warm Springs Indians (Scollon and Philips, Chapters 2 and 12). But silence can also have a negative value when it is seen as the failure of positive politeness—the need to be involved with others. This can occur in any culture but seems to be the unmarked case in cultures which may be characterized as relatively 'noisy' such as among Italians (Saunders, Chapter 9), American blacks (Gilmore, Chapter 8), the Igbo (Nwoye, Chapter 10), and New York Jews.

Nonetheless silence can be seen as positive or negative by members of any culture, as it is measured against what is expected in that context.

Looking at Maltz's (Chapter 7) findings about silence in worship with the double vision of negative and positive politeness, Quakers see noise as an imposition—a violation of negative face—and Pentecostals see noise as an expression of worship—observance of positive face. On the other hand, Quakers see silence as allowing the individual space to receive the Holy Spirit—observance of negative face. Pentecostals see silence as insufficient praise and participation—failure to observe positive face.

Interestingly, it is the model of religious practice that formed the basis for Durkheim's (1915) original schematization of positive and negative religious rites, which Goffman's (1967) notion of deference broadened to apply to everyday life, in turn forming the basis for Brown and Levinson's (1978) schema of negative and positive politeness. The Quakers typify what Durkheim identified as the negative religious rite—the avoidance of the profane to prepare for reception of the sacred, silence as what Maltz terms 'expectant waiting'.

Although silence can be seen as negative politeness—being nice to others by not imposing, or, as Maltz suggests, disengagement—the conventionalization of silence as an expression of negative meaning can result in engagement. Thus some of the teachers in Gilmore's (Chapter 8) ethnographic study refer to children's silent sulks as 'temper tantrums'. In keeping with Saunders' account of the use of silence in cases of serious anger, an American observed that his Italian lover became disproportionately (to him) concerned when he became silent.

SILENCE AS REFLECTION OF COGNITIVE AND SOCIAL PROCESSES

The ambiguity of silence in interaction derives as well from another duality in the nature of all communicative signs. It can be seen from the perspective of the producer or the receiver. When Walker (Chapter 4) reports that witnesses are told to pause before speaking in order to plan their answers, it is the production function of speech that is in focus. But when lawyers distrust the testimony of hesitant witnesses, it is the effect on the hearer that is at issue.

This duality reflects an even deeper one underlying it. In addition to distinguishing between the function of the pause for speaker as opposed to hearer, Walker's 'two faces of silence' highlight its cognitive versus social uses, each of which has a potential dual function, for speaker and hearer. Thus the cognitive function of pausing to give the speaker time to think may be mirrored in giving the hearer more time to comprehend. (This may contribute to the fact that spoken language is easier to comprehend because it is less dense than written language read aloud, a situation in which the creator took more time to produce the discourse than the hearer has to comprehend it.)

The social consequences of pausing in terms of impressions made on the hearer may be mirrored in the speaker's adoption of a pausing (or, seen from a less deliberate point of view, hesitant) style for the purpose of appearing as one sort of person rather than another, a phenomenon that Robin Lakoff (1975) suggests accounts for the fact that women tend to hesitate more than men. That is, speakers may consciously or unconsciously wish to present themselves as 'hesitant' in order to be more likable, or to be conventionally polite, or to be feminine, or for other social reasons.

Thus, a greeting card exhibits on its face the words, printed in handwriting rather than typeset, 'I just want to tell you that . . . that . . . that . . .' Inside, the writing concludes, '. . . I love you'. The representation of hesitation, like the representation of handwriting rather than typeset letters, is supposed to give the receiver of the card the sense of spontaneity and hence sincerity (which is at odds with the impression normally made by a mass-produced greeting card).

Chafe (Chapter 5) focuses on the cognitive function in discourse production: 'The speaker's chief goal is to get across what he has in mind, . . . the adequate verbalization of his thoughts.' But choices a speaker makes about how to verbalize thoughts also result in impressions made on others about the kind of person the speaker is, and what s/he thinks about the setting and the addressee—all that makes up what Bateson (1972) calls the metamessage. In other words, a speaker deciding how to verbalize a thought will probably do so in different ways depending on whether s/he is talking to a child, a parent, a boss, or an audience of a thousand in a lecture hall, and depending on how s/he is disposed toward that audience and toward the subject. Chafe is certainly correct to note that most speakers in most situations would be far more distressed to be told 'You didn't get across what you had in mind,' than 'You spoke ungrammatically (or disfluently),' but they would probably be equally or more distressed to be told, 'You got across what you had in mind, but I think you are a jerk.'

The cognitive/social duality underlies, in fact, Allen's (1978) positive and negative aspects of silence cited at the outset: a chance for personal exploration vs. failure of language. Personal exploration is the existence of cognitive activity underlying silence; the failure of language refers to its social function.

SILENCE AS A JOINT PRODUCTION

A last observation to be made about the nature, meaning, and function of silence in interaction is that, again like other features of discourse, it is always a joint production. Jack Kroll quoted Jane Fonda's remark about her father to prove that Henry Fonda embodied the strong silent male stereotype.[3] Kroll assumed that it was Henry Fonda who owned that silence; it was he who was not talking. Goodman, in the column cited, gave joint ownership of the silence to the Company Man and his daughter. Yet another woman told me that when her husband returned from driving his teenage daughter somewhere, he felt awful because they had driven in silence. She cited the silence as evidence of the daughter's hostility toward her father.

These varying interpretations of a similar phenomenon highlight the fact that when there are two or more participants in a conversation—in other words, when there is conversation—anything that happens or doesn't happen, is said or unsaid, is the result of interaction among the two—what McDermott and Tylbor (1983) call collusion. At any point that one person is not talking and thereby produces a silence, no one else is talking either—or there wouldn't be a silence.

---

[3]This image itself has a positive and negative aspect. Thus the mirror image of the strong silent man—something positive (strength) underlying—is the withholding man—something positive omitted (interpersonal rapport)—an aspect of the male stereotype which is widely referred to and complained about by women.

SILENCE IN CONVERSATION

How, then, does the ambiguity of silence influence conversation? My discussion of examples from New York Jewish conversational style rests on a theory of meaning in conversation and method of conversational analysis developed under the influence of John Gumperz, which I shall sketch here only briefly. (For detailed discussion of theory and method see Gumperz 1982, Tannen 1984.)

The Analysis of Conversational Style

Gumperz demonstrates that speakers use paralinguistic and prosodic features to indicate how they mean what they say—that is, to 'frame' (Bateson 1972) their message—and to establish cohesion, that is, to indicate relationships among words in a sentence and sentences in a discourse. The features of speech used in this way include intonation, pitch, amplitude, pacing, rate of speech, pausing, rate of turntaking, choice of words and phrases, topics preferred and avoided, genres (storytelling, joking, lecturing), and ways of serving the constraints of these genres.

Ways of using these features generally seem self-evident and obvious. It seems, for example, self-evidently appropriate to some speakers to raise their voices when angry, to use a certain voice quality when joking, to tell stories about certain topics with certain points in mind. However, in communicating with others, intentions must be deduced from these cues; they are not known, as one's own intentions are (more or less) known. Intentions of others can be deduced only by reference to norms, and one uses one's own norms in interpreting others' speech. In other words, I assume that you mean what I would have meant if I had said the same thing in the same way at such a time. This principle of interpretation works fine in communication with others who share assumptions and habits. It fails, however, in communication with others who have different habits and expectations. Hence there arises miscommunication among speakers of different backgrounds. Moreover, judgments are made not about how others speak but about their abilities and/or personalities.

Thanksgiving Dinner Data

I have been engaged in extended analysis of a taperecorded, transcribed conversation which took place over Thanksgiving dinner among six participants—three native New Yorkers of Jewish background (of which I was one), two Californians of non-Jewish background, and one native of England (who had one Jewish parent) whose style was clearly distinct but more closely approximated that of the Californians than that of the New

Yorkers. I had begun that study with the intention of analyzing each participant's conversational style—how s/he used the features I have noted in interaction. It soon became clear, however, that I could not equally study the styles of all those present. For one thing, the three New Yorkers at times were the only speakers, but there was no time that the non-New Yorkers spoke to each other with no New Yorker participating. Furthermore, according to the recollections of the non-New Yorkers, the New Yorkers had 'dominated' the conversation. (The ensuing analysis demonstrates that the perception of 'dominance' and the intention to dominate are not always congruent.)

It became clear after analysis of the data that the three New Yorkers tended to use certain features in certain ways that had one effect—a positive one—when used with each other, and another effect—a negative one—when used with the non-New Yorkers. I will briefly indicate what those features were and suggest that they may be understood as an outgrowth of a negative attitude toward silence in casual conversation.

New York Jewish Conversational Style

The features characterizing the styles of the New Yorkers in this conversation included:

1. Fast rate of speech[4]
2. Fast rate of turntaking
3. Persistence—if a turn is not acknowledged, try try again
4. Marked shifts in pitch
5. Marked shifts in amplitude
6. Preference for storytelling
7. Preference for personal stories
8. Tolerance of, preference for simultaneous speech
9. Abrupt topic shifting

These features are combined in conversational devices. For example, the machine-gun question typically exhibits fast rate of speech, marked high or low pitch, reduced syntactic form, and personal focus, as seen in my questions to Chad, intended to show interest in him.[5]

---

[4]Scollon (1982) points out that rate of speech has at least two distinct components, tempo and density. I use the term to refer to both.

[5]In transcription, three dots (...) represent a half second pause; each additional dot (.) represents anothers half second of pause. ? = rising intonation. Period (.) = falling intonation. : = lengthening of vowel sound. acc = fast; p = soft; f = loud. ' = high pitch on word; r = high pitch on phrase. ´ = primary stress; ` = secondary stress; underline = emphatic stress. /?/ = incomprehensible utterance.

(1) Deborah: ⌐Yoù live in LÁ?

(2)   Chad: Yeah.

(3) Deborah: ⌐Y'visiting here?

(4)   Chad: Yeah.

(5) Deborah: What do you ⌐dó there?

(6)   Chad: uh: I work at Studio Prosuh- ... First Studios. ...

```
              ⌐a:nd
(7) Deborah: └Yòu an ártist?
```

(8)   Chad: No: no.

(9) Deborah: Writer?

(10)   Chad: Yeah:. I write ... ádvertising copy.

The questions got little response because their machine gun nature made Chad feel under fire, and his resistance to answering them made me instinctively throw out more as I tried harder to draw him out.

Another device was mutual revelation, which operates on the principle: 'I tell you about me; you tell me about you.' Yet another is the storytelling round, in which each speaker tells a story with a point similar to that of the preceding one, with no introduction, and the point is dramatized rather than stated. Expressive reaction is a loud, fast, and paralinguistically gross response to someone's point, like 'Wow,' 'You're kidding!'

Many of these devices have the effect of filling up conversational space. Among the most salient features of the style are fast rate of speech, fast turntaking (i.e. minimal pause between speakers), and loud voices. This can be seen in the excerpt from the transcript presented above. There are no hesitations in my speech, many in Chad's. My question (7), "You an artist?", overlaps with Chad's answer (6) to my question about where he works.

The persistence device—the tendency of speakers to introduce freely new topics that are unrelated or tangentially related to prior talk—is another salient feature of the style. In one interchange, for example, the three New Yorkers each pursued their own topics: one talked about the food, another talked about the tape recorder on the table, and I talked about how our immigrant parents and grandparents felt about Thanksgiving. The British guest responded to my topic (though in a way that I thought missed my point). There were instances in the conversation of New Yorkers pursuing their own topics as many as seven tries before dropping them for lack of listener response. There were no instances of non-New Yorkers pursuing topics for more than two tries, if they were not picked up.

The persistence device grows out of the conventionalized assumption that others want to hear anything one has to say, and is necessarily associated with a tolerance for overlapping and diffuse talk. The jumping from topic to topic was noted by all non-New York participants when the tape of the conversation was played back to them later, to the effect that it seemed odd to them; in fact, they remembered this feature of the talk even before they heard the tape. It was not remarked upon by New York participants, either when I asked what they remembered or when I played the tape for them. Furthermore, it was clear from their responses as well as their comments during playback that the New Yorkers did not mind when a comment they made was ignored. In contrast, the non-New Yorkers felt that if they said something it should be attended to.

An example of a segment of fast-paced, overlapping interchange follows:

(1) Deborah: Próbly not. Dju go to the Coliséum?
                      acc

(2) Chad: No.

(3) Deborah: Probly he didn't go to the West Side⌉
               acc, p

(4) Steve: ⌈Cóliséum?!
                                       f

(5) Deborah: Thàt's where the beginning of the West 'Síde is.
               acc

(6) Steve: Oh right.

(7) Peter: ⌈Wwhàt's the Coliséum.
     Steve: ⌊/?/

(8) Deborah: Fifty ninth and uh:

(9) Chad: [*sings*] Ea:st Si:de, We:st Si:de.

(10) Peter: What ís it.

(11) Deborah: What ís it? It's a big exposítion center.

(12) Steve: And office building.
     David: ⌈/?/

(13) Peter: ⌊By fifty ninth. And Columbus Circle.
(14) Deborah: ⌊mmm⌋

                    ....

(15) Steve: Rremember where ⌈W I N S used to be?

(16) Deborah: No⌉

(17) Steve: ⌊Then they built a big huge skyscraper there?

(18) Deborah: No. Whère was thát.

(19) Steve: Right where Central Park West met Broádway. That
               acc

⌐building shaped like that. [*Makes a pyramid with hands*]

(20)   Peter: └Did ⌐I give you too much? [*re turkey*]

(21) Deborah: └By Columbus Círcuit? ... that Columbus Círcle?

(22)   Steve: └ Right on Columbus Círcle.

Hére's Columbus Circle, ... ⌐here's Central Park West,

(23) Deborah: └Nòw it's

the Huntington Hártford Museum.

(24)   Peter: └Thàt's the Huntington Hártford, right?

(25)   Steve: Nuhnuhno. ... Hére's Central Park West, hére's

Deborah: └Yeah.

Broadway. We're going nórth, thìs way? ... and

Deborah: └ uhuh ┘

here's thís building hère. The Huntington Hártford is

is ⌐on the Soúth side.

(26) Deborah: └on the óther- across. Yeah, rightrightrightright

⌐And nów that's a new building with uh:┐

(27)   Steve: └And there was ...   └ and┘   └there was a-

stóres here, and the upper second floor was W I N Ś.

Deborah:└ oh: ┘

... And we listened to:

(28) Deborah: Now it's a round place with a: movie theatre.

(29)   Steve: Now- there's a roun- No. The next .. néxt block is but

... but ... <u>this</u> is a huge skýscraper right there.

Deborah: └ oh ┘   └ oh, yeah.

......

(30) Deborah: hm┐

(31)   Steve: └It's amazing.

(32) Deborah: I never <u>knew</u> where W I N Ś was.

(33)   Steve: That was my <u>haunt</u> cause I went down for children's concerts.

One way to understand these features is to understand that the New Yorkers would have been uncomfortable with silence in this setting. Hence it is better to toss out a new topic rather than risk silence as an old one peters out. There is an economy by which participants are free to ignore comments, enabling others to toss them out as exuberantly as they like. In the economy practiced by the non-New Yorkers, comments are coercive: listeners had to pay attention to them. Therefore speakers were inclined to be much more tentative about offering topics, hesitating when starting and beginning vaguely, in order to temper that coercive effect.

FAST TALKERS AND SLOW TALKERS

A psychologist at UCLA, Gerald Goodman (Esterly 1979), has identified the conversational style I have been describing, although he does not identify it as such. He calls fast-paced speakers 'crowders' and considers them a conversational menace. He offers a course—at a price—to teach crowders patience. Goodman eloquently articulated the effect fast talkers have on those unaccustomed to their style:

> There's a dehumanizing aspect to being crowded; there's a lack of respect involved. Interrupting arises from a variety of factors—anxiety, a desire to dominate, boredom, the need to express freshly stimulated thought . . . People walk away from conversations with crowders feeling upset or dissatisfied or incompetent, though they may not understand why. (p. 68)

Goodman allows only one positive interpretation of fast talking: the 'need to express freshly stimulated thought'. All the other reasons he can think of for it are negative, associated with the evil motive 'domination'. Moreover, he equates the effect of domination on the hearer with the speaker's intention to dominate.

Goodman is expressing an interpretation of fast pacing similar to that evidenced and expressed by the three non-New Yorkers in the dinner conversation I analyzed. It is the feeling of being imposed upon, in violation of Robin Lakoff's (1973) politeness rule 'Don't impose', and in violation of negative face. However, universal as this need is, the question of what constitutes an imposition is culturally relative. Hence the 'dehumanizing aspect' Goodman observes, the vague feeling of dissatisfaction and incompetence, is not a response to only one specific linguistic feature used by others, but to any linguistic feature used in an unexpected way. It is the lack of sharedness of style that is disconcerting. Fast talkers walk away from those same conversations feeling similarly uncomfortable, most likely having interpreted the slower pacing as a failure of positive politeness: the need for interpersonal involvement, in other words, a violation of Lakoff's politeness rule, 'Maintain camaraderie'.

What we have, then, is two senses of politeness: the need to show involvement and the need not to impose, that is, to be considerate. Taciturnity and volubility can be seen as ways of honoring and not violating one or the other of these needs. The question for each speaker (and, in a larger sense, for each culture) is whether it is better to risk offense by saying too little or too much—put another way, too much silence or too little? The 'mainstream' American notion of politeness prefers to risk saying too little; in other words, considerateness is valued relatively more than involvement.[6]

Goodman notes the opposition between fast pacing and silence. He recommends: 'It may come as a bulletin to crowders that one of their options is S-I-L-E-N-C-E'. Here he has hit upon something important. But I wonder—and don't yet know—whether slow talkers would consider their pauses to be silence. Because, no doubt, one person's silence is another's pause. A silence is differentiated from a pause only by the intentions and conventions of the speaker. Silence and pause can be distinguished only by reference to prior experience: how long does a person typically pause within the stream of speech, and before taking a turn at speech? Teachers, for example, know the problem of determining whether a student who has been called on is pausing because s/he doesn't know the answer (silence as omission of something), or because s/he is formulating the answer (silence representing underlying action).

WHEN ARE SLOW TALKERS FAST TALKERS?

Differences in attitudes toward and uses of silence between Southern Athabaskan Indians (Apaches) and non-Indian Americans have been demonstrated by Basso (1979). Scollon (Chapter 2) notes that the image of the silent Indian is associated with an attitude toward silence as negative, the malfunction of a conversational machine which ought to proceed with a steady hum. He suggests that Athabaskans are found by non-Indians to be 'passive', 'sullen', 'withdrawn', 'unresponsive', 'lazy', 'backward', 'destructive', 'hostile', 'uncooperative', 'anti-social', and 'stupid', largely because of their greater use of silence with outsiders making these judgments. He notes experimental research by Feldstein, Alberti and Ben Debba (see also Crown and Feldstein, Chapter 3) that women who took shorter pauses than their conversational partners see themselves as: 'warmhearted', 'easygoing', 'cooperative', 'attentive to people', 'outgoing', 'talkative', 'cheerful', 'adventurous', 'socially bold'. Women who took longer pauses than their conversational partners felt themselves to be 'reserved', 'detached', 'critical', 'distrustful', 'skeptical', 'taciturn', 'sober', 'shy', 'restrained', 'rigid', 'prone to sulk', 'changeable', 'self-reproaching', 'tense', 'frustrated', 'easily upset'. These women also took shorter speak-

[6]My interpretation of silence-resistant or short-pause styles as conventionalizing politeness as display of involvement, and of silence-favoring or long-pause styles as conventionalizing politeness as display of considerateness corresponds in a number of ways with Kochman's (1981) of black and white styles, which he discusses in terms of 'rights of sensibilities' and 'rights of feelings.'

ing turns. Scollon notes the similarity of these negative self-attributions to negative stereotypes of Athabaskans and suggests that 'for our society, a slower pace in exchanging turns is a highly negative quality'.

These findings seem to conflict with my findings based on the Thanksgiving conversation (and reinforced by Goodman and Kochman). I found that the speakers who tended to speak more quickly than their fellow conversationalists, and those who tended to speak more slowly, both had negative views of the others' intentions. The faster speakers, indeed, felt the slower ones to be withholding, uncooperative, and not forthcoming with conversational contributions. But the slower speakers, for their part, felt the faster ones to be dominating; they found it hard to get a turn to speak. The negative attributions of the slower speakers by the faster ones do indeed correspond to those Scollon and Feldstein et al. found for slower speakers—but the participants characterized as 'slower' in my conversation were the kind of 'mainstream' Americans who evaluate Indians negatively for talking slowly, and who are, in the spirit of Goodman, condemning faster talkers as dehumanizing. (A corollary to the negative attributions of the slower speakers toward the faster ones can be seen in Basso's [1979] demonstration of negative stereotypes among Apaches of white people as insincere and preposterously gregarious.)

Furthermore, the slower speakers in my study were able to talk positively about their habits and negatively about those of the others with a self-assurance that the faster speakers did not evidence. The necessary result of differing pacing with respect to turntaking was that faster speakers spoke more. This happened in two ways. First of all, one who expects more pauses between turns is still waiting for that amount of pause when a faster speaker perceives the pause to be bordering on silence and starts to talk. Second, those who wish to avoid silence in conversation, who place greater value on the show of involvement, prefer overlap—that is, simultaneous talk. Often listeners talk at the same time as speakers, not to wrest the floor but to show involvement, appreciation, enthusiasm. However, with speakers who do not use this style, what was intended as a cooperative overlap often became an interruption. That is, the overlap-resistant speaker, instead of being encouraged by the vocalization of the listener, thought that the listener wanted to take the floor away and therefore stopped talking. The resultant change of turns felt and looked to all concerned like an interruption—even to the unwitting 'interruptor' who might not know how it happened but knows an interruption when s/he sees one—and knows it is valued negatively, and knows who has to take the blame for it.

When listening to fast-paced, loud, overlapping segments of the conversation among the New Yorkers, the slower speakers responded with disbelief (for example, 'I don't see how you guys can all talk at the same time'). But the participants themselves, on hearing the tape of those portions of the conversation, also reacted with negative feelings; in their case, embarrassment ('Do we really sound like that?'). Interruption is negative by definition. Someone in our society can accuse, 'Don't interrupt', but not, 'Don't just sit there. Interrupt!'

CONCLUSION

The findings of my study, then, were that slower-paced speech is more positively evaluated by 'mainstream' American speakers than faster speech, and longer switching pauses preferred. How could this be, in light of the findings of Feldstein et al., as corroborated by Scollon, that slower paced speech and shorter switching pauses are more positively evaluated by the same group? The answer was really quite simple. A call to Feldstein revealed that his study had been conducted at the City College of the City University of New York, and the subjects were primarily New York Jewish women, directly confirming my findings that New York Jewish speakers prefer a faster-paced style.

But what of Scollon's own findings, to the effect that the slower paced and more silence-filled speech of Athabaskan Indians is negatively evaluated? The answer there, I think, is the relativity of judgments of rate. Slower-paced style is negatively valued, but slow and fast have meaning only with reference to expectations. 'Slow' is, in other words, 'slower than I expect', which, regardless of absolute rate, results in the impression of having nothing to say or being unwilling to speak. 'Fast' is 'faster than I expect', which, regardless of absolute rate, results in the impression of crowding. Allowing for individual differences, such expectations are culturally based.

And, finally, when is a pause a silence? When it is longer than expected, or in an unexpected place, and therefore ceases to have its 'business as usual' function and begins to indicate that something is missing. When does talk become oppressive—that is, perceived to be in violation of appropriate silence? When that talk is causing the pause or silence to be shorter than expected, or omitted where expected.

Thus, while there certainly are broad cultural differences with respect to the unmarked valuation of silence and noise (as seen, for example, in Maltz's [Chapter 7] demonstration of contrasting valuation of noise and silence in religious worship by Quakers and Pentecostals), nonetheless, the most significant differences are those reflecting how much pause is deemed appropriate for a given function and in a given context. A pause becomes a silence, and a silence is negatively valued, when it is too long or appears at what seems like the wrong time and the wrong place.

REFERENCES

Allen, Carolyn. 1978. Failures of word, uses of silence: Djuna Barnes, Adrienne Rich, and Margaret Atwood. Regionalism and the Female Imagination 4:1, 1–7.

Basso, Keith. 1979. Portraits of 'The Whiteman'. Cambridge: Cambridge University Press.

Bateson, Gregory. 1972. Steps to an ecology of mind. New York: Ballantine.

Brown, Penelope and Stephen Levinson. 1978. Universals in language usage: Politeness phenomena. Questions and politeness, ed. by Esther Goody, 56–289. Cambridge: Cambridge University Press.

Cliff, Michelle. 1979. The resonance of interruption. Chrysalis 8.29–37.

Colette. 1971. The pure and the impure. Baltimore, MD: Penguin.

Colette. 1972. The innocent libertine. Baltimore, MD: Penguin.

Durkheim, Emile. 1915. The elementary forms of the religious life. New York: The Free Press.

Erickson, Frederick. 1982. Money tree, lasagna bush, salt and pepper: Social construction of topical cohesion in a conversation among Italian-Americans. Analyzing discourse: Text and talk, ed. by Deborah Tannen, Georgetown University Round Table on Languages and Linguistics 1981. 43–70. Washington, DC: Georgetown University Press.

Erickson, Frederick. 1984. Rhetoric, anecdote, and rhapsody: Coherence in a conversation among black American teenagers. Coherence in spoken and written discourse, ed. by Deborah Tannen, 81–154. Norwood, NJ: Ablex.

Esterly, Glenn. 1979. Slow talking in the big city. New West 4:11 (May 21), 67–72.

Ferguson, Charles J. 1976. The structure and use of politeness formulas. Language in Society 5.137–151.

Goffman, Erving. 1967. Interaction ritual. Garden City, NY: Doubleday.

Gomes, Louis Antone Jr. 1979. Social interaction and social identity: A study of two kindergarten children. Ph.D. dissertation, Harvard Graduate School of Education.

Goodman, Ellen. 1979. Close to home. New York: Simon & Schuster.

Gumperz, John J. 1982. Discourse strategies. London: Cambridge University Press.

Kochman, Thomas. 1981. Black and white styles in conflict. Chicago: University of Chicago Press.

Labov, William and David Fanshel. 1977. Therapeutic discourse. New York: Academic Press.

Lakoff, Robin. 1973. The logic of politeness, or minding your p's and q's. Papers from the Ninth Regional Meeting of the Chicago Linguistics Society, 292–305.

Lakoff, Robin. 1975. Language and woman's place. New York: Harper & Row.

Lakoff, Robin Tolmach. 1979. Stylistic strategies within a grammar of style. Language, sex, and gender, ed. by Judith Orasanu, Mariam Slater, & Leonore Loeb Adler. Annals of the New York Academy of Science 327. 53–78.

McDermott, R. P. and Henry Tylbor. 1983. On the necessity of collusion in conversation. Text 3:3.277–297.

Reisman, Karl. 1974. Contrapuntal conversations in an Antiguan village. Explorations in the ethnography of speaking, ed. by Richard Bauman & Joel Sherzer, 110–124. Cambridge: Cambridge University Press.

Sadock, Jerrold. 1982. Are there languages without idioms? Paper presented at Formulaicity Conference, University of Maryland, July 17, 1982.

Sapir, Edward. 1949. Speech as a personality trait. Selected writings of Edward Sapir in language, culture, and personality, ed. by David Mandelbaum, 533–543. Berkeley: University of California Press.

Scollon, Ron. 1982. The rhythmic integration of ordinary talk. Analyzing discourse: Text and talk, Georgetown University Round Table on Languages and Linguistics 1981, ed. by Deborah Tannen, 335–349. Washington, DC: Georgetown University Press.

Tannen, Deborah. 1984. Conversational style: Analyzing talk among friends. Norwood, NJ: Ablex.

Tannen, Deborah and Piyale Comert Oztek. 1981. Health to our mouths: Formulaic expressions in Turkish and Greek. Conversational routine, ed. by Florian Coulmas, 37–54. The Hague: Mouton. Rpt from Proceedings of the Third Annual Meeting of the Berkeley Linguistics Society, 1977, pp. 516–534.

Chapter 7

Joyful Noise and Reverent Silence: The Significance of Noise in Pentecostal Worship

Daniel N. Maltz

Berkeley, California

One of the most common uses of silence is to express reverence, awe, or the respect that comes with being left speechless, of having to, as Basso (1970) puts it, 'give up on words'. Analysts of the meaning of speech and silence have often used this observation to comment on the appropriateness of silence for use in religious contexts. Basso (1970:215), for example, uses as one of his examples of how 'in our own culture . . . an individual's decision to speak may be directly contingent upon the character of his surroundings' the injunction, 'Remember now, no talking in church', and Bruneau argues that '[t]here are many places, objects and events to which silence is the expected response. *Churches,* courtrooms, schools, libraries, hospitals, funeral homes, battle sites, insane asylums, and prisons, for instance, are often places of silence' (Bruneau 1973:41, emphasis added) and 'Religious rituals in many Christian orders, regardless of the conception of highest authority, are replete with movement toward silence' (Bruneau 1973:37). Similarly, many Americans tend to think of a moment of silent prayer as a culture-free or theologically unbiased expression of religiosity.

But this equation of religion with silent reverence contains a cultural bias, a bias not shared even by all variants of British and American Protestantism. Within Pentecostal churches throughout the world, including even the relatively subdued Scottish Pentecostals among whom I did fourteen months of anthropological fieldwork (Maltz 1978), noisiness rather than silence is the most common as well as the preferred form of religious worship. Singing to the accompaniment of loud musical instruments, praying audibly in public, preaching and testifying, prophesying and speaking in tongues all characterize Pentecostal worship.

My purpose in this paper is to use these observations about Pentecostal forms of worship as opposed to two other variants of British-American

Protestantism to throw light onto some of the variations possible in the interpretation of noise and silence and some of the similarities that underlie these variations.

NOISE AND SILENCE AS RELIGIOUS STYLES: THE CASE OF MICHAEL

Noisiness is practically a defining characteristic of Pentecostal worship. Non-Pentecostal Christians who occasionally visited one of the Pentecostal churches in Edinburgh often complained that they found the service too noisy. The Pentecostal response is to defend the emphasis on noisy worship as in the following description of worship by a Canadian Pentecostal:

> At the altar or in the prayer room, the people will be praying and praising God audibly. All this seeming noise and confusion is most disturbing to a stranger or a member of another church. However this seeking of God in audible prayer together as a company of God's people is not new, but as we have endeavored to point out in our study of the New Testament church, is the accepted normal spiritual activity in the worship of God. To never lift the voice to praise God is an abnormal Christian experience! (Brown 1966:209)

The attitudes of Edinburgh Pentecostals are best summarized by the Biblical verse 'Make a joyful noise unto the Lord' [Psalms 98:4 and 100:1] which was posted prominently on the wall of one of the smaller Pentecostal meeting halls and by the chorus to a popular hymn from *Redemption Hymnal* (the hymn book shared by all of the major British Pentecostal denominations):

> There's a shout in the camp, Hallelujah! Glory to God!
> There's an echo in Heaven, Hallelujah! Glory to God! (Miles 1955:258)

An editorial on worship in a British Pentecostal magazine puts it succinctly, 'The coming of the Spirit makes the tongue of the hitherto dumb to sing. There is no such thing as a silent Pentecostal' (Linford 1973:2).

The tension between the noisiness of Pentecostal worship and the more restrained forms of worship in other Protestant denominations can be understood in greater depth through an examination of the following extracts from the diary of Michael [a pseudonym], the son of a Congregational minister in southern England who had been 'born-again' and 'received the Holy Spirit' while a student in Yorkshire. During 1972–73, when the diary was kept, he was completing his undergraduate degree in social welfare at the University of Edinburgh while attending services at both a small Pentecostal assembly where he was leader of the young people's meeting and a much larger evangelical Presbyterian church.

December, 1967 [from a testimony given at a church meeting in England]
Another side to my life was lack of self confidence in certain things, possibly caused by my upbringing at home and school. Thus I was shy and embarrassed of saying if I like a girl since someone might laugh so I never told anyone about that idea. I was shy of it being known I went to church. In fact inherent in my system was a resistance which would prevent me from doing anything as dramatic or as eyeopening as confessing Christ . . .

February 11, 1973
Whether in meetings when there is silence, this is a drain on the speaker I don't know. He can certainly feel whether he has his audience with him, or not. Thus in prayer meetings Mr. N. has often to exhort, when encouragement doesn't work, the congregation to respond vocally. [I] am 'guilty' of silence in his meetings, yet deem myself justified in making everyone speak in my meetings . . .

February 15, 1973
I didn't praise God with my whole heart in the services today; as many did with their whole heart. Some discovered or reached heights of spirituality in their worship, it seemed. . . But was I just spectating tonight, a fringe member, unwilling for the 'sacrifice' of praise?

April 15, 1973
I felt strong resistance to returning to Canongate Pentecostal Church [a pseudonym] after my month's absence . . . attending Holyrood Abbey in the morning and CPC in pm reflected distinct differences in worship; the former more in line with my quietness, thoughtfulness, and order; the latter a free, unstructured, unplanned (dancing in the spirit, messages in tongues, simple choruses) . . . My tendency to favour the more quiet may reflect a class bias, which doesn't justify staying away from CPC.

April 22, 1973
In the evening service the lads and girls attended again. They were noisy and disrepectful and left half-way through. (They had been worse during the Thursday evening service.) . . . 'What is the limit to which God and the gospel can be mocked?' was asked. 'This is God's house, therefore it should be kept holy' is a deeply rooted approach. We need to distinguish between what is noisy and what is bad that is noisy. For noisiness per-se is not bad—for God wants people to be noisy in praising him (as Mr. N. said even tonight). For them to greet each other as they enter is not bad; if we can do the same.

April 23, 1973
[I need to contemplate] making a social and non-judgmentative distinction between 'noisy' and 'quiet' churches suiting different types of people [and] the legitimacy of standing to sing choruses and clapping if people want to and for this to be a custom, so that we all join in including me.

May 6, 1973
I need to understand what are the norms of behaviour for worship and then to take part in worship on that basis. Just because I like to be quiet, this is no excuse for quietness when the norm is talking out loud; for instance if to say 'Amen' is a cue to the speaker that he is making contact; and does not indicate rudeness; then the speaker needs people (i.e. me) to say amen. If people stand up for choruses on certain occasions; there is no reason for me to remain seated just because this is how choruses are normally sung. Here the norm is to clap hands for choruses then since church worship is a social activity, let all the congregation do so together, unless it is legitimate sometimes not to clap.

May 20, 1973
What I learnt tonight in relation to the testimony I gave: I had talked of changes taking place in my personality over relatively long periods of my Christian life. I talked of my shyness in terms of healing and the role the church does and could play . . . I suppose I have even begun to talk of my quietness as a burden the Lord wants me to bear, even though it makes for a considerable social handicap.

September 1, 1973 [reflecting back on his 1967 testimony (see above)]
Note also the non-elimination of the problem of shyness, which I then believed I could overcome. In fact I did overcome it considerably only more recently have I become so shy again. I now find creative possibilities in being a quiet person—one who can listen, observe, study etc. . .

These excerpts serve to display a great deal of the complexity in the meaning of Pentecostal noisiness. Because of Michael's unusual perspective as a social analyst and potential social activist as well as a believing Christian, he explores the issues on several levels at once: the religious, the sociological, and the personal. On each of these levels he displays a personal ambivalence which helps illustrate the complexity of the meanings of the contrast between noisy worship and quiet worship. Religiously, he continually notes a clear-cut distinction between the two modes of worship with a certain ambivalence about the advantages and disadvantages of each. Quiet worship appeals to him as the 'normal' way of doing things, as allowing thoughtfulness, order, and the expression of 'holiness'. Noisy worship, on the other hand, he sees as having the positive values of expressing support of the leader, involving a deeper display of commitment on the part of the worshipper, and leading to greater 'heights of spirituality' for the participant.

As a social analyst, Michael explains the distinction between noisy and quiet worship in terms of social class, personality differences, and the variation in 'custom' from one community to another. In all three of these domains he expresses his sense of alienation from the rest of the congregation by emphasizing his distinctiveness from everyone else: he is upper-middle class, they are working class; he is quiet, they are noisy; their norms aren't his norms.[1] But his personal sense of differentness is in conflict with his professional plans to work with church groups for working-class teenagers. So he feels himself compelled to try to empathize with and support both what he perceives as the general working-class milieu of the church as a whole and, in particular, the neighborhood young people ('the lads and the girls'), who attend the church's Saturday night coffee bar and periodically appear at church services, in their conflicts with the minister and the rest of the congregation.

Finally, on the personal level, Michael is aware of a strong preference he feels for quiet rather than noisy worship, but he is ambivalent about the meaning of this preference and his evaluation of it changes over time. In a positive vein, he sees his quietness as a reflection of his thoughtfulness. In a negative one, he perceives his preferences as personal prejudices and conceptualizes his shyness as a personality flaw, particularly in relation to his professional need to learn to feel comfortable speaking publicly in front of a group. For much of his life as a young Christian he perceives his shyness as a personal weakness which his religious conversion and particularly his participation in Pentecostal worship is helping him to overcome. But eventually, after becoming disenchanted with the Pentecostal message, he resigns himself to accepting shyness as a personal burden with 'creative possibilities'.

NOISE AND SILENCE AS RELIGIOUS CRITIQUES: A THREE-WAY COMPARISON

Michael's discussion of the relationship of noisy and quiet styles of worship to aspects of culture and personality illustrates the subtlety with

---

[1] Michael tends, in my opinion, to greatly overemphasize the extent of his distinctiveness in the Pentecostal churches of Edinburgh. Although by no means a majority, students and graduates of colleges and universities with middle-class occupations were not uncommon in the churches, and Michael's shyness and personal reserve did not make him unique either. The dimension on which he was probably most unusual was his advocacy of social activism, but even here there was little uniformity of values among active Pentecostals.

which the tension between these two worship styles can be utilized in the spiritual self-exploration of a single, somewhat marginal, individual. Discomfort over his own ambivalence about styles of worship, however, has led Michael to interpret all preferences for one worship style over another in simple reductionist terms, as static reflections of differences in class and personality. But not all religious actors are so ambivalent about their own preferences, and changes in Protestant worship style have often been the result of conscious acts of religious protest. The flow of Protestant history, particularly that of its more radical branches, has been more aggressively critical, argumentative, and rebellious than a reductionist perspective of this sort tends to acknowledge.

Because variations in Protestant worship consist largely of differences in rules for the use of speech in religious contexts (Samarin 1973), changes in modes of worship are primarily changes in conceptions of when and where speech and silence are appropriate, of what kinds of speech acts are appropriate in what contexts, of who should speak when, and who should remain silent. Because changes in Christian worship involve more than simple adaptations to changing cultural contexts, arguments about worship have often been important arenas for conscious protests against the religious status quo, critiques of dominant assumptions about proper modes of worship, and demands for more satisfying ways of expressing one's relationship with God. For several centuries, changing ideas about the proper use and interpretation of speech and silence have been an important part of many of the religious disagreements between Protestant groups. To better understand the role of speech, silence, and noise in some of these conflicts of Protestant history, it is useful to examine in detail some of the changing assumptions about Protestant worship that are revealed through a careful comparison of three major movements of radical religious reform in British and American history—the Puritan movement of the sixteenth and seventeenth centuries, the Quaker movement of the seventeenth century, and the Pentecostal movement of the twentieth century. Although sharing a common religious heritage, each of these three movements criticized the sociolinguistic traditions of its predecessors, proposed new standards for the religious use of speech and silence, and added its own modifications to the basic Christian paradigm of preaching the Word.

Puritans
Of the three major strands of Protestantism to arise at the time of the Reformation—Lutheranism, Anglicanism, and the Reformed-Presbyterian complex (Marty 1972:41–55)—it was the third which was most radical in its critique of liturgical forms of worship. Changes in worship initiated by these sixteenth-century radical reformers involved issues of

speech and silence in at least three major ways. First, there was a shift in the dominant mode of worship. Ceremonial forms were abolished and replaced by a focus on the verbal activities of prayer, preaching, and congregational singing. In a single step, 'the ear replaced the eye' (Maxwell 1955:49). Second, there was a shift in focus from an altar-centered religion focusing on the actions of a priest to a pulpit-centered religion focusing on the preaching of a minister. Third, there was a shift in the rules of participation with the restoration of congregational singing, a linguistic shift to the use of the vernacular, and the encouragement of congregation members 'to share in the service as active participants; . . . no longer [as] passive observers' (Maxwell 1955:50).

In general, these Calvinist reforms established the basic paradigm of Christian worship that came to dominate most variants of Protestantism in both Great Britain and America. In an important sense, 'Calvin set the pattern of worship, though not always of doctrine, for Baptists, Congregationalists, Methodists, and Disciples, and of course Presbyterians, in the entire English-speaking world' (Jones 1954:128). This basic Protestant paradigm placed primary emphasis on the role of the minister as a preacher of God's word, maintaining a relatively passive but somewhat variable verbal role for members of the congregation.

The Puritan movement, as the radical wing of the Reformation in Britain, can be conceptualized as primarily a further elaboration and refinement of this new Protestant paradigm of worship: 'Among other things, Puritanism referred to a particular set of religious beliefs about language that focused on preaching as the principal event in religious practice' (Kibbey 1973:1). As a critique of the religious establishment, Puritans continued in the Calvinist tradition of abolishing 'popish' formalism. They attacked the official policies of the Anglican church on the use of reading in worship, including both reading the Bible aloud in church and responsive readings (in which the minister and congregation read alternate passages). The written word alone, even when read in church, they argued, could not convert anyone (Kibbey 1973:5). Responsive reading they ridiculed as the pointless 'tossing to and fro of tennis balls' (Kibbey 1973:5). They took the Calvinist argument against formalized worship a step further than their predecessors, however, rejecting not only traditional ceremonial forms but also all attempts to create an established liturgy, an endeavor they regarded as a kind of 'idolatry, in that it equated the liturgy with the Bible and infringed Christian liberty' (Davies 1972:149). In the place of prescribed prayer or formal liturgy, they advocated a form of public worship that left to the Holy Spirit responsibility for teaching 'all the people of God, what and how to pray' (Davies 1972:149).

Praying and preaching were not, of course, the only forms of religious speech practiced by the Puritans. Lay Puritans supplemented the preaching of their minister with, among other things, the singing of hymns and, particularly in New England, the delivering of conversion narratives by candidates applying for church membership (Kibbey 1978; Morgan 1963:89). In those Puritan churches that placed particular value on spontaneity, short extemporaneous speeches known as 'prophecies' were delivered by lay members of the congregation to supplement or, in the absence of a minister, even replace the minister's sermon (Morgan 1963:27–28, 99). Preaching, however, remained the central act of Puritan religious speech, 'the principle means ordained by God for instructing people in the great truths revealed by the Scriptures' (Morgan 1963:7); and listening quietly to the Word being preached remained the most important sociolinguistic act of the lay Puritan.

What the Puritans added to the Calvinist paradigm of worship was a greater emphasis on the role of the Holy Spirit. This Puritan refinement of the Calvinist conception of religious speech, especially as expressed in the thought of John Cotton, has been analyzed in detail by Ann Kibbey (1973), whose discussion provides the basis for the following summary. As the Puritans understood preaching, it was a speech event involving four major elements: the Word, the preacher, the Holy Spirit, and the hearer of the preached word. Of these four, the least important was the preacher, since the efficacy of preaching did not come primarily from the speaker. The power to create faith came instead from the speech itself, but not so much from the words alone as from the extent to which the Holy Spirit was present within them. Divine inspiration, in the Puritan view, was understood not as the Holy Spirit being located within the speaker but within the spoken word, thus making the Spirit-filled word as animate a participant in the speech event as either the speaker or the hearer. The primary focus of the speech event was the interaction between the Holy Spirit and the hearer. It was the Spirit, not the speaker, that was responsible for communication. Thus the central human role in the whole event was that of the hearer, and listening to the word being preached became the most important religious act of Christian worship.

In several important ways, the Puritans set the stage for later developments in the history of radical Protestantism. They critiqued other earlier forms of worship and raised the possibility of criticizing even verbal worship with charges of excessive formalism; they elaborated the paradigm of the Protestant preacher, focusing on the role of the Holy Spirit; and they developed a model of religious communication in which the concepts of speech and silence were understood in relation to notions of God's word, the Holy Spirit, inspired preaching, and inspired listening. In relation to all of these developments, both seventeenth-century Quakers and twentieth-century Pentecostals were clearly heirs to the Puritans. They challenged the inadequacies of other worship forms, they elaborated the paradigm of the preacher, and they further explored the theology of the Holy Spirit. Yet when compared to one another on the issue of speech and silence, these two movements clearly advocated moves in opposite directions—the Quakers toward expectant silence, the Pentecostals in the direction of joyful noise.

Quakers

The rise of Quakerism in the mid-seventeenth century involved a significant transformation and reinterpretation of the basic paradigm of Protestant worship:[2] 'though Quakerism represented a fundamental departure from Calvinistic Puritanism . . . it was in many respects an outgrowth of the Puritan movement' (Bauman 1970:69). Quakers retained continuity with the radical reformative outlook of the Puritans in their conception that 'man's place was to worship God singlemindedly, to throw off the empty forms and worldly degeneration that clogged men's lives, and to follow the teachings of Christ to salvation' (Bauman 1970:70), but they applied this notion of 'empty form' not merely to the liturgical formalism of the established churches but to the verbal formalism of the Puritans as well. For Quakers, the Puritans as well as the Anglicans were the religious establishment to which they were responding. Their response to the Puritan paradigm of religious speech included a decreased emphasis on the role of preaching, a reconceptualization of 'the Word of God,' and a shift in the focus of worship from a preacher at the pulpit to a congregation 'waiting on the Spirit' (Creasy 1972:328).

It is not that Quakers rejected the role of preaching completely. Early Quaker preachers were, in fact, denounced by their enemies for their 'railing' and 'fanatic' spirit (Bauman 1974:151). Quakers believed strongly in spreading their doctrine, which they labeled 'The Truth', to others, but they were at least as concerned with the spiritual state of the preacher as with the words he preached. They recognized that even preaching could become meaningless formalism if the minister spoke from a human rather than a spiritual motivation, that forceful rhetoric appealing to intellect or emotion was spiritually ineffective 'because these were faculties of the earthly man, not of the Spirit' (Bauman 1974:151). Because words could all too easily be used on 'trivial, irreligious, or untruthful matters . . . which gratified the earthly and not the spiritual side of man' (Bauman 1975:257), the primary Quaker attitude toward speech was one of distrust. They rejected the role of an ordained ministry as advocated

---

[2] Unfortunately, Bauman's most extensive discussion of Quaker concepts of speech and silence (Bauman 1983) was not available in time to be incorporated into this chapter.

by other churches and viewed ministry in general as a risky business (Bauman 1974).

While following the other radical Protestant reformers in elevating the 'Word of God' to a central place in Christian thought and practice,

> Quakerism developed in reaction against the prevailing Protestant doctrine which held that the Scriptures were *the* Word of God, given once and for all . . . [arguing instead] that Scriptures constituted *a* Word of God, one instance (or composite of instances), albeit a most important one, of divine revelation, and that revelation was an ongoing and progressive process to be realized in every man (Bauman 1974:145).

This reconceptualization radically transformed the Puritan model of communication. If the Holy Spirit was no longer located solely within the word of Scripture (as in the Puritan conceptualization) and direct divine revelation was possible for every individual, the preacher was no longer an essential part of religious worship, and attention was shifted to the doctrine of the 'Inner Light'.

The concept of an 'Inner Light' involved two distinct kinds of imagery: spatial (inner vs. outer) and visual (light). The contrast between 'inner' and 'outer' was used to distinguish the spiritual domain from the worldly domain, the spirit within from the individual's outward bodily nature. Uninspired speech was conceptualized as glorification of the outer self, and the central concern of the religious Quaker was to become attuned to the Inner Light through a suppression of this outer worldly self, a state of suppression referred to as 'silence' (Bauman 1970:2). The shift in central imagery for talking about Christ from the 'Word' to the 'Light' implied a shift between two senses, from hearing to seeing; and the fact that the light was 'inner' made clear that even this visual imagery was meant to be taken metaphorically. Whereas a focus on listening to the Word implied the necessity of speech, attending to the 'Inner Light' could be done in perfect silence. What Quaker emphasis on the 'Inner' Light and seeking an experience of the 'in-dwelling' Light of Christ did *not* imply, however, was either an individualistic rejection of social interaction or a denial of the basic Protestant conception of religious worship as primarily communicative,

> for illumination by the Light brought the worshipping Friend into union with the Divine and, through Him, with all others who are attuned to the Light . . . [and, from a Quaker perspective] the Inner Light was actually a medium of communication and direction (through which the attentive soul might come to know God's will) manifested positively in a strong inward sense that a certain action be taken to meet a particular situation, or negatively in the conviction that a course of action which had been contemplated be eschewed. (Bauman 1971:36)

The concept of 'silence' was a central aspect not only of the spiritual behavior of the individual Quaker, but also of the primary form of corporate Quaker worship, the 'silent meeting'. The underlying idea of a silent meeting was not that of purposefully avoiding speech but rather of gathering together in a group to jointly 'wait upon the Spirit'.

> The keynote of Quaker worship [was] not the quest for mystical absorption, nor preoccupation with individual meditation and private devotions. It [was], rather, the profoundly simple intention, by a gathered group, of opening itself to the presence of Christ. (Creasy 1972:328)

Sermons and an ordained ministry were absent and no verbal utterances at all were necessary but,

> there was no 'resolution not to speak' and few meetings were actually conducted in complete silence. There were, in fact, a number of *openings* in which speech was not only appropriate but necessary. . . If, after a period of silent waiting and experiencing of the strength and urgency of his message, [a] Friend felt certain that his words came from the Light, he was obligated to speak them aloud. (Bauman 1974:149)

What is most striking about the religious uses of speech and silence for the Quakers is the almost paradoxical relationship between these two modes. Neither silence nor speech were ends in themselves. The purpose of religious speech was to aid the individual in the quest for silence (Bauman 1974) and the function of silence was awaiting an inspired word. Clearly the Quaker model of religious communication involved not merely refraining from speech, but the speaking of inspired utterances as well. Equally clearly, it was neither the production of nor the hearing of these inspired utterances that was given a central place in this model, but rather the silent waiting for inspiration to come.

Pentecostals

Twentieth-century Pentecostals present a striking contrast to the Quakers of nearly three centuries earlier. Although both are responses to the same Reformist Protestant paradigm of worship with its emphasis on a sermonizing minister and a hopefully attentive congregation, and both look to the inspiration of the Holy Spirit to overcome harmful formalism, they focus on different problems with the paradigm and thus respond differently. Whereas the Quakers saw churches in which the Spirit was drowned out by the mechanistic and uninspired preaching of an ordained ministry, Pentecostals see dead churches in which the 'Full Gospel' is not being preached and the Holy Spirit is not being given free rein. To Pentecostals, traditional forms of Protestant worship tend to be characterized as overly 'silent,' 'lifeless,' 'cold,' 'dry,' 'formal,' and 'tradition-bound' (Anderson 1979:212; Ladlow 1973:3). And if silence and lethargy are the weaknesses of the established churches from a Pentecostal point of view, then their solution is a shout of enthusiasm, a joyful noise, and a fresh empowerment of the Holy Spirit.

Noisiness in Pentecostal worship is a response to non-Pentecostal silence, and this response expresses a number of distinct themes in the Pentecostal vision of how a Christian should behave in a silent world: by making commitments public, by expressing joy, by participating in congregational worship, and by giving free rein to the Holy Spirit.

First, noisiness serves an an expression of commitment. Like other evangelicals and fundamentalists, Pentecostals find the Bible to be obviously true and yet are aware that much of the world denies these truths or sits by silently ignoring them. To the secular claim that 'God is dead,' they feel motivated to sing back the chorus lines 'God's not dead. No. He is alive.' Unlike those who through silence deny or ignore Biblical truths, they feel obligated to stand up and be counted. It is important to display one's religious commitments publicly and audibly through public testimonies (accounts of personal religious experience) in church and witnessing (presenting the gospel message) to outsiders. Certain public verbal acts, particularly testimony and speaking in tongues, can act as what Gerlach and Hine call 'bridge-burning acts' (Hine 1968:97–118; Gerlach and Hine 1968:32, 1970:124–127; McGuire 1977; Hoffnagel 1978:118, 157), publicly forcing oneself past the point of no return in one's commitment to evangelical Christianity and/or the Pentecostal movement. In the Scottish churches, for example, a public testimony is required at the time of one's [adult] baptism, members of the congregation may be called upon to give testimonies during other services (sometimes as a means of forcing a public commitment), and young Christians are often pressured by ministers or other leaders to commit themselves publicly through street-corner or door-to-door witnessing, often to a not very receptive public.

Just as individuals should be willing to face the ridicule of the secular world by publicly expressing their commitment to Christ, so should church worship services be unconstrained by social as opposed to spiritual pressures. The subdued forms of worship to be found in non-Pentecostal churches are suspected of compromise with or capitulation to worldly standards of decorum and propriety. Noisiness in worship serves an an indicator that Pentecostals are not constrained by and even openly reject secular notions of respectability (see Manning 1980:183 on Pentecostalism and respectability). Accusations of deviancy such as foolishness, craziness, and fanaticism may be valued by church members as indications of their separation from the values and standards of 'the world'. In the serpent-handling churches of Appalachia, for example, James Birckhead argues that 'saints capitalize on the notion that they "are crazy" as an in-group identity marker' and proudly proclaim that 'this is the most persecuted church around because, unlike other churches, the will of God is done' (Birckhead 1976:Chapter 4). Similarly in Britain, Roger Homan describes Pentecostal attitudes as follows:

> Pentecostals do not ridicule their differentness but they enjoy and endorse it. One of the ministerial styles most frequently observed in old-time pentecostal assemblies in England was characterized by the profession of crudeness and ignorance and had the function of rejecting by example sophistication, learning, and propriety (Homan 1981:221).

They know that their noisiness is an object of ridicule by outsiders and celebrate this difference by making fun of their mockers as in the following performance by a Pentecostal preacher for the entertainment and edification of his congregation:

> Those pentecostals don't half make a row. (Laughter). Have you ever heard them sing in those, what do they call it, assemblies? (Laughter). They don't half kick up a din with their old glory time. (Laughter). I tell you something, saints, there's no place I'd rather be on this earth than with God's children in His house, giving Him the praise. (Amen) (Homan 1981:221).

Second, Pentecostal noisiness serves an an expression of joy. Pentecostals in Edinburgh were fond of contrasting the joyfulness of their services with the dour solemnity of more traditional Scottish churches in which the fear of hell was stressed over the joy of salvation and of direct encounter with the Holy Spirit. The following excerpt from a minister's message—recorded in Edinburgh, Scotland in September 1972—illustrates this point well:

> There was a young boy last night in Bathgate, young 15 or 16, converted in the campaign and it was really an amazing conversion because when I spoke to him after the service he said 'something's happened to me when that man was preaching' . . . He said to me, he says 'You know, I think it's wonderful in this church.' He says 'In other churches that I've been to, everything's so quiet. When the prayers are being said, there's a dead creepy silence. When the people were praying tonight, people were expressing something that was inside them.' He says 'Do you do this at every service?' I says 'Yes, at every one.' And he says 'Could I do that as well 'cause I just felt like shouting out, during, when that man was preaching.' And I says 'Well you shout out whenever you want. That's the Holy Spirit, freedom and the liberty of the Holy Spirit.'

The act of rejoicing refers not only to the use of verbal exaltations but also to the frequent singing of adorational hymns or fast-tempoed choruses, often accompanied by a wide variety of musical instruments. Unlike some of the stricter Presbyterian denominations which prohibited all use of musical instruments both in and out of church contexts, Pentecostals welcomed instruments of all kinds including organs, drums, tambourines, violins, pianos, and guitars and incorporated them into the worship service. Following in the tradition of the Salvation Army and other holiness denominations, Pentecostals saw no reason why the liveliest tunes should be 'left to the world' and made use of these tunes in their joyful worship.

The expression of joy is not merely permitted in Pentecostal worship but openly encouraged. As described by Homan (1978) on the basis of his extensive research in a large number of Pentecostal congregations in England, learning to think of rejoicing as a normal, even necessary, part of Christian worship is a significant part of the socialization of newcomers to the Pentecostal milieu:

> An individual not manifesting 'joy' is not enabled to feel part of the assembly and experiences a sense of omission from the high-points of assembly life: he is 'missing something'. The neophyte learns appropriate behaviour in order to avoid the feeling of exclusion and in response to the incentive to affiliate represented by the outward expressions of 'joy' which constitute a dominant theme in meetings. . . . 'Joy' is the prerogative and mark of the committed pentecostal Christian: like other evangelicals, pentecostals often say that salvation can be discerned on the face. 'Joy' is variously expressed in happy fellowship, a radiant smile, contributions of praise and not least in music. (Homan 1978:513)

For a Pentecostal used to joyful worship, having to sit quietly in one's pew can be a painfully constraining experience. An elderly woman, who had long been an active Pentecostal, once explained to me why she was never fully satisfied by the Saturday night meetings she attended at a nondenominational mission hall. Although she enjoyed the services and had no objections to the content of the sermons, she found it terribly constraining, she explained, to have to remain silent during the service rather than being able to respond to the preaching with verbal exaltations such as 'Praise the Lord' and 'Glory be to Jesus'.

Third, Pentecostal noisiness is a result of and an expression of congregational participation. As described by Hollenweger (1972), probably the world's leading scholarly authority on the worldwide Pentecostal movement,

> [t]he most important element of Pentecostal worship is the active participation of every member of the congregation, even if this amounts to

several thousand people, in dancing, singing, pilgrimages, praying individually and collectively (called 'prayer in concert'), playing all kinds of instruments from the hand-harmonica to triangle and drum, from the saxophone to the violin, evaluating and judging the sermon by inspiring shouts or critical remarks and questions (Hollenweger 1972:312).

Although some of the specifics vary from one cultural setting to another (Scottish Pentecostals discourage dancing and 'prayer in concert'), the general theme of open participation serves several functions throughout the Pentecostal community including giving a sense of spontaneity and unplannedness to the flow of the service; challenging the legitimacy of the human authority of the minister in contrast to the divine authority of the Holy Spirit; preventing congregation members from slipping into the role of observers rather than participants in spiritual experiences; creating a sense of 'fellowship' that comes from sharing words, thoughts, and experiences; and allowing individuals to exchange ideas, thoughts, and inspirations. Despite regional and local variations in the extent to which preaching is monopolized by a few or open to the full congregation, individuals may verbally contribute to the flow and content of the service in almost all Pentecostal churches with Bible readings, short messages, singing (including solos), personal testimonies, announcements, verbal gifts (including tongues, prophecy, and/or interpretation), and prayer. Some contributions arise spontaneously from the participant, others in response to being called from the pulpit. The following excerpt from a description of a Sunday evening service in Recife, Brazil is fairly typical of the participatory nature of Pentecostal services:

As members continue to arrive Brother S, a presbyter, leads the singing, occasionally calling for requests from the congregation. At a little past seven Brother B, a deacon, is called forward to read a passage from the Bible which will serve as the lesson for the evening . . . When B has finished reading from the Bible, he announces the names of visitors and asks those in the congregation who wish to welcome the guests to raise their hands and say yes. Hundreds of hands wave in the air and a resounding 'Sim!' echoes through the church. Brother S then calls on several men to come forward and 'speak about the Lord'. As each leaves his seat and makes his way forward, the congregation sings a refrain from a hymn until he has reached the pulpit. Most of the men read a Bible verse on the importance of prayer or evangelization. One brother tells of a miraculous cure in Casa Amarela (a Recife *bairro*). Another tells of his youngest brother who has been baptized by the Holy Spirit at three years of age. 'I held him in my arms and could feel the force of the Lord.' A few people in the congregation begin speaking in tongues. . . Brother S makes the appeal (*chamada*) for new converts. He begins the appeal by calling on the non-believers present to raise their hands . . . The man who first responded to S's *chamada* is called forward to kneel before the pulpit. The congregation rises and delivers a fervent prayer, each one speaking in his own words. . . (Hoffnagel 1978:142).

A final and probably most important meaning of noisiness in Pentecostal worship is the idea of 'giving free rein to the Holy Spirit', of allowing God to express Himself or demonstrate His presence by taking control of the speech of congregation members. This idea is probably best expressed in the characteristically Pentecostal act of speaking in tongues, producing a spiritually inspired utterance that is unintelligible to the speaker. Although all Pentecostals regard tongues (and prophecy if it is practiced) as a case of God speaking through a human vehicle, the significance of a specific act of speaking in tongues will vary both from one church to another and from one occasion to another in a single church. The three primary meanings of tongues, emphasized to different extents in different variants of Pentecostalism, are as a sign, for rejoicing, and for edification. As a sign, tongues is a mere indication of the presence of the Holy Spirit, that the speaker is at that moment under the protection of, being baptized by, or being filled with the Holy Spirit. As rejoicing, tongues provides a speaker with words for speaking to God in prayer when his or her own words are inadequate. Such a message is understood by God but not by the speaker or audience. Finally, tongues may be used in some forms of Pentecostalism to convey a message from God to a group of Christians through a human channel. In such cases, the gift of tongues is accompanied by the companion gift of interpretation in which the message is 'interpreted' into a language intelligible to congregation members.

Because of the multifaceted nature of Pentecostal noisiness, the encouragement of noise can be used to express a number of different Pentecostal critiques of other churches depending upon the specifics of the local religious context and the theological preferences of the specific congregation. The noisiness of public witnessing and other 'bridge-burning' acts expresses the conversionist nature of evangelical Christianity as opposed to other more retreatist, secretive, or exclusivist religious forms. The joyfulness of noisy worship is commonly opposed to the restraint and solemnity of Calvinist worship. The spontaneity and apparent confusion of congregational participation acts as a check on and critique of an overemphasis on human as opposed to divine authority. Finally, the noisiness of the verbal gifts and other divinely inspired speech indicates a form of worship in which the individual Christian is so filled by the Holy Spirit that 'his cup runneth over'. In general the Pentecostal conception of the noisiness of ideal worship is that of the individual Christian filled to overflowing with the Holy Spirit so that words bubble over in the form of rejoicing, prayer, preaching, testimonies, or verbal gifts.

NOISE AND SILENCE AS RELIGIOUS SYMBOLS: THE LIMITS OF RELATIVITY

As demonstrated in the previous section, three radical religious movements, although all part of a single cultural tradition, each used noise and silence in a strikingly different way to critique and protest the dominant religious assumptions of its time. Puritans stressed inspired preaching in response to ritualistic reading and recitation. Quakers stressed the 'silence' of inner religious experience in response to the superficiality and externality of mere talk. Pentecostals, in contrast, responded to the spiritual silence of a religiously indifferent world by advocating the making of a 'joyful noise.' The fact that radical Protestants of the seventeenth century advocated less noise in Christian worship while those of the twentieth century advocate more noise appears to be a cultural relativist's dream. Even within a single historical tradition, the meanings of noise and silence appear to reverse themselves in a matter of a few centuries. The relationship of noise and silence to their meanings appears to be arbitrary; one person's silence seems to be another person's noise.

The cultural relativist approach, typified by Samarin's (1965) discussion of the 'language of silence,' seems content simply to illustrate the existence of variability in the interpretation of noise and silence and in the 'functions to which silence is put' (Samarin 1965:118). But by stopping at this point, the relativist approach forces one to the conclusion that as symbols 'noise' and 'silence' have no inherent relationship to the meanings with which they have been attributed, and such a conclusion is highly misleading. To apply it to the meaning of noise and silence for Puritans, Quakers, and Pentecostals is to confuse two meanings of the word 'symbol,' a confusion clarified by considering Sapir's (1934) classic distinction between two types of symbols: 'referential symbols,' the meanings of which are arbitrary and conventionalized, and 'condensation symbols' which are richly packed with nonarbitrary meanings. For the early Quakers and contemporary Pentecostals, 'noise' and 'silence' are what Ortner (1973) calls 'key symbols' and Turner (1964) calls 'dominant symbols'. Their meanings are taken very seriously; a multiplicity of meanings are attributed to them; believers feel strongly about them, contemplate their meanings, and expand upon these meanings. In sum, they fit Sapir's notion of 'condensation symbols': the link between these symbols and what they are understood to signify is anything but arbitrary.

Two sources of inherent meaning of these two symbols can be usefully distinguished—their logical properties and their experiential nature—roughly equivalent to what Turner (1964:30) refers to as the ideological and sensory poles of symbolic meaning and Fernandez (1974:120) distinguishes as structural ('the shape of experience') vs. textual ('the feelings of experience') sources of metaphoric meaning.

Logically, noise and silence represent a continuum of noisiness from zero (silence) to infinity (absolute noisiness). Several meanings may be attributed to the two symbols on the basis of this logical relationship. First, noise and silence both contrast with ordinary social behavior. In this sense, their meanings are the same and both can be used to express that which contrasts with the ordinary. Bruneau makes this point in noting that:

> Often, undifferentiated repetition is similar in communicative function to undifferentiated silence. For instance, it may be more than coincidence that recent protest is often marked by serious silence or repetitious chanting. Both can be interpreted easily as ambiguous and undifferentiated. (Bruneau 1973:20)

Thus Quakers and Pentecostals each protest the worship styles of mainline Protestants, one with silence, the other with noise. Baer (1974, 1976) (in the only other study I know of to explicitly compare Quaker and Pentecostal modes of worship) makes a similar point about the potential equivalence of noisiness and silence as nonordinary modes of behavior:

> the 'strangeness' of glossolalia to most people, not least of all ministers and seminary professors, has blinded them to a fundamental functional similarity between speaking in tongues and two other widespread and generally accepted religious practices, namely Quaker silent worship and the liturgical worship of Catholic and Episcopal churches. My thesis is that each of these three practices permits the analytical mind—the focussed, objectifying dimensions of man's intellect—to rest, thus freeing other dimensions of the person, what we might loosely refer to as man's spirit, for a deeper openness to divine reality. (Baer 1976:152, slightly revised from Baer 1974:220)

Thus out-of-the-ordinariness can be used to express transcendence as well as protest.

But this logical continuum implies more than an equivalence between its extremes with both being opposed to moderation. A second logical property of noise and silence is that they are opposed to one another. It is this property (among others) which Baer overlooks in his unconvincing attempts to explain the failure of all religious participants to recognize that glossolalia, liturgy, and silence are functional equivalents:

> It may well be that these three types of religious practice complement and build upon each other. . . Or, it could be the case that glossolalia for many people in our culture represents a more decisive break with the

hegemony of the analytical mind than either Quaker silence or the liturgy of the church and thus opens the way to spiritual growth beyond what the individual has previously experienced.(Baer 1976:161, slightly revised from Baer 1974:227)

What is significant about the logical opposition between noise and silence, as shown in the extended discussions above, is that each of them can be used to express opposition to the other. Thus silence is an appropriate response to a world perceived as noisy, and noise is an appropriate response to a world perceived as silent.

Third, silence is absolute while noisiness is relative. There's only one kind of silence but many kinds and degrees of noise. Thus advocating noisiness as ideal behavior leads to additional problems beyond those implied by advocating silence. Quaker silence raises problems of purpose and appropriate timing, but Pentecostal noisiness raises questions about how much noise and what kind of noise as well.

Fourth, the relationship between noise and silence is not just a relationship between opposites but between a presence and absence of something such that silence but not noise can be represented as an absence. Thus silence is in one sense a derivative concept: whatever noisiness is seen to entail, silence is a lack of it. Speaking is one of the main expressions of noisiness and speaking—the oral transmission of utterances from a speaker to a hearer—has as least three important implications, each of which contrasts with silence: communication, social interaction, and social engagement.

As communication, the act of speaking implies that there is a message to be sent and an audience to receive the message. Silence deemphasizes the message and the needs of the audience. The more stress a particular movement places on the need for communicating a message, the more likely it is to emphasize the role of speech [or its written equivalent]. Even the Quakers thought of speech as the appropriate means for communicating their message to the outsider, and more evangelistic movements stress the theme of 'spreading the word' a great deal more.

As interaction, speech implies the existence or creation of an interpersonal relationship. Silence deemphasizes social relationships. The Pentecostal's very human model of the Christian's 'personal relationship with Christ' is expressed through a very human type of speech interaction. The Pentecostal speaks personally to Christ and seeks a verbal message from Him in return. Quakers, in contrast, conceptualize their relation with divinity in less conversational, less interpersonal terms and seek instead an experience of the Spirit of God within oneself.

As engagement or involvement, speech is contrasted with the disengagement of silence. Quakers and Pentecostals, with their very different valuations of speech, apply the idea of engagement to different aspects of the external world. For Quakers, speech is engagement in the human and worldly and thus to be suppressed. For Pentecostals, religious speech is engagement in social relations with divinity and contrasts with ignoring or denying these relations by remaining silent.

Experientially, the meanings of noisiness for the hearer can be distinguished from those for the producer. For the hearer of noise, noisiness is a forced awareness of something outside or beyond the self and silence an opportunity to ignore the external (or at least its auditory aspects). For the noise producer, noisiness (including speaking, singing, and shouting) involves inner emotions, thoughts, feelings, and other aspects of the self being projected outward, whereas silence is the repression, suppression, or containment of these inner forces. The meanings attributed to these processes of internalization and externalization will vary depending on the ways in which the self is conceptualized, the external physical and spiritual worlds are understood, and dichotomies such as body/spirit and inner self/outer self are comprehended. Quietness can be interpreted as 'awaiting the Spirit', meditation, self-control, withdrawal, shyness, or emotional coldness depending upon one's assumptions about spiritual and psychological reality. Similarly, noisiness can be interpreted as emotionalism, becoming a 'vessel for the Spirit', self-indulgence, enthusiasm, or lack of self-control. The tendency to impose one's own assumptions about psychological reality on the interpretation of the behavior of others leads many nonreligious observers to think of Quakerism as introspection and Pentecostalism as emotionalism, characterizations which contradict the reported experiences of members in both cases.

As condensation symbols, 'noise' and 'silence' are constrained in their meanings by universal logical and experiential attributes. But these constraints do not imply that their meanings are inflexible. Meanings vary across cultures, over time, and from one situation to another. Meanings vary for a number of different reasons: changes in other parts of the cultural system, changes in historical context. changes in the way meaning is applied to specific situations, and changes in the richness of meaning that symbols are assumed to possess.

First, because the meanings of noise and silence are in part defined in terms of other cultural concepts, changes in the meanings of these other concepts will affect the meanings of 'noise' and 'silence'. Thus, if silence is a lack of interaction with the 'world', changes in the conceptualization of 'the world' will affect the meaning of silence. Second, since noise and silence are central elements in debates about the way the world is and the way it should be, the way one's opponents conceptualize noise and silence affect one's responses. Third, since noise and silence are used to interpret specific incidents and behaviors, some of their meanings will shift depending on the specific situations they are being used to interpret. Thus even among Pentecostals, who advocate noisiness in worship, certain types of disruptive behavior may be condemned as too noisy [see excerpts from Michael's diary for April 22 quoted above]. Finally, Sapir's distinction between condensation and referential symbols refers not to two types of symbols but to two ends of a continuum of ways in which a symbol is assumed to mean. Even a prototypical referential symbol like an Arabic numeral can be treated as a condensation symbol by a numerologist, or a highly meaningful condensation symbol like the Christian cross treated as a mere emblem of identity. Similarly, noisiness and silence which early in the history of Quakerism and Pentecostalism were understood as deeply meaningful condensed representations of what worship was all about can become over time mere emblems used simply for distinguishing one church from another.

CONCLUSION

My basic argument in this chapter has been that the potential meanings of noise and silence are not arbitrary. They are constrained by both logical and experiential aspects of the phenomena themselves. What varies are the contexts in which the symbols are interpreted, the situations in which they are applied, and the seriousness with which multiple-meanings are explored. It is possible in some contexts to reduce potential condensation symbols to mere referential symbols by ignoring many of their potential interpretations. In almost all symbolic situations, in fact, at least some potentially logical interpretations are rejected as inappropriate or simply ignored. But where noise and silence have been elevated to a place of central significance as key symbols and the general milieu is one of extreme concern with exegesis as is certainly the case in Bible-centered Christianity, noise and silence remain multireferential condensation symbols highly constrained in their meanings by their inherent logics.

The different types of data explored in this paper reveal a variety of different aspects of this relationship between the potential and actualized meanings of noise and silence. The introspection in Michael's diary is heavily dependent upon his recognition of noise and silence as being logically opposed. Silence is seen as inwardly-oriented, thoughtful, but also passive. Noisiness is seen as outwardly-oriented, interactional, and involving active participation. He accepts this dichotomous view of human behavior and personality because it fits so well with the distinction between two extreme worship styles. The distinction between two styles of worship becomes a way of thinking about himself, who he is and who he can and should be. He recognizes quietness as defining his natural personality, sees the potential values of noisiness and equivocates over the value and/or possibility of changing his inherent nature. As multi-referential symbols, 'noise' and 'silence' serve as a kind of personal therapeutic system. It is by thinking about differences in their inherent meanings that he thinks about and tries to deal with his interactional problems.

By asking why some people prefer to worship quietly while others prefer to do so with great noise, Michael is able to provide an extremely elaborate exegesis of the symbolic richness of 'noise' and 'silence' in his personal Christian experience. But a fuller understanding of the range of possible Christian interpretations of 'noise' and 'silence' requires the asking of more sophisticated historical, sociological, and theological questions. The comparison of three different approaches to the same problem of religious meaning in the historical section of this paper illustrates the way in which a single pair of religious symbols can be combined with the same cultural paradigm of Christian preaching to produce different religious conclusions depending upon the way in which the historical context is perceived and which of the potential meanings of 'noise' and 'silence' are actualized. The inherent logical contrast between noisiness and silence allows reformers to stress silence as a protest against noisiness or advocate noise as a protest against silence. The basic Calvinist paradigm of Protestant worship separates the functions of speech and silence, dividing them between the positions of speaker and hearer: the preacher speaks, the congregation listens quietly. Quakers and Pentecostals protest this sociolinguistic division of labor with alternative strategies. Quakers emphasize the spiritual role of the silent listener, Pentecostals increase the speaking parts for congregation members so that even listening to a sermon preached becomes a noisy, participatory act.

Viewing these variants as logical alternatives rather than parts of a historical process provides still other insights into the inherent meanings of noise and silence. Each variant has a kind of inherent compelling logic of its own. Although both Quakerism and Pentecostalism envision Spirit-led meetings as the antidote to sterile formalism, the Quaker stress on silence and the Pentecostal stress on noisiness imply far more than simply differences in modes of worship. They indicate radically different conceptions of the Holy Spirit, the self, communication, and relations with outsiders. In general Quakers look inward while Pentecostals look outward. Quakers seek the spirit within each individual; they contrast an inner spiritual self with an outer natural one; they stress the silent wait for inspiration over the inspired utterances which result; and they have an ambivalence about the preaching necessary to evangelize among outsiders.

Pentecostals, in contrast, conceptualize the Holy Spirit as external, capable of engaging in intimate interaction with the individual, but only by burning up and replacing one's inner sinful nature and using the outer form of the individual Christian as a 'vessel'. They have no concept of an inner light, only of the possibility of being 'filled' by an external Holy Spirit. The presence of the Holy Spirit is indicated as it was at Pentecost [Acts 2] by loud and even seemingly drunken behavior. Pentecostal spiritual experience leads not to quietness and withdrawal from outsiders but towards an increasing zeal to evangelize and publicize one's experiences.

Finally, there is a sense in which noisiness and silence are in a kind of argument with one another independent of the preferences of individuals or groups. Each one needs the other to be recognizable, and every move towards one implies new problems in relation to the other. Each refinement and reform of Protestant worship in terms of noise and silence leads to additional complications, tensions, and critical responses. Each paradigm shift implies the need to work through a new set of logical corollaries. Each new thesis implies a new antithesis. Almost as soon as the Calvinist paradigm of worship was developed, the Puritans were led to question the rigidity of its form, to ask how spiritual communication was taking place, and to analyze the implications of noisy preachers and quiet congregations. The Puritan emphasis on the role of the hearer led logically to Quaker challenges to the legitimacy of having preaching at all. But the Quakers were then left with their own ambivalences: over evangelizing (which rapidly decreased in importance among most Quakers after the first generation) and over the role of prophetic or inspired speech in a religious system which stressed waiting for inspiration over using it.

Pentecostalism is in many ways simply a new solution to the same problem concerning the Protestant model of worship that aroused the Quakers and Puritans: the relation between speaking, God's word, and the Holy Spirit. And their valuation of noisiness as a sign of the presence of the Holy Spirit raises the same old problem that bothered the early Quakers: How can you tell inspired noisiness from human self-indulgence? Their solution to self-indulgent noisiness is also the same as the Quakers: 'waiting on' the Holy Spirit. But this is not a case of history repeating itself. It is simply a case of parallel expressions of the inherent logic of noise and silence. When a Pentecostal 'waits on the Spirit,' it need not be silently. It can be with audible prayer, in tongues, or by reading the Bible either silently or aloud. And waiting for divine inspiration, for a Pentecostal, is not the focus of group worship but a preliminary to it, often to be done at home before coming to church. There is, after all, 'no such thing as a silent Pentecostal' (Linford 1973, cited above).

ACKNOWLEDGMENTS

The original idea for this paper derives from a comment by Jane Fajans, who, while doing summer fieldwork in Scotland in 1973, first made me aware of the striking contrast between the quietness of Quaker worship and the noisiness of Pentecostals. An earlier and much shorter version of the paper was presented at the 1978 annual meeting of the Southwestern Anthropological Association in a session entitled 'Anthropological Perspectives in the Study of Christianity.' Julie Rake, Ruth Borker, and Renato Rosaldo all provided useful comments and suggestions at that time. For assistance in the long and painful process of enlarging the paper and 'turning it inside out,' so that its primary focus was 'noise and silence' rather than the anthropology of Christianity, I thank Deborah Tannen, Ruth Borker, Don Brenneis, and Jim Snyder. Finally, there are two individuals without whose cooperation the present version of the paper could never have been written. One is 'Michael', who kindly provided me with access to his personal diary. The other is Ann Kibbey of the English Department at Yale University who allowed me to make use of her unpublished material and provided extensive comments, criticisms, and bibliographic suggestions on an earlier version of this paper.

REFERENCES

Anderson, Robert Mapes. 1979. Vision of the disinherited: The making of American Pentecostalism. New York: Oxford University Press.

Baer, Richard Arthur Jr. 1974. The moods and modes of worship. Theology Today 31 (3). 220–227.

Baer, Richard Arthur Jr. 1976. Quaker silence, Catholic liturgy, and Pentecostal glossolalia—Some functional similarities. Perspectives on the new Pentecostalism, ed. by Russell P. Spittler, 150–164. Grand Rapids, MI: Baker Book House Co.

Basso, Keith Hamilton. 1970. To give up on words: Silence in Western Apache culture. Southwestern Journal of Anthropology 26 (3). 213–230.

Bauman, Richard. 1970. Aspects of 17th century Quaker rhetoric. Quarterly Journal of Speech 56 (1). 67–74.

Bauman, Richard. 1971. For the reputation of truth: Politics, religion, and conflict among the Pennsylvania Quakers 1750–1800. Baltimore: The Johns Hopkins Press.

Bauman, Richard. 1974. Speaking in the light: The role of the Quaker minister. Explorations in the ethnography of speaking, ed. by Richard Bauman & Joel Sherzer, 144–160. Cambridge: Cambridge University Press.

Bauman, Richard. 1975. Quaker folk-linguistics and folklore. Folklore: Performance and communication, ed. by Dan Ben-Amos & Kenneth Goldstein, 255–263. The Hague: Mouton.

Bauman, Richard. 1983. Let your words be few: Symbolism of speaking and silence among seventeenth-century Quakers. Cambridge: Cambridge University Press.

Birckhead, R. James Patrick. 1976. Toward the creation of a community of saints. Unpublished PhD Thesis, University of Alberta.

Brown, Victor Gordon. 1966. The Church: Historical and contemporary. Petersborough, Ontario: College Press.

Bruneau, Thomas J. 1973. Communicative silences: Forms and functions. The Journal of Communication 23 (1). 17–46.

Creasy, Maurice A. 1972. Quaker worship. The Westminster dictionary of worship, ed. by John Gordon Davies. Philadelphia: The Westminster Press.

Davies, John Gordon (ed.). 1972. The Westminster dictionary of worship. Philadelphia: The Westminster Press.

Fernandez, James William. 1974. The mission of metaphor in expressive culture. Current Anthropology 15 (2). 119–145.

Gerlach, Luther Paul and Virginia Haglin Hine. 1968. Five factors crucial to the growth and spread of a modern religious movement. Journal for the Scientific Study of Religion 7 (1). 23–40.

Gerlach, Luther Paul and Virginia Haglin Hine. 1970. People, power, change: Movements of social transformation. Indianapolis: Bobbs-Merrill.

Hine, Virginia Haglin. 1968. Personal transformation and social change: The role of commitment in a modern religious movement. Unpublished MA Thesis, University of Minnesota.

Hoffnagel, Judith Chambliss. 1978. The believers: Pentecostalism in a Brazilian city. Unpublished PhD Thesis, Indiana University.

Hollenweger, Walter J. 1972. Pentecostal worship. The Westminster Dictionary of Worship, ed. by John Gordon Davies, 311–312. Philadelphia: The Westminster Press.

Homan, Roger. 1978. Interpersonal communication in Pentecostal meetings. Sociological Review 26 (3). 499–518.

Homan, Roger. 1981. Crises in the definition of reality. Sociology: The Journal of the British Sociological Association 15 (2). 210–224.

Jones, Ilion T. 1954. A Historical approach to evangelical worship. New York: Abingdon Press.

Kibbey [Levy], Ann Marilyn. 1973. Puritan beliefs about language and speech. Unpublished paper presented at the 72nd Annual Meeting of the American Anthropological Association, December 2, 1973.

Kibbey, Ann Marilyn. 1978. Personal communication, July 4, 1978.

Ladlow, Gerald W. 1973. Ecstatic praise. Redemption Tidings 49 (19). 3–5.

Linford, Aaron. 1973. Worship. Redemption Tidings 49 (40). 2.

Maltz, Daniel Nathan. 1978. The bride of Christ is filled with His Spirit. Women in ritual and symbolic roles. ed by Judith Hoch-Smith & Anita Spring, 27–44. New York: Plenum Press.

Manning, Frank Edward. 1980. Pentecostalism: Christianity and reputation. Perspectives on Pentecostalism: Case studies from the Caribbean and Latin America, ed. by Stephen Glazier, 177–187. Washington, DC: University Press of America.

Marty, Martin E. 1972. Protestantism. Garden City: Image Books.

Maxwell, William D. 1955. A History of worship in the Church of Scotland. Oxford: Oxford University Press.

Maxwell, William D. 1972. Reformed worship. The Westminster dictionary of worship, ed. by John Gordon Davies, 331–333. Philadelphia: The Westminster Press.

McGuire, Meredith Black. 1977. Testimony as a commitment mechanism in Catholic Pentecostal prayer groups. Journal for the Scientific Study of Religion 16 (2). 165–168.

Miles, C. Austen. 1955. There's a shout in the camp. Redemption hymnal. Eastbourne, Sussex: Elim Publishing House.

Morgan, Edmund Sears. 1963. Visible saints: The history of a Puritan idea. Ithaca: Cornell University Press.

Ortner, Sherry Beth. 1973. On key symbols. American Anthropologist 75 (5). 1338–1346.

Samarin, William John. 1965. Language of silence. Practical Anthropology 12 (3). 115–119.

Samarin, William John. 1973. Protestant preachers in the prophetic line. International Yearbook for the Sociology of Religion 8. 243–257.

Sapir, Edward. 1934. Symbolism. Encyclopedia of Social Sciences 14: 492–495.

Turner, Victor Witter. 1964. Symbols in Ndembu ritual. Closed systems and open minds: The limits of naivety in social anthropology, ed. by Max Gluckman, 20–51. Chicago: Aldine Publishing Company.

Chapter 8

Silence and Sulking: Emotional Displays in the Classroom

Perry Gilmore
University of Pennsylvania

INTRODUCTION

Although recent years have witnessed a steadily growing body of ethnographic data concerning classrooms, the realm of emotions has largely been ignored. The sociolinguistic emphasis in classroom research has been primarily focused on verbal aspects of communicative (Hymes 1964) or interactional (Mehan 1976) competence (see, for example, Cazden, John, and Hymes 1972; McDermott 1977; Mehan 1979; Gilmore and Glatthorn 1982; Spindler 1982; Edwards and Furlong 1978; Bellack, Kliebard, Hyman and Smith 1966). This body of ethnographic literature illustrates that beyond academic competence there is a need for students to demonstrate interactional competence in social settings in order to do well in school. These studies have primarily demonstrated that not only the academic knowledge must be present but that the student must also know when and how to display that knowledge according to socially acceptable rules of classroom interaction.

Though this sociolinguistic research has certainly enriched the study of schooling and expanded our awareness of important dimensions of the interactions surrounding learning events in school, it has somehow failed to address some of the most essential aspects of classroom life.

Urban classrooms are often scenes of clashes of will. Many of the most crucial social interactions in school settings are highly charged with emotion and regularly interpreted with regard to 'attitude'. The ways in which these confrontations are interpreted and treated by teachers and students will strongly affect the nature of the attitudes conveyed as well as any learning which takes place in classrooms. The research presented in this chapter was part of a three-year study conducted in a predominantly low-income, black urban community and elementary school. The study sought to identify and explore school and community perceived problems concerning literacy achievement. The research focus was on cultural patterns of literacy-related social interactions in and out of school. These were examined to ascertain their consequences for the acquisition and display of school-recognized literacy practices. The data were collected in and out of school and consist of personal observations, interactions, and interviews documented over a three-year period with field notes, audio tape recordings, and collections of relevant 'artifacts'.

A major problem identified in the study site and voiced repeatedly by teachers (about 50 percent black and 50 percent white), parents, administrators, and children in the community was 'attitude'. A 'good attitude' seemed to be the central and significant factor for students' general academic success and literacy achievement in school. In this particular setting, talk about 'attitude' was dramatically more prominent than talk about 'intelligence'. In fact, it was made clear to staff and parents as well as students, that in cases of tracking and/or selection for honors or special academic preference, 'attitude' outweighed academic achievement or IQ test performance.

The specific dimensions and features, and actual meanings of 'attitude' can of course differ from one setting to another. To document them in this particular setting was one of the goals of the investigation. The approach taken here was concerned with how attitudes are *communicated, understood,* and *interpreted.* The functions and uses of the concept as it is constructed in this particular context were considered.

By observing actions and reactions to behaviors seen as related to attitude and by noting the language used to describe or evaluate such behaviors, a profile of the constructed meanings was developed. A picture began to emerge of what linguistic, paralinguistic, and social behaviors 'count' as attitude and of how these behaviors were affected (both in performance and interpretation) by the different contexts in which they occurred. The process of identifying a domain of the concept of attitude required the discovery and description of the related folk categories used by the participants.

A student with a 'good attitude' was described in terms like 'completing homework', 'being cooperative', 'no discipline problems', 'good attendance', 'being punctual', 'having involved parents', 'good work habits', and the like. The descriptions were extensive and quite varied in terms of the dimensions of behavior they encompassed.

Further, in talking to many of the staff, and in the initial phases of general observation in the school and community, it became apparent that 'attitude' was delicately woven into a broader context of what might be labelled 'propriety'. Proper standards of what is socially acceptable in conduct or speech appeared to be a consistent concern in both the community and the school.

At times in talking about students, other descriptions were offered that seemed related to the use of 'good' and 'bad' attitude. The label 'street kid' or 'child of the streets' seemed to be used to describe students who were not neatly groomed, did not have 'involved parents', had little supervision at home, were often absent or late, did not complete homework, and the like. These 'street' kids were often the same children who were characterized as having 'an attitude' or a 'slight attitude'. (In these cases the use of the term 'attitude' alone conveys the notion of a negative or bad attitude.) On the other hand, labels like 'cultured', 'lady-like', 'nice kid', 'respectful', which seem to imply politeness and propriety, were used synonymously with 'good attitude'.

A 'good attitude' appeared to be central to inclusion in special high track classes referred to as an Academics Plus Program. The Academics Plus Program is described by staff as a rigorous, 'back to basics' curriculum in which academic achievement and excellence is the primary goal.

To qualify, a student not only has to be working at a certain grade level, but also to display a 'cooperative attitude'. The program is in effect a tracking procedure for attitude as well as academic achievement. Teachers sometimes talk about the process as one of 'weeding out bad attitudes'. A student working at a relatively low grade level might be admitted to the program if his or her behavior indicated a desire to work and be cooperative. In such a case, a 'good attitude' outweighs limited academic achievement. In other reported instances, a bright child who might be achieving academically, but whose behavior is characteristic of a 'bad attitude', would not be admitted. In such a case, 'attitude' again outweighs academic achievement. Less than a third of the population in each intermediate grade level (3–6) was selected for the special academic program. It was clear to the staff, the children, and the parents that although the participation in the Academics Plus Program did not guarantee literacy success and general academic achievement, it certainly maximized the chances for it. And the key factor for admission was something everyone called a 'good attitude'.

Students who were viewed as having 'good attitudes' were consistently viewed as being 'good kids'. The label became a part of the constitution of the individual's basic character and indicative of the individual's worth. Yet when the behaviors subsumed under the label 'attitude' were examined, the data indicate that they consist largely of a set of paralinguistic and kinesic communicative adornments which are associated with a particular ethnic style or socioeconomic class, rather than a set of character traits reflective of the nature of individuals. The following discussion will describe the nature of student silences; the way they were used, interpreted, and treated with regard to attitude in dialogic interactions in the classroom.

ENACTING ATTITUDES: PORTRAYALS AND MASQUERADES

All situations carry with them a sense of what feelings are appropriate to have. Hochschild (1979:552) addresses this issue when she discusses 'emotion work' which she describes as 'the act of evoking or shaping as well as suppressing feeling in oneself'. Hochschild suggests that there are 'feeling rules' which are learned and used as baselines in social exchanges. Classrooms provide an excellent setting in which to capture the pedagogy involved in 'emotion work' and the teaching and learning discourse that surrounds 'feeling rules'. In classrooms such rules are frequently articulated.

Consider the emotion work embedded in this brief classroom interaction taken from my field notes:

> There is a loud chatting and calling out and several students are out of their seats while the teacher is trying to explain how to do the assignment. The teacher suddenly shouts in a loud and angry voice, 'Sit down, sit up . . . (more softly) and don't look surprised or hurt cause we've gone over this before.'

The teacher first shows anger, shouting at the class to 'sit down' and 'sit up' (i.e., get in your seats and sit tall at attention). When several students portray looks of 'hurt' or 'surprise', she tells them it is not acceptable to feel or, more accurately, to look as if they feel that way. In this particular instance the teacher may have been mediating her expression of emotion by telling the class that it wasn't a serious enough emotion to be hurt by. The teacher reminds them that they know the rules they were breaking (e.g., calling out, walking around the room while she was talking to them as a class, side-chatting loudly). This reminder is conveyed in the phrase 'we've gone over this before'. Therefore she is able to justify her own angry response while instructing the class about the appropriate emotional response she expects them to *have* and, even more significant—to *show*.

Thus a three part lesson is being learned by the students: (1) there is an appropriate set of feelings to have in a given context; (2) there are conventional ways (e.g., postures, facial expressions and the like) that are used to express the feelings you have to the other participants in the setting; and (3) if you are *not* actually feeling the appropriate feelings in a given situation, you can, and are in fact expected to, enact the conventionally accepted bodily and facial configurations that correspond with the given emotion. *Emotional masquerading*, knowing when and how to disguise inappropriate feelings, is an essential aspect of classroom survival.

Silence and nonverbal behavior are particularly important in classroom interactions because much of student emotional communications must take place without talk. The traditional classrooms I observed support the generalization that most of the talk is by the teacher (Anderson 1978), and that 'children's time is spent overwhelmingly in listening and reading' (Cazden 1979). 'Silent communication' was frequent between students and teachers. My classroom observation specifically focused on interactional silences, that is, the features and boundaries of silence in face-to-face interactions other than pauses for thought. (This excluded, for example, the silence which may have occurred while doing independent assigned seatwork such as reading or writing exercises.)

SILENCE DISPLAYS

In the following two examples from my field notes each student replies to the teacher's question with silence. In one case the silence is acceptable, in the other it is not. (See Sample A.)

These two examples suggest that it is not merely the silence that is or is not appropriate, but the way in which the silent performance is adorned with bodily configuration and gestures. In the first example the gestural adornment is interpreted by the teacher and by the student's peers who were also part of the audience, as a public confession as well as a public apology. The teacher was allowed to remain in authority and the social structure was not disrupted. In the second example, however, the nonverbal postures and facial expressions were interpreted quite differently. This assorted package of bodily signals was seen as defiant, a public challenge to the teacher's authority. The child was sent to the principal's office a few minutes later.

Ritual displays have been described as behaviors which provide a 'readily readable expression of (an individual's) . . . situation, specifically his intent' as well as 'evidence of the actor's alignment in the situation' (Goffman 1976:69). It seems reasonable then to view the behaviors described under the label 'gestural adornments' in the examples above, as *silence displays*. These silent responses are, in fact, conventionalized acts which are choreographed predictably and perfunctorily in portraying alignments and attitudes. The reader can, no doubt, make an accurate guess as to which of the two students above would be designated as having a 'bad attitude'.

In order to better understand the ways in which student silence dis-

144   GILMORE

SAMPLE A
EXAMPLE 1 (ACCEPTABLE SILENCE)

Speaker	Utterance	Gestural Adornment
Teacher:	What were you doing?	
Student #1:	(silence)	Looks up at teacher with slightly bowed head, eyebrows turned up with slightly quizzical look, shrugs shoulders, raising arms with elbows bent and palms up
Teacher:	Okay. But don't do it again.	

EXAMPLE 2 (UNACCEPTABLE SILENCE)

Speaker	Utterance	Gestural Adornment
Teacher:	What were you doing?	
Student #2:	(silence)	Chin up, lower lip pushed forward, eyebrows in a tight scowl, downward side glance to teacher, left hand on her hip which is thrust slightly forward
Teacher:	Answer me.	
Student #2:	(silence)	same
Teacher:	I asked you a question . . . Answer me . . . I said answer me!	
		walks toward student

plays are interpreted, the discussion will consider student and teacher silence displays. The following section will compare and contrast the ways in which teachers and students use, understand, and respond to each other's dialogic interactional silences. The discussion of teacher silence is presented below in order to provide the conversational context for the primary focus of interest here, which is student silence.

TEACHER SILENCES

The example below (see Sample B) illustrates the uses a classroom teacher may make of silence as a display which is mutually understood by all participants in the scene and can and does affect behavior.

A closer examination of some of the features of teacher silence may be useful at this point. Silence displays are often marked with shift in body orientation such as looking up from a book, standing up, turning to or walking near an individual who is 'breaking a rule'. Teachers will sometimes give a scolding look or shake their head 'no' during the silence.

SAMPLE B

Some of the functions and uses of teacher silences are depicted in the following interactions.

FIELD NOTES, EXCERPT A

The class has returned from lunch. The teacher has led them in two lines, boys and girls, up the stairs from the cafeteria to the classroom. Once in the room students get seated, chat, go to the water fountain, and the like. There is considerable movement and noise in the room. The teacher stands in the front of the room holding the book *Sounder*, her fingers separating the pages along with the book marker. On the board the schedule is listed in chalk: Sounder, Abraham Lincoln, Language Arts, etc.

Teacher: When I see . . . when I see every mouth stopped and everybody turned around to me, I'll know we're ready to start our schedule.

(Teacher stands silently staring around the room.)

.
.
.

(Students continue to chat and move around the room.)

.
.
.

Teacher: Maria is ready.

.
.
.

Teacher: I'm not gonna wait forever until I start putting names up there.*

.
.
.

(Students are quiet and the teacher begins to ask review questions about the book they read yesterday.)

The teacher begins to read from the book in an animated and involved tone. Occasionally she stops reading, sometimes in the middle of a sentence, and looks up silently to some individual student

(continued)

SAMPLE B (*Continued*)

who's been side chatting. Once the student is quiet again she continues to read. Several students are talking in small clusters around the room. The teacher stands and walks near two students who've been playing with rulers, having a small duel under their desks. The teacher takes the rulers from them as she continues reading from *Sounder*. The teacher sits in front of the room again reading, punctuating her performance with questions about characters, feelings, vocabulary words, and the like. The class gets noisy again.

(Teacher puts book down to her lap and then stands silently.)

.

.

.

Teacher: All right, I'll wait again.

.

.

.

(Teacher stands silent. When class is quiet she sits and softly begins reading again.)

*Names are put on the board for good and bad behavior and are rewarded or punished accordingly.

When extremely frustrated, the silence may be accompanied by a tight jaw or blushing. In all cases I've observed, the teachers wear a serious facial expression. The display has never appeared accompanied by a smile. Sometimes, in fact, an abrupt change in facial expression from smile to stern seriousness will mark the silence display. For example, I observed a teacher chatting in a smiling and relaxed way with her students as they were lining up on the playground after recess. Abruptly, as if suddenly changing a dramatic theater mask, the teacher silently looked out over the lines wearing an angry warning look. The quickness of the change, with no apparent provocation by the students, suggests that the change in facial expression was not so much a change in the teacher's emotional state as a change in the message she was trying to convey, that is, now it was time to get quiet and orderly.

In addition to body signals and facial expression, another physical characteristic of the use of a silence display is the manipulation of and use of physical gestures that mark the display. I have observed teachers turn out the lights or write a name on the board during the silence. An interesting fact about silence as a conventional communicative signal is that it runs a high risk of going unnoticed, especially in the circumstances in which teachers frequently use it (i.e., when classes are noisy).

Not surprisingly, silences are often marked not only with gestures, body orientation and the like, but with signals that actually carry sound.

Often teachers will initiate a silence display by slamming a door (in some cases even opening the door first in order to do so), slapping a book down on the desk, or clapping their hands. Teachers often keep props for this purpose. One teacher I observed kept a wooden club on her desk which she would bang. Bells and whistles are often used. Verbal markers (from shouts to silent whispers) are also effective in drawing attention to silence. Examples of such verbal markers include: 'I'm waiting', 'I've had it!', 'Johnnie knows why I'm standing here.', 'I've had it for the day. We're just going to sit.', 'uh oh (standing with hands on hips),' 'okay,' We're not ready.', 'Brian . . I need your attention.', 'Freeze', and so on. Several such verbal markers are illustrated in the sample protocol above (e.g., 'Margo is ready.', 'I'm not going to wait. . .'). Sighs are also used as aural signals along with silence.

The teacher's silence display appears to carry a mutually understood meaning for all classroom participants. It seems to mean 'pay attention to me' and/or 'what you're doing is not acceptable to me.' The appropriate student response is silence and attention. Usually the display is most effective as a transition device, a way to get attention and class cohesion for a new lesson or activity, marking the beginning of a new frame. It is very frequently used at these 'junctures' (Mehan et al. 1976). The other most obvious use is for maintaining an orderly interaction. Silence can be used not only to initiate but also to regain and maintain the orderliness of the lesson structure.

The length of time the teacher keeps the silence varies considerably from a brief pause in a sentence to a prolonged period of five to ten minutes or more. At times the silence will be ended as soon as the teacher gets the desired attention. On other occasions the silence will continue conspicuously after the class's silence is accomplished, thus prolonging the message and probably also prolonging the mood.

Silence as a means of 'keeping control' is frequently recommended to novice teachers, both in training institutions, staff development seminars, and in the nature of helpful hints passed on from veteran teachers in informal faculty dining room and hallway chats. Teachers have also commented that silence and waiting are a good way to 'fight' the pressure and the fast pace of the classroom, an effective device to 'slow down the activity', a way to 'interrupt' or 'stop the pressure', 'a relief', 'a way of withdrawing and regaining focus' for all participants. This is probably true especially of long silences produced and prolonged by strong disapproval, frustration, and a sense of loss of control.

Teacher silences and regulation of volume in general seem to facilitate the pacing and cadence of classroom interactional rhythms. They are dramatic devices by which a teacher, as the pivotal person in a traditional classroom, can actually freeze a frame, keep the class hanging, so to speak, by silently waiting. In this way teachers may play with and elongate a naturally permitted silence in order to convey a message about appropriate student behavior. Teachers might refer to 'the stare' or suggest that giving someone 'the eye' will serve as an effective reprimand. Indeed these silent 'looks' are effective controlling devices, especially if they have interrupted a normal stream of talk. In sum, then, by withholding their turn at talk, while simultaneously maintaining the conversational floor, teachers exercise strong control of the interaction.

STUDENT SILENCES

Unlike the teacher silence which has only one audience—the students—student silence can be a communicative device directed at fellow students as well as the teacher. The primary concern in this discussion is to examine silence as a way of displaying emotion, but brief mention of the other uses of interactional silence should be made. In traditional classes of 25 to 30 students, where discourse usually takes the form of two interlocutors engaged face-to-face—one the teacher, the other, 25 students who must behave as one speaker, it is not surprising that much of the student silence is cooperative and in the role of listener. The uses of silence range from attentively being involved in the focused activity to disguising, silently, side activities such as reading under the desk, note passing, and the like. Much of the silence of students falls into this category. This listener silence 'fits in' the participation structure of the situation and is, in fact, where most students hide during the major part of the school day. This type of hiding is so effective that a teacher or indeed a classroom researcher may have to make strong effort if these students are to be noticed. Except for occasionally short answers, the primary role of these invisible students is to facilitate the discourse by remaining silent.

The student silences that are most visible occur in teacher-student confrontations such as those shown in Examples 1 and 2 above. Usually these encounters are ones in which the student is being reprimanded, and often take place in front of other class members. In these cases I have observed two kinds of student silence displays, which can be called *submissive subordinate* and *nonsubmissive subordinate*. The first, submissive subordinate, is only observed with interactions with the teacher or other adult authority, never with peers. This display is marked with body gestures such as a bowed head, quizzical expression around the eyes, a smile, even a giggle, if the offense is not too serious, a serious but relaxed facial expression, and so on (recall Sample A, Example 1). Sample C describes such a display.

By contrast, the nonsubmissive subordinate display of silence, which I have chosen to label *stylized sulking,* carries with it a very different

SAMPLE C
FIELD NOTES, EXCERPT B

Johnny plays with his hat. The teacher interrupts the lesson and tells him to stop playing with his hat. Johnny looks down, bowing his head briefly, then looks up at the teacher, his eyes raise first then his head follows. His eyebrows curl questioningly and he smiles a rather tentative but affectionate smile. The teacher continues speaking and as she verbally threatens that he might stay after school the smile disappears quickly from his face during her utterance.

bodily configuration (recall Sample A, Example 2). The protocol below (see Sample D) will illustrate the difference.

This example (Sample D) demonstrates some of the power and control that can be exercised by a student with a silent display of emotions. It appears to be an effective face-saving device for one who must be subordinate. The bodily configuration is easily noted, as the teacher's detailed comments illustrate, but very difficult to modify in a face-to-face encounter.

As mentioned earlier, the performance of this display is often highly stylized and differs for boys and girls. Girls will frequently pose with their chins up, closing their eyelids for elongated periods and casting downward side glances, and often markedly turning their heads sidewards as well as upwards. Girls also will rest their chins on their hand with elbow support on their desks. Striking or getting into the pose is usually with an abrupt movement that will sometimes be marked with a sound like the elbow striking the desk or a verbal marker like 'humpf'. Again, as with the teacher silence, it is necessary to draw some attention to the silence, and with the girls it seems to be primarily with a flourish of getting into the pose.

Boys usually display somewhat differently. Their 'stylized sulking' is usually characterized by head downward, arms crossed at the chest, legs spread wide and usually desk pushed away. Often they will mark the silence by knocking over a chair or pushing loudly on their desk, assuring that others hear and see the performance. Another noticeable characteristic of the boys' performance is that they sit down, deeply slumped in their chairs. This is a clear violation of the constant reminder in classrooms to 'sit up' and 'sit up tall'. Teachers will often talk about 'working on' sitting up, feet under the desk, lining up, and so on. The silence displays go against all the body idiom rules of the classroom. Even when less extreme postures are taken, however, the facial expression remains an easily read portrait of emotion.

For both boys and girls, 'getting into the sulk' does not seem to be verbally marked the way that teachers' silences are. Getting *out* of a sulk presents certain challenges to boys and girls alike however. I have ob-

SAMPLE D
FIELD NOTES, EXCERPT C

Ann has been kept after school along with several others. Each student is being called to the teacher's desk individually to discuss what they did wrong that day. Ann is called to the teacher's desk as Willa, Ann's friend, is dismissed. Ann stands at the desk with her chin up, her face tight and fixed, her eyelids closed for elongated periods and her gaze shifts mostly downward to a side glance, only briefly and rarely looking to the teacher. Ann taps her foot as she stands silent and distant.

Teacher: When you stop tapping your toe and looking like that, I'll talk to you.

(Ann is silent. Her mouth is set tightly and her lids are lowered and taut—'mean eyes'—she continues to tap her foot.)

.
.
.

The teacher asks her why she's here and with no change in affect she answers cryptically that she was 'yelling in the hall'.

Teacher: You're angry?

Ann: Yeah.

Teacher: (inaud.) . . . let people know you're angry without being nasty, tapping your toe, calling people names . . .

.
.
.

(Ann unchanged remains silent.)

.
.
.

Teacher: You're tapping your finger too—I can see you're still angry . . . come on (almost pleading tone).

.
.
.

(Ann same.)

.
.
.

Teacher makes several other attempts (including a reminder that she's keeping her friend Willa waiting—and Willa is sick), but Ann remains silent and retains her body configuration with no sign of leak. Teacher asks if she would like to sit down and think about it. Ann says 'yeah' and leaves the teacher's desk.

Ann gets a drink, chats with her friend, Willa, while teacher talks to John.

After a few minutes pass Ann walks past the teacher's desk to get a handout they were to take home.

Teacher: (smiling) Oh, you lost it already.

Ann: (smiles) Yes.

(Teacher hands Ann the folder containing the handout.)

Ann and Willa are chatting. Ann is smiling. Both girls stand near the teacher's desk and all talk and laugh, kidding with Ben, Gary, and John about 'boyfriends'.

Teacher: (to Ann) Your whole body and face are different now . . .

Teacher continues to comment on her affect change and asks again what was going on before. Now Ann goes into a fluent narrative about her argument with Sam. The teacher responds saying 'but that doesn't tell me about all this other stuff . . . tapping your toe . . .'

They continue to talk briefly, then the teacher asks if she will try to behave tomorrow. Ann mumbles 'yeah' and the teacher smiles saying, 'Can you say it differently?' Ann smiles and says, 'Yes, Miss Davis', as she turns to leave.

---

served several instances where it might be valid to say that someone got 'stuck in a sulk'. Sample E illustrates such a situation.

A confrontation by the teacher to a sulker in a sulk does not seem to modify either the body signals or the mood. It appears that the sulk only melts when the teacher changes or breaks the frame by shifting attention and releasing the performer: for example, in Table 8.4, when Ann was

SAMPLE E
FIELD NOTES, EXCERPT D

Teacher has dismissed the class for lunch. Darnel and Robert remain behind. Their names had been put on the board because they were misbehaving—arguing and hitting each other. The teacher walks over to Darnel and leaning her hands on the desk and on the back of Darnel's chair she bends down slightly and speaks softly to her. Teacher asks about what happened between them and Darnel answers in a tense and quick tone that Robert hit her first and she hit him back. Darnel's face is tight as she speaks and she side glances to Robert then closes her eyes and looks back to the teacher then down to the floor.

The teacher responds in a soft voice that there are other ways to have responded. 'When he hits you, say something . . . ignore him'. Darnel sits up abruptly and responds 'He called me a gorilla face. I said if you see one . . . slap one'. Robert, sitting a few seats away, turns to her calling, 'I didn't call you . . .' Darnel shouts 'Yes you did'. The teacher steps in and stops the exchange, 'Okay

(*continued*)

that's enough'. After a brief silence the teacher says 'Looks to me like you two are still angry'. Teacher tells Robert to go sit over next to Darnel. As Robert stands and is escorted by the teacher to a chair next to Darnel, the teacher tells them both that they should 'talk to each other' explaining that they work *together* in a classroom.

Robert sits hard into the chair and slumps down with legs extended and arms crossed at his chest. His face is set hard and he stares down at the floor silently. Darnel, too, stares down at the floor with her cheeks sucked in a bit and her lips pushed out in a pout. They both hold their silence.

The teacher goes around the room marking work that the class left out on their desks. Robert and Darnel continue to hold their silence as well as their body configuration. Ten minutes of the lunch period have passed. Darnel takes a small box from inside her desk and holds it in her lap fingering the decorations on it.

The teacher walks over to them after a few more silent moments pass. 'Isn't there anything you want to say?' Both students look at the floor silently. Both wear pouting, scowling expressions on their faces. The teacher takes the box from Darnel and puts it back into the desk. The teacher continues to talk to them, trying to persuade them to talk to each other, express their feelings verbally. 'There are ways of telling someone you're angry without pushing, shoving . . .' Darnel responds in a defensive quick tone, 'He hit me in my sore eye'. The teacher tells Darnel to tell him that. Darnel resumes her pose looking down at the floor silently. The teacher says to Robert leaning over Darnel, 'When you hit her in her sore eye it made her furious'. The teacher comments that they are missing lunch. 'Don't you want to tell her something?' Both children are silent.

Time passes. The teacher marks papers. The two students sit silent. Darnel takes the box from her desk and fingers it in her lap.

The teacher is marking Robert's paper. 'Robert, would you come here a minute?' Her comment briefly shifts the scene and Robert walks over to her and they go over his paper as she points out his handwriting is confusing. She asks 'What kind of a steak was it?' Robert is silent and his face is tight and angry. The teacher talks quietly looking at his paper and not looking up at his face. She explains that he wrote *beefsteak* as *feet* and *feet steak*. He responds quietly (inaudible to me) and his face softens. As Robert walks back to his 'seat' (the one assigned to him in order to talk with Darnel) the teacher asks 'Now is there anything you want to say to Darnel?' Robert does not respond. He sits down and Darnel sits quietly fingering the box. The teacher addresses Darnel, 'I told you to put that box away'. Then, to Robert, the teacher adds, 'Why don't you tell her you're gonna stay away from her and she better stay away from you'.

Robert and Darnel sit silent. Both wear scowling expressions on their faces. More time passes.

The teacher who is again marking papers says, 'Okay. Go to lunch. There are five minutes left. Don't sit near each other'.

---

allowed to go away from the teacher's desk; when Robert began to talk about his paper; or when the teacher or student actually leave the room. To confront a sulk seems to be a no-win situation. One way teachers deal with this type of display is to send the offender to the principal's office. Affection, teasing, and humor were observed as effective means of breaking a frame or melting a sulk, even when it is an intense or prolonged one.

SAMPLE F
FIELD NOTES, EXCERPT E

The teacher sitting on Rodney's desk calls Willa up to her. Several other students are standing near the teacher also. Willa approaches sulking. The teacher in a light tone smilingly says 'What's the face?' and continues asking 'What happened in math?' Then the teacher pulls Willa close and affectionately touches, smiles and jokes with her saying in a friendly teasing key '. . ya put your head down and put your lips out at me . .' She continues to talk and hold Willa and Willa begins to smile and laugh and answers in a friendly tone.

Sample F illustrates the use of teasing and affection effectively used to modify a sulk that had been continuous through three lessons, lasting for a period of close to one hour.

Peer reactions to stylized sulks are often expressed but do not seem to modify the behavior in any way. The display is directed at the teacher and only secondarily for peers. Though a teacher's affection might end a sulking display, a friend's affection doesn't seem to have that power. I have observed a girlfriend stroke her 'neighbor's' back while she sulked over repeatedly not being called on or not being excused to go to the bathroom. Though the friend's affection did not affect the display it did indicate a judgment of support for the emotions being portrayed. In contrast, when peers judge the display to be inappropriate they laugh at, tease, and point at the performer of the display.

Sample G shows another reaction to a third party by someone in a sulk.

SAMPLE G
FIELD NOTES, EXCERPT H

The teacher calls on individuals for oral reading in an entire class activity. Nine children have had turns. As each child finishes reading and the next turn is left open, most of the others raise their hands to be called on. At one of these pauses between turns Towanda, one of the five new students who have just moved to the class, raises her hand again as she has for the last several times. While her hand is up for a turn the teacher calls on another saying, 'Go on Tanika'. Towanda lowers her hand and makes a sulking face at the teacher. As her head lowers to look down at the passage in her book her eyes follow the same path at a slight delay, lingering first in a 'mean' stare at the teacher. When her eyes meet mine accidentally in their path to the print on her desk her face is in a tight sulk still expressing her disappointment of not getting a turn. Towanda is new to the class and does not know me at this time. I'm not sure she has any idea who I am or what I'm doing in the class. When our eyes meet, I'm not sure who did it first or whether it was simultaneous, but we both smiled. I may have done it first to let her know she had not been 'caught' being disrespectful by someone who would then judge or punish her. She might have smiled in response or initiated the smile to show that it wasn't a serious or lasting nonverbal statement. She may have also smiled simply because it seemed she was 'caught'—a slight shoulder shrug accompanying the smile suggested that reaction.

The teacher has put one boy's name on the board. He sits deep in his chair, arms crossed at his chest looking down. The teacher dismisses the class to go take the CAT Math test in the library. She tells the sulking boy that she's not going to make him take the test 'cause you're too upset'. He maintains his pose until she goes to work with a new girl also not taking the test. While the teacher works across the room with the other child, the boy drops the body posture, sits up and close to his desk, and begins to read.

Towanda demonstrates her own ability to instantaneously switch her emotional display from sulk to smile and indicates a kind of meta-awareness of what kinds of deliberate control she can exercise over this type of communication of gestural expressive emotion.

How do students use the sulk? What functions does it seem to perform? One of the major results of the silent display is that it clearly gets attention. Although teachers refer to it differently as 'pouting', 'fretting', 'acting spoiled', 'being rebellious', 'acting nasty', 'having a temper tantrum', and so on, all notice it and usually respond. Often the student benefits. Consider Sample H.

Students often get in trouble in classrooms for fighting with each other. I have observed several silent devices for avoiding confrontation. If a student has been in an argument with another student—for example, getting into a sulk that attracts the teacher's attention—this will often result in the teacher moving the other's desk or sending him or her out of the room or the like. Sulking among peers is generally short-lived. In these cases of prolonged peer-peer sulking, the audience appears to be the adult in control.

The student silent display seems then to have the same mutually acknowledged meaning for participants as did the teacher display—'pay attention to me' and/or 'what you're doing is not acceptable to me'. In many of the observed instances of its use the communicative device seems to work. However it appears to be a highly risky display, for though there may be some immediate rewards, the long term message that seems to be a by-product is that children who use it too often and inappropriately get labeled as having 'bad attitudes', and are tracked accordingly.

TEACHERS AND STUDENTS

The analysis indicates that because of the different statuses of students and teachers, their silences are performed in situations and with styles that reflect their dominant and subordinate role, although the uses and meaning of their silences are actually very similar.

In both cases, submissive and nonsubmissive, the student silences are clearly subordinate. Among peers the display is not always infrequent but is always short-lived. Long sustained displays such as those with the teacher reported in Sample H simply do not occur with peers, even when the peers are in the role of teacher.

It is especially of interest that the shape of the student silence can be turned around so that it can have antithetical messages depending on when it is used and what body idiom and gestures it is wrapped in. The paradox in school is that at the same time silence is reified as a sign of 'good control' and an indicator of a 'well-run organization', it is also a punishable offense if used at the wrong time and in the wrong way.

Silence is valued, equated with good emotion management (i.e., self-control) and rewarded when achieved. In the school cafeteria prizes are given to those who are quiet and controlled at lunch and 'talkers' are punished publicly by having to stand at the wall and/or stay after school. In the crowded conditions and organizational structure of most urban schools, teachers are often judged by their colleagues and superiors by the orderliness of their lines, the silence in their classrooms, and the 'mannerliness' of their students.

The other side of the paradox is the silence a student displays when, for example, he or she does not answer a teacher's question. Nonsubmissive silences most often follow a teacher's request for a confession in public, for example, 'What were you doing?' An answer in most cases would cause loss of face in front of peers. Stylized silent sulking is frequently used as an ego-saving measure, and often turns the loss of face back to the teacher.

STYLIZED SULKING: ITS MEANING AND TREATMENT IN CONTEXT

The behavioral event of stylized sulking is a characteristic response in face-to-face clashes of will between student and teacher. These were conventional displays of emotion that appeared regularly in my field notes and were prominent and noticeable in classroom interactions. The displays were themselves discrete pieces of behavior which conveyed information. They were dramatic portrayals of attitude. They were postures that told a story to the teacher and to onlooking peers. They were face-saving dances. Students who frequently used the displays were also students who were often identified as having 'bad attitudes' and as a result were tracked out of academic programs.

Stylized sulking was performed by both sexes though there was some variation in the style of its performance according to sex. Performances were individual, not group behaviors. Though on occasion one might come upon a situation where a group of students simultaneously were expressing the same sulking bodily configuration and facial expression it would not be a cooperative endeavor, but a coincidence of corresponding emotions and displays. Stylized sulking as a school-related problem seems age-related. Though these displays were not performed exclusively by students in the intermediate grades (4–6) they were significantly more prominent then.

Sulking was primarily performed in a silent channel and an angry key. It seems, in fact, a last holding place to express defiance. For those students who do cross the line, the predictable verbal accompaniment transforms the crime from one of 'bad attitude' to one of insolence and insubordination. These latter labels usually are associated with treatments more extreme than low track classes (e.g., suspension, psychological guidance, and the like).

Stylized sulking was usually performed to an authority figure. The individual sulker is subordinate in status to the receiver of the display. Though the display, which is often used as a face-saving device, is certainly meant to be seen by onlooking peers, the primary audience is the adult in control. Sulking generally appeared in settings where an authority figure was in control and usually in direct conflict with the performer. Classrooms, hallways, lunchrooms, and the like are predictable settings for this kind of display. Further, the behavior appeared more in classes which have not 'weeded out bad attitudes'. In settings where propriety had been selected for, such as Academics Plus classes, few if any sulking events were observed. Certain agreed upon expectations of attitude and behavior in the Academics Plus classes changed the classroom context in a way that made sulking no longer adaptive. The demeanor was no longer appropriate for the teacher or the peer group in the setting. Though the act of sulking itself was rarely, if ever, mentioned and was almost never consciously a part of the assessment of a student's attitude, students who sulked repeatedly had negative characteristics attributed to them as a result. Stylized sulking was not consciously, but nonetheless, quite effectively selected out, in the process of identifying 'good attitudes'.

Another concern focuses on how stylized sulking was treated in this community. As mentioned earlier though the entire student population observed was black, the faculty is both black and white (50 percent/ 50 percent). The data suggest that there are, in general, commonly held views about these displays that are different for most blacks and whites. The data consisted of views directly expressed about stylized sulking, observations of the ways in which black and white teachers behaved in response to these displays, and finally comments made by the faculty and parents about the differences they themselves were conscious of concerning the way white teachers and black teachers generally responded.

In general it was felt that white teachers tended to be more 'lenient' and 'permissive' where this type of communication was concerned.

A black teacher was more likely to discipline a dramatic sulking display, sending the child to the office, calling the parent, or in some way immediately chastising the student. Black parents often scolded or threatened to hit children for such displays. In church and community contexts an 'attitude' was quickly conveyed in such displays and children were told to leave or modify their behavior. A white teacher, on the other hand, might be more likely to ask a child to verbalize his or her feelings as well as directly refer to the feelings the display seemed to communicate (e.g., I can see you're feeling angry). In general, whites were seen as less likely to discipline these 'temper tantrums'. Acceptance of the behavior tended to escalate student use of it, creating classrooms which were viewed as having 'bad attitudes.'

Stylized sulking seemed to be seen as a 'cultural' variation of expression and communication. Sulking, in the highly stylized way it is performed by many of the students, was viewed by both black and white teachers as part of a stereotypic communicative style of blacks. Much the way Jewish or Italian gestural style might be characterized, so too this behavior might easily be interpreted as a black gestural performance.

Black parents and teachers suggested that white teachers might be more tolerant of such behaviors because they were 'intimidated by black children and their parents'. White teachers tend to talk about student 'hostility' and the need to be more verbal about feelings. As a result of the controversy over the use of nonstandard varieties of English and in the recent concern with bilingual and multicultural education, there has been a growing sensitivity to and awareness of cultural variation in communication. Often by allowing these behaviors, white teachers believe they are expressing acceptance of cultural diversity—'It's part of their culture.'

Black teachers and parents frequently express concern that this permissiveness and lenience are signs of 'low standards' or of 'not caring about' these black kids and whether they learn the necessary skills, attitudinal and academic, which are seen as prerequisites to success. White teachers, too, express similar concerns about 'low standards', often looking to black teachers for appropriate models for reaction. Humor, teasing, and affection were instructionally effective strategies used by both black and white teachers in response to sulking displays. These behaviors tended to minimize the intensity of the confrontation and the tone of insubordination on the part of the student.

Upon closer examination, however, sulking itself is not actually uniformly treated or uniformly performed. Some children seem to have perfected this type of display routine in a very highly stylized way. In observations of language acquisition in poor white working-class families, Peggy Miller (personal communication) found that mothers would tell their babies under two years old to make 'mean eyes' as part of a communicative routine. In the black community in which this study is being conducted, expressed norms of appropriate interactional demeanor include 'looking ready to fight' (Davis 1981) and 'not taking shit' (May 1981).

The stylized sulking could be interpreted as one behavioral element of a 'tough' demeanor, yet how sulking behavior gets interpreted appears to be highly dependent on contextualization cues. One child's sulk is read as 'anger and hostility', while another, appearing to display the same or very similar physical characteristics, is merely 'being dramatic' or 'needing attention'. Very similar behaviors are interpreted in very different ways. In one case the behavior can be glossed as style and in another case, 'bad attitude'. In a similar fashion, there are teachers and parents who appear to play with stern face silent stares and look as a dramatic performance. One student commenting on one such teacher said, 'At first I thought she was real mean till I realized she was just foolin' around. She has a good sense of humor.' I observed this particular teacher's class on the day when parents were invited to come in and take the place of their children as students for the day. She, in comic fashion, performed both verbal and nonverbal means of parodied strict control. Silent looks of disapproval seemed humorously inappropriate when directed at a class full of adults. Not only was it clear that it was playful, but the parents' cooperative engagement in the game sanctioned the appropriateness of it in their view as a means of control for their children.

It appears that student sulking can be interpreted positively or negatively depending on when and how the display is performed in a particular context. Certain children can signal the message 'this is play' (Bateson 1972), but for the most part it is a behavior that carries the image of incorrect deference and demeanor and is usually interpreted as indicative of a 'bad attitude'.

Goffman has commented that 'the human use of displays is complicated by the human capacity for reframing behavior' (1976:71). Rituals become ritualized and transformations can be transformed. Performances become styled and coded in distinguishable ways as a result of cultural influences. Not only do cross-cultural examples detail the range of styles for expressing emotions, but considerable ethnic diversity can be observed in our own society. In the recent popular movie, *Four Seasons,* one particularly hot-headed and explosive character in stereotypic fashion defended her temper by repeatedly declaring with corresponding gestures, 'I'm Italian!' Comedians (like the teacher mentioned above) typically draw on these styles and use these displays in parenthesized fashion as a resource for humor. Most popular for young audiences is actor Gary Coleman's quotable line and memorable posturing of 'stylized sulking' on the weekly situation comedy on network television, *Different Strokes*. When he says to his big brother 'What chu talkin about, Willis' his eyes are narrowed and his demanor is clearly tough and black. But the display is contextualized in such a way that it is a parody of being tough and black. It is rekeyed in such a way that it becomes clearly lighthearted and funny. The same display conveys a quite opposite meaning. Moods as well as ethnic styles are being played with.

Geertz (1973) describes what he calls a stratified hierarchy of meaningful structures as he details the subtle yet distinct differences between twitches, winks, fake-winks, parodies of winks, and rehearsals of parodies of winks. In much the same way this example of stylized sulking can be 'unpacked'. It can be performed by design for comic effect as well as threatening effect. One of my undergraduate students has recounted stories to me of ways in which she and a friend, the only two black girls at a private girls' school, used verbal and nonverbal displays associated with 'street' behavior of blacks in order to frighten the white girls. The context of these displays and the ways in which they are framed determined the way they were interpreted. Possibly they sometimes take the form of ethnic 'in' jokes, which are understood to be okay when no ethnic outsiders are present.

In addition to expressing emotion, displays provide evidence of an actor's alignment. Sulking displays therefore must also be considered in this latter regard. In general, sulking displays can function as face-saving devices which maintain dignity through individual autonomy when confronted by an authority in control. The display indicates the actor's refusal to align him or herself with the authority figure. The stylized sulking characteristic of black communicative repertoire seems to be interpreted as a statement of alignment with the student's own ethnicity and socioeconomic class.

CONCLUSION

The preceding discussion was concerned with identifying the domain of the concept of attitude in the particular community being studied. The focus on attitude was stimulated by the significance it held for the participants in the setting. Attitude was the key element for student success in school. It was the identifying ingredient for stratifying and tracking students. The 'success' track in this particular school was an Academics Plus program. A 'good attitude' was a prerequisite for admittance. When discussing the program with a group of new incoming parents, the principal made it clear that if parents made sure the kids came with a 'good attitude' the school would do everything in its power to assure their reading and writing skills and their chances for getting into 'better' schools (magnet and academic schools in the city). This exchange was clear to all the participants. It was a trade of appropriate attitudes for literacy. Literacy is a commodity which is in the school's domain, and the school makes decisions as to when it will be parceled out.

The preceding exploration indicates that the concept of attitude itself is abstract. It has different meanings to different individuals and in different contexts. Yet if the exchange was to be understood in terms of its social significance as well as its behavioral manifestations, attitude had to be understood in terms of not only the way it was talked about but also the way it functioned.

The key event of silent stylized sulking was the 'window' through which underlying cultural themes were explored. The event was considered in terms of the immediate shape of its performance, the metaphoric nature it suggested, and the social meanings it held for the participants. Stylized sulking was selected for specific attention for several reasons. It was prominent and controversial. It was consciously associated with assessments of attitude. The display was seen as representative of bad attitudes and was squelched by tracking which effectively selected the behavior out. Finally, the behavior was seen as part of black gestural and communicative style and repertoire.

Expressive forms such as stylized sulking can essentially be viewed as metaphors for the human condition. The expressive forms used by the students can be seen as individual autonomy in the face of authority. The ritual display of stylized sulking was examined as a metaphor for the everyday life of these students' social world. Through the use of this metaphor it became apparent that a 'bad attitude' was closely associated with a conveyed message of black alignment.

The fact that a prominent behavioral event which was significant with regard to assessing attitudes was associated with a display of black culture raises an important question. Is there a trade of blackness for success in the study site? The answer is a complicated one.

One of the problems that seems to have confused much of our literature and likely blinded us with regard to improving education where 'at risk' populations are concerned is that we have glossed diverse settings and groups of people with simple and misrepresentative terms. There is no homogeneous black community. The community in which the study was conducted was recently black (in the last fifteen years), having been largely Jewish and Irish before. A general theme in the neighborhood was one of upward mobility. The community was widely supportive of and responsive to the school as an institutional leader.

Though in classrooms, in church, and at home students would be reprimanded for using nonstandard vernacular or stylized sulking displays, the theme of black pride was very strongly dominant in the school community. Many of the teachers and parents had taken trips to Africa, taught black history, and participated in various African cultural activities. Several families in the community were from Africa (ten children in all). Teachers focused curriculum projects on black history and black pride themes. In regular assembly programs student choruses sang out in clear and vibrant tones 'to be young, gifted and black, that's where it's at'.

These examples are offered in order to demonstrate that indeed the school and the community are not attempting to squelch blackness or pride in being black. The examples indicate that, to the contrary, black pride and black history are prominent themes in the school and community. The example of sulking seems more to be associated with a certain class of black communicative repertoire that has typically been a marker for failure in our society. Like nonstandard vernacular, these behaviors will tend to close rather than open doors for black children who are trying to be successful in our society. No matter how legitimate a linguistic or behavioral analysis of such behavior is, the key factor of legitimacy is how these behaviors are interpreted in the social world in which they are performed. For these children, most of their parents and teachers agree—the cost is too high. Symbols of black 'street behavior' such as vernacular and stylized sulking are seen as ethnic and socioeconomic markers which interfere with success and may even limit access to socially valued commodities such as literacy.

ACKNOWLEDGMENTS

The research reported here was supported by a grant from the National Institute of Education, to Dell Hymes, principal investigator. I am grateful for the support and comments offered throughout the course of the study by Dell Hymes and David M. Smith. I want to thank Erving Goffman for the original stimulus to examine sulking displays and for his critical comments on an earlier draft of this work. Ray McDermott and Bambi Schieffelin also offered helpful comments.

REFERENCES

Anderson, Elaine S. 1978. Learning to speak with style: A study of the sociolinguistic skills of children. Stanford University: Unpublished doctoral dissertation.
Bateson, Gregory. 1972. A theory of play and fantasy. Steps to an ecology of mind. New York: Ballantine Books.
Bellack, A., H. Kliebard, R. Hyman, and F. Smith. 1966. The language of the classroom. New York: Teachers College Press.
Cazden, Courtney B. 1979. Language in education: Variation in the teacher-talk register. Language in Public Life, Georgetown University Round Table on Languages and Lin-

guistics. 1979, ed. by James E. Alatis & G. Richard Tucker, 144–62. Washington, DC: Georgetown University Press.

Cazden, Courtney, Vera John, and Dell Hymes (eds.). 1972. Functions of language in the classroom. New York: Teachers College Press.

Davis, Ave. 1981. Harriet Tubman School: Community perspectives. Part of final report to National Institute of Education, Dell Hymes, principal investigator.

Edwards, A. D., and V. J. Furlong. 1978. The language of teaching. London: Heinemann Educational Books, Ltd.

Geertz, Clifford. 1973. Thick description: Toward an interpretive theory of culture. The interpretation of cultures. New York: Basic Books.

Gilmore, Perry and Allan Glatthorn (eds.). 1982. Children in and out of school. Washington, DC: Center for Applied Linguistics.

Goffman, Erving. Gender advertisements. Studies in the Anthropology of Visual Communication 3 (2). Fall 1976.

Hochschild, Arlie. 1979. Emotion work, feeling rules and social structure. American Journal of Sociology 85 (3): 551–575.

Hymes, Dell. 1964. The ethnography of speaking. Anthropology and human behavior, ed. by T. Gladwin & W. C. Sturtevant, Washington, DC.

McDermott, Ray. P. 1977. The ethnography of speaking and reading. Linguistic theory: What can it say about reading, ed. by R. Shuy. Newark, DE: International Reading Association.

May, Linda. 1981. Spaulding School: Attention and styles of interaction. Part of Final Report to NIE, D. Hymes, principal investigator, University of Pennsylvania.

Mehan, Hugh, Courtney Cazden, L. Coles, S. Fisher and N. Maroules. 1976. The social organization of classroom lessons. University of California, San Diego: Center for Human Information Processing.

Mehan, Hugh. 1979. Learning lessons: The social organization of classroom behavior. Cambridge, MA: Harvard University Press.

Spindler, George (ed.). 1982. Doing the ethnography of schooling. New York: Holt Rinehart Winston.

PART IV

SILENCE IN CROSS-CULTURAL PERSPECTIVE

Chapter 9

Silence and Noise as Emotion Management Styles: An Italian Case

George R. Saunders
Lawrence University
Appleton, Wisconsin

Italians enjoy (or suffer from, depending on the point of view) a popular stereotype as emotional, expansive, noisy, 'warm' or 'hot' people.[1] This paper will not attempt to refute that stereotype, but will argue that some Italians can also be very silent and that, in fact, exuberant noise and grim silence are in some respects functional equivalents. In particular, both silence and noise may be used in the management of strong but problematic emotions, although the two expressive styles are called into play in somewhat different circumstances. Radcliffe-Brown suggested long ago that in ambiguous social relationships (those that are simultaneously 'disjunctive' and 'conjunctive'), people may institutionalize a stylized form of interaction or noninteraction, as in 'joking relationships' and 'avoidance relationships' (1952:90 ff.). My thesis here is analogous: where there is ambivalence about the expression of emotion, noise and silence may be used as stylized strategies for its management. Furthermore, in the Italian case, the more serious the potential for conflict, the more likely it is that people will choose the silent mode.[2] Understanding

---

[1]An earlier version of this paper was presented at the 1981 meeting of the American Anthropological Association in Los Angeles, in a symposium entitled 'Emotional Styles in European Families'. My thanks to the audience and participants—particularly John Russell—for helpful comments in that session, and to Melford Spiro, F. G. Bailey, and Deborah Tannen, who subsequently read the paper and made several suggestions.
[2]In this case, I am referring to the psychological or social distress that the conflict would cause to the person, not to any 'objective' seriousness of the issue. This point is discussed later in the paper. It is also worth noting that the association of silence with the potential for serious conflict is apparently not universal, although also not unusual. In his analysis of black and white American styles in conflict, Kochman (1981:43) describes an interracial argument in which the white is clearly frightened by the noisy verbal attack, but the black (more like an Italian, perhaps) reassures her with the comment, 'You don't need to worry; I'm still talking. When I stop talking, then you might need to worry.'

silence and noise as alternative expressive styles, however, requires prior consideration of some psychological and cultural aspects of family life.

THE SETTING

The fieldwork which provides the data for this paper was conducted in an alpine Italian village called Valbella.[3] Located near the French border in the Maritime Alps of northwestern Italy, Valbella has a population of about 2,300 (in 1980). Since World War II, the economic base of the village has shifted from primary reliance on agriculture (small dairy farms) to wage labor, particularly in government jobs and in industrial concerns located around the provincial capital of Cuneo, some 30 kilometers from Valbella. In the 1980s, the village retains its 'mountain' ('rustic') atmosphere and identity with a curious mixture of pride and self-deprecation. It is not a 'sleepy hamlet', but there is a kind of melancholy in its contemporary bustle. Valbella has been depopulating steadily since the 1880s, when it held close to 8,000 inhabitants, and the age cohorts of the remaining population have shifted upward. In recent years, social services and recreational amenities have become increasingly difficult to find in the village itself, and younger families continue to move into the provincial capital or other urban areas in the Piedmont region.

Whatever the realities of the past and the present, contemporary Valbellans tend to regard the future of the village with pessimism. Most appreciate the improved standard of living of recent years, but they lament the loss of 'community', the emigration of their young people, and—perhaps most of all—they worry about the loss of commitment to traditional values concerning the family. The family is the symbolic focus of profound emotion for Valbellans, and it is in the family context that problems of emotion management become especially significant.

EMOTIONAL DEPTH

There is considerable justification for accepting the characterization of Valbellans—like other Italians—as profoundly emotional people, despite the difficulty of devising a scientifically adequate means of measuring

---

[3] I began fieldwork in Valbella (a pseudonym) in the summer of 1972, spent a year there in 1974–75, and returned again in the summers of 1979 and 1980. The fieldwork has been supported at various times and in various measures by a Fulbright Scholarship, a National Institute of Mental Health Traineeship through the University of California in San Diego, and a Lawrence University Faculty Research Grant. The fieldwork also constitutes part of a five-society study of 'Culture and Goals in the Nuclear Family', going forward under the direction of Marc Swartz and with the collaboration of Joshua A'konga, Michael Murphy, and J. M. Weatherford.

emotional depth. Since the issue is important for the analysis of expressive styles, I will at least attempt a 'back door' argument to support
the assertion that Valbellans are people who feel deeply, and for whom
emotion and its expression may be simultaneously satisfying and problematic.

It is difficult to find, in either the psychological or anthropological
literature, much discussion of the process of development of emotional
depth. Though there has been some excellent recent anthropological
work on emotion, most has dealt either with the cultural patterning of
emotional displays (cf. Super and Harkness 1982), or with cultural differences in the cognition of emotion (the ways in which different groups
conceptualize emotion states) (White 1981; Lutz 1982). Psychologists
have also dealt with the cultural variation in facial expressions of emotion, with problems of identifying discrete emotions in different cultural
settings, with the functions of emotions in biological and cultural evolu-
tion, and so forth (see Izard 1980 and Boucher 1979 for reviews of relevant work). The theoretical problems in describing and accounting for
cultural differences in the depth of emotion, however, remain relatively
untouched. On the other hand, emotional 'shallowness' has been the
subject of considerable investigation. In anthropology, two main lines of
analysis are relevant to my argument, though they are pertinent by contrast with the Valbellan case. The first derives from Margaret Mead's
attention to the emotional 'casualness' of Samoans and the emotional
withdrawal of the Balinese (Mead 1949; Bateson and Mead 1942). The
second concerns low levels of emotional responsiveness resulting from
culturally patterned parental rejection of children (Rohner 1975). An
examination of the cultural patterns associated with the development of
emotional 'shallowness' may be instructive by contrast with those of
Valbella.

In her first book, *Coming of Age in Samoa,* Mead focused on the
affective noninvolvement of Samoans. She characterized them as people
in whom 'the lack of deep feeling' is 'conventionalised until it is the
framework of all their attitudes toward life' (1949:118). She relates this
generalized low level of affect to the socialization style: 'From the first
months of its life, when the child is handed carelessly from one woman's
hands to another's, the lesson is learned of not caring for one person
greatly, not setting high hopes on any one relationship' (1949:118). She
also advances the hypothesis, implied in the quote above, that emotional
depth is related to the intensity of the child's attachment to a single
caretaker (see also Bowlby 1971; Kaufman 1975).

Later, when Mead and Bateson conducted fieldwork in Bali, emotional
depth was again one focus of their research. In the Balinese case, however, the distinction between the subjective experience and the expression

of affect becomes crucial. The Balinese teach their children to avoid expressing emotion in ordinary interpersonal relations, but Mead implies that the feelings are nonetheless present. As she points out, 'The Balinese distinguish clearly between fear and the expression of fear, and it becomes a commonplace to hear people say fiercely to cowering or crying children, "*Da takoet*" ("Do not act afraid"), and this is the only reassurance which is ever attempted. Nobody would say, "*Da djerih*" ("Don't *be* afraid"). No one even attempts to furnish enough reassurance so that the child's internal fear may be dispelled' (Mead 1942:31). Mead seems to suggest that the Balinese children withdraw into themelves and concentrate their feelings there, while remaining emotionally unresponsive to outer stimuli. This point is also made in Hildred Geertz's analysis of the Javanese, who find 'the events of the inner world more engrossing than those of the outside world' (1974:251; see also C. Geertz 1973:135–140). Depth of emotion is demonstrated, however, at culturally stipulated occasions. For example, affective expression is permitted in the theatre, and the theatre is a centrally significant Indonesian institution (Geertz 1973, 1980; Peacock 1968). Geertz has also suggested that the Balinese 'live in spurts', which implies that emotional disengagement is not constant. Perhaps it would be appropriate to suggest that Balinese emotions are generally latent but occasionally active; if this is the case, Valbellans will be seen to be in direct contrast.

In the Balinese case, it is clear that no simple characterization of levels of emotion is adequate. Mead and the Geertzes alike seem to suggest that the controlled and restrained behavioral style in fact works to minimize the subjective experience of affect. Mead says, for example, 'Life is without climax. . . And there is always the danger that one may not be aroused at all.' Furthermore, 'Life is a rhythmic, patterned unreality of pleasant, significant movement, centered in one's own body to which all emotion long ago withdrew' (1942:48). And Geertz says that the Balinese 'use . . . emotion for cognitive ends' (1973:449), in a phrase that sounds almost like the psychoanalytic concept of an 'intellectual defense'.

Levy has noted a similar tendency to minimize emotionality in Tahiti, and he describes a number of techniques by which Tahitians 'dissociate' or 'distance' themselves from affect. They evade potentially evocative situations, refuse to look at or think about troubling things, and they isolate strong feelings in parts of their bodies that are dissociated from their psychological selves. Significantly, one of the mechanisms by which they manage emotion is the custom of remaining silent while taking time to work out (*feruri*) their thoughts (1973:496). Levy also suggests directly that Tahitian methods of controlling emotion are effective; their emotional casualness is genuine, because these institutionalized ways of coping with potential emotion actually allow Tahitians to maintain a calm internal state.

The theme of low affect levels has also appeared in studies in New Guinea and Africa. Heider has characterized the Grand Valley Dani as a 'low energy culture', and has particularly focused on the lack of interest in sex as an indicator of emotional nonengagement. In general, he says, 'There is certainly affection, but rarely grand passion; annoyance but rarely an angry explosion' (1979:81). More specifically, concerning sex, he notes that the Dani observe a four to six year postpartum sexual abstinence, that there are no strong sanctions supporting the taboo, that there are no alternative sexual outlets during this period, and that—the *coup de grace*—the Dani are not particularly bothered by it. In short, they just don't care much (1976:188ff.).

The process of 'socialization for low affect' is the focus of Goldschmidt's treatment of emotional superficiality among the Sebei of Africa. He writes: 'I should make it clear that I am talking about low affect levels, not hostility, anxiety, or anger. It is psychological disengagement that is the characteristic mood, a lack of involvement of individuals with one another in all relationships' (1976:65–66). Goldschmidt traces the psychogenesis of this personality characteristic to the lack of involvement of mothers with their children, describing the 'absent eyes and idle hands' of women who seem not to notice their children even as they tend them. Again, the contrast with mothering in Valbella will be striking.

A different kind of emotional shallowness is described in the work on 'maternal deprivation' and parental rejection of children. Goldschmidt's care in pointing out that he is not talking about hostile people is perhaps specifically designed to distinguish the Sebei from societies with 'rejecting' parents, because in the latter case 'flattened affect' does not seem to preclude high levels of hostility and anxiety. In fact, studies on this theme seem to differ from those of the Mead tradition in at least three ways. First, 'shallowness' is seen as pathological or quasipathological, as in the Spitz studies of maternal deprivation (1945; 1946). Second, it seems to refer not to generalized lack of emotion, but rather simply to lack of *positive* emotion. Rejected children, at least as portrayed in Rohner's (1975) ambitious cross-cultural analysis, seem quite capable of profound negative feelings. Third, the etiology of this lack of positive responsiveness is to be found in the hostility of the parents toward the child. While this attention to flattened affect is unquestionably justified, it is nonetheless unfortunate that its converse, emotional depth, is taken as a given, unitary phenomenon, and all variations from that utopia are seen as quasipathological. As the Munroes put it, 'the capacity for positive affective relations is a mammalian maturational phenomenon that fails to develop only under conditions of severe social deprivation in infancy' (Munroe and Munroe 1975:47). From this perspective, only the negative cases are of interest; the varieties of positive emotional depth are ignored.

It is apparent, at least, that the 'flattened affect' of rejected children is quite distinct from the emotional casualness of Tahitians, the Dani, Samoans, and the Balinese and Javanese, and the emotional depth of Valbellans could be taken as the polar opposite of either of these types of affective shallowness (or perhaps as the third corner of the triangle). Again, there is little discussion in either anthropology or psychology of how deep feeling is encouraged by particular socialization styles, but these two kinds of studies at least provide some clues. They suggest that emotional depth is somehow related to the warmth of the parent–child relationship, to the attentiveness of the parents to the child's needs, and to the intensity of the attachment of the child to a single caretaker. In virtually all respects, the socialization styles of Valbellans contrast with both the 'casual' and 'rejecting' styles, and Valbellans seem, in fact, to be people with a profound emotional life.

EMOTION IN VALBELLAN FAMILIES

Parent-child relationships in Valbella are highly personalized and intense, and though children may receive attention from many adults, affect does not appear to be diffused. On the contrary, the mother-child relationship remains the focus of deep and frequent verbal and symbolic attention to emotional states. This is in keeping with evidence cited by Bowlby that 'in the early months of attachment the greater the number of figures to whom the child was attached the more intense was his attachment to mother as his principal figure likely to be' (Bowlby 1971:250). This relationship is dramatized by the symbolic attention given to it, and it becomes paradigmatic for emotion in general. Casual admiring comments like 'Oh, you beautiful child, you must make your mother very happy', or 'You'll break your mother's heart some day' serve to remind the child (and others) of the fact that this relationship counts above all others. Mothers often point out to their children their emotional interdependence; it is as if the feelings of mother and child are interchangeable. In short, life in Valbella develops around an intense attachment to a single, loving adult.[4] This attachment is commented on constantly in Italian culture, and it provides the foundation for affective depth.

---

[4]I do not mean to imply that others—fathers, grandfathers, grandmothers, and older siblings—are not also involved affectionately with the child, but no other relationship seems to receive the same symbolic loading as that with the mother.

The intensity of the interaction of adults and children in Valbella is striking, especially by contrast with the Sebei. Goldschmidt describes Sebei mothers as 'remote' and 'disengaged' in their interactions with infants (1976:67), and his pictures show the child doing the work of searching for the breast while the mother stares into space or talks to her companions. In Valbella, in contrast, the infant is often picked up briskly and held with its face a few inches away from the face of its mother, who looks the child in the eyes and talks to it in a loud and emotional voice. The child is shaken playfully, hugged and squeezed so hard it hurts, tossed in the air and caught in loving arms. The physical contact is accompanied by intense eye contact and verbal patter, much of it with emotional content. The mother tells the child how much she loves her or him, and about the joy and pain she has experienced or anticipates in the future because of the child.

In addition, mothers in Valbella encourage the continuing dependency of their children, and there is much symbolic merging of mother and child.[5] This fusion of mother and child is one of many channels for teaching the child the relevance of the emotional states of others, and for encouraging a kind of ego-centered empathy based on the merging of oneself and others.

Parent–child relationships in Valbella are also emotionally labile, despite the firm foundation of warmth and affection. Warmth easily becomes heat, and parents are often offended and angered by their children. Children thus learn that—though satisfying—emotional life is also problematic, and nothing can be taken for granted. This point is important: the rhythm of affective interaction is irregular and jumpy, and as the responses of others become less predictable, children learn to retreat to the security of silence. We will return to this point.

On the whole, children in Valbella experience an intense, loving, warm relationship with their parents, and especially their mothers. Such love, however, does not preclude the development of hostility and anger or of anxiety. Indeed, these seem to be key components of Valbellan personality, despite the fact that they are also, in Rohner's terms, highly emotionally responsive. Emotional responsiveness, for Rohner, is 'a person's ability to express freely and openly his emotions, for example feelings of warmth, affection, and other positive emotions. Emotional responsiveness is revealed by the spontaneity and ease with which a person is able to respond emotionally to another person. Emotionally responsive people have no difficulty forming warm, intimate, involved, and lasting

---

[5]See Gilmore and Gilmore (1979) on the problems of disidentifying with the mother in southern Spain, and Saunders (1981) for a general discussion.

attachments' (1975:177). This is an excellent description of Valbellans. They are capable of deep attachments (although husband–wife relationships are not always intimate and loving), and they deal with other people on a highly personal level. Rohner's suggestions are misleading, however, in that he seems to treat hostility and anger as nonemotions. People who show 'negative' emotions are lumped together with those who are 'emotionally insulated'. They are 'generally characterized by restricted emotional involvement with others. They usually have strong needs for affection but are unable to return it' (1975:85).

I would argue that a number of aspects of socialization in Valbella facilitate the development of 'emotional responsiveness' alongside of hostility and anxiety. Valbellans are deeply emotional, but the emotions are both positive and negative. This is, in general, a 'high-energy' culture, and Valbellans, in contrast to the Sebei, socialize their children for high affect. They give them warmth and love and encourage their attachment, but they also frustrate them, tease them, and discourage their independence.

It is worth noting that Valbellans characterize themselves as highly emotional people (although they do not see themselves as so emotional as Sicilians and southern Italians). In the positive versions of their self-stereotyping, they are compassionate, generous, passionate, sensuous, and tremendously attached to their families. In the negative versions, their emotionality inclines them to act without reasoning and sometimes to hurt other people (and themselves) in ways that they later regret. It is this potential that makes the management of emotion essential in some cases.

Other studies of Italians have given similar attention to both the profundity and the problematic nature of emotion. Pancheri, for example, in a comparative study of emotions of Roman Italians and German-speaking Swiss from Bern, came to this conclusion: 'In the Italian population there is a clear prevalence of basic traits of anxious depressive type: feelings of sadness, a pessimistic view of the future, psychomotor retardation, restlessness, and irritability seem to be more characteristic of the normal Italian population than of the normal Swiss population' (1975:560). The high value given to intensity of feeling among Italians is also supported in a study by Young and Ferguson (1981:199 et passim). These themes are likewise prevalent in the work of Anne Parsons on southern Italian families, and she particularly emphasizes the degree of emotional involvement of individuals in family life and the high tolerance of emotional instability (1969:100–112 et passim).

The socialization of children involves training for both the expression and the control of emotion. One aspect of this training—the strong emphasis on formal, respectful relations with strangers and unrelated adults—is particularly relevant for learning to be silent in problematic situations. Children are taught to deal with greetings and direct questions from unrelated elders by replying in rote, formal, respectful phrases, and then to be silent (*stare zitto*). This is an important aspect of the *educazione* of the child, and these formal, rote interactive patterns are functionally equivalent to learning the value of silence in problematic situations (cf. Basso 1972). There has been much written about the importance of 'shame' in Mediterranean cultures (Pitt-Rivers 1966; Campbell 1964), and silence is the idiom of shame. A properly educated child learns to remain embarrassedly silent as long as the situation remains ambiguous. Once the stranger has been appropriately 'familiarized', or has made direct overtures to the child, of course, the child is free to act out, to seek attention, and to express interest and emotion. The 'silent style', then, is learned in childhood along with the dramatic, noisy style; and it is specifically introduced in the context of ambiguity, strangeness, and potential difficulty. Through silence and formal, rote courtesy, people maintain emotional neutrality, and this is important in ambiguous situations.

More commonly, however, Valbellans engage in a running commentary on emotional experience, with obvious enjoyment of the exploration of affective intensity. In playful dramas, adults help children experience and express emotions. When a child cries in anger, adults often name the emotional state for the child, help the child focus on the source of the anger, and instruct the child to dramatize the emotion. 'Oh, you're so angry at the bad old toy. It doesn't work right, does it? Bad, bad toy. Come, give me your fist, and we'll hit that bad old toy.' Adults clearly enjoy stirring up emotions in children, both positively and negatively. They delight children by surprise presentations of gifts, special foods, and other treats; and they enrage them with teasing. My interpretation of such scenes is that children are learning to pay attention to emotions and to find satisfaction in their dramatization. This cultural patterning of emotional experience and expression leads Valbellans—I suspect like other Italians—to revel in their emotions, to play with them, to dig deeply into them.

Drama is another element in the popular stereotype of Italians, and both popular and scholarly analysts have made much of their dramatic sensibilities. Barzini refers to it as 'the importance of spectacle' (1964:61). There is no question that Valbellans appreciate dramatic performances in many contexts, and display of emotion in everyday life is one form of theatricality. F. G. Bailey (1983) has argued that rhetoric, especially in the grandiloquent fashion so popular in Italy, is a stylized and sophisticated extension of emotion which, among other things, may function to inhibit the use of reason. Of course, silence may also be theatrical, as Bock has nicely shown (1976). The dramatization of emotion (through either noise or silence), however, brings us back to the problem of the Balinese case—the difficulty of interpreting the correspondence between internal states and the performance itself. Are Valbellans emotional when they act emotional, or are they simply good actors? Though the problem has yet to be resolved adequately by either psychologists or anthropologists, a few suggestions are in order.

Dramatic performances may simultaneously mask and express emotional states, and the cultural approval of theatricality allows a great deal of flexibility in the psychological and social use of a performance. That is, people learn to express emotion easily, and they have a well-developed competence in acting out emotional states, but this does not necessarily make the emotion any less genuine or deep. William James suggested that we cry not because we are sad, but rather that we are sad because we cry (cited in Bruner 1966:12). Though there are problems in such a formulation, it does remind us of the complex feedback among the subjective experience of emotion, the functioning of the autonomic nervous and visceral systems (and the limbic system), and expressive motor movements. Recent work also emphasizes the importance of the cognition of emotion, which is both cultural and psychological. As Kleinman notes, 'The affects engendered by these stimuli, such as anger, anxiety, depression, guilt, etc., are known to the person in whom they are evoked only via cognitive processes: perception, labeling, classifying, explaining, valuating. Thus affects exist as such for the individual only after they are cognized' (1980:147). Dramatization directly involves such conceptualization of emotion, and thus both depends on and contributes to the subjective experience.

In effect, I would argue that where you see emotion, there *is* emotion, but the emotion you see is not always the emotion that is there. That is, where people act emotional, they are feeling emotion (or at least they generate emotion as they perform), but neither the content, the source, nor the object of the emotion can necessarily be accurately inferred from the performance. Ekman and Friesen (cited in Levy 1973:273) have also pointed out that feelings expressed by the face are closest to conscious control and most easily self-monitored; less controlled, less conscious emotional states are expressed through the trunk and the extremities. Valbellans use a great deal of large motor movement to express their feelings, including action of the arms, shoulders, and even the lower body; they also use varied and dramatic facial expressions. Affect may then be expressed in several different ways by different parts of the body, and may reflect different levels of consciousness of the different components of the emotion. The relatively unconscious aspects *may* be those that most accurately locate the source and the object of the feeling.

Levy also argues that willful dramatization of emotions is a way of controlling them as well as expressing them, and I think that this is often precisely the case in Valbella. Culture approves of the expression of emotion, and people know how to perform an affective state, but sometimes social relations require the management of these emotions. In the noisy dramatization, the emotion is deep and genuine, but its precise nature is not necessarily accurately apprehended by either the actor or the audience. As we all know, we may cry either when we are happy or when we are sad. The performance allows one the satisfaction of expressing deep emotions, but the stylized, dramatic form of the expression makes it possible to do so in a 'safe' way, and to disguise (or at least make ambiguous) its true content.

Can silence and stillness then be taken as lack of emotion? Certainly it is often precisely that. But silence is more complicated than noise. A great deal of communication can take place without words, of course, but we are interested here not in nonverbal communication, but in the emotion behind nonverbal *non*communication. Remembering that the face is easiest to monitor, we might expect that strong emotions would show themselves elsewhere, and in fact I think that silent Valbellans often 'wear' their emotions not on their tongues or in their faces, but rather in their general posture, their incessant activity, and in their physical relationships with their animals, automobiles, and other objects in their environment. Still, when people are silent, it certainly might be because they are feeling nothing, and so it is always more difficult to infer emotionality from silence. At this point, let me simply assert that silence *may* be an indication of conflicting or problematic emotions, emotions which must be monitored, controlled, or inhibited in expression because of their potential consequences.

EXPRESSIVE STYLES AND EMOTION MANAGEMENT

So far I have argued the following points. First, in Valbella, the relationship of child and parents typically provides a deep foundation for intense emotional experience. Second, for the most part, emotional experience and expression are satisfying and enjoyable for Valbellans. Third, children are trained to act out emotions, and do so competently and easily, but they are also trained to approach ambiguous or problematic situations with silence. Fourth, Valbellan culture approves of emotional display, but also respects the right of individuals to remain silent. Fifth, performance or dramatization of emotion may in certain senses create the feeling itself, and certainly helps the actor and others label and conceptualize it. In doing so, however, it also makes it possible for the actor to mask the true content of the emotion. Silence may similarly constitute such a performance, and may disguise deep but anxiety-provoking feelings.

The most important point, however, has to do with the management of problematic emotions within the family context. Family relationships carry an exceptional affective load in Valbella. People are very attached to their families, and it is in the family context that the most profound emotions are engendered. On the other hand, people believe that family relationships are fragile and can be broken. When hostility is evoked in the family, it is anxiety-producing, precisely because people depend so much, psychologically, on their families. There is no tragedy like the breakup of a family, but there is also no anger like that found in family relationships. Accordingly, emotion management is essential in family interactions.

In Valbella, the major issues that evoke anger in the family appear to be dependency and authority. These are core areas for intrapsychic as well as interpersonal conflict. They are closely related, and to some extent the encouragement of dependency and the exercise of authority are simply motherly and fatherly expressions of the same impulses. Authority relations are central to a man's self-concept and identity, and the dependence of her children on her is fundamental to a woman's identity. Since these are core psychological issues, having to do with definitions of self, challenges in these areas may lead to conflicts that are especially difficult to undo.

Structurally, the points at which these two problems are most likely to result in conflict are when the children are adolescents and young adults. The challenges that teen-agers present to the authority of the father are particularly dramatic in the contemporary situation, where the 'generation gap' has been accentuated by the occupational, educational, and communicational dynamism of the postwar period. The basic problems are traditional, but general economic and cultural change have shifted the balance of power from the father to the children, and thus the potential for serious damage to family relations is substantial. Similarly, the traditional problems of mother-in-law and daughter-in-law relationships (Saunders 1979), though mitigated by the trend toward nuclear family households, still offer considerable opportunity for psychological and social tension.

The extremes of emotion, then, are experienced in the family context, but it is also in that context that the expression of negative emotions is most problematic. Two culturally patterned expressive styles help in the management of emotional conflict. The first involves effusive, vociferous emotionality, but focused on issues of little real consequence to the actors. I will call this the 'noisy-avoidance' interactive style. The second pattern involves an unrelenting silence, a reluctance to talk at all, and a profound respect for the silence of other members of the family. There are other expressive styles as well, of course, but these two seem to be regularly employed in Valbella. In some families, the two styles are alternated, or some members use one style and others the other. For the most part, however, there seems to be a fairly consistent pattern within families, with slight variations to fit particular moods and situations. The noisy-avoidance style has the cathartic effect of allowing the expression of real affect, but by focusing it on inconsequential issues, permits the participants to return relatively quickly to an emotional equilibrium, and thus avoids destructive effects on family relations. The silent style allows people to avoid confrontation when fully satisfactory solutions to the issue are unlikely.

In a number of the families with which I worked on a regular basis, the 'noisy-avoidance' style seemed more or less institutionalized.[6] That is, when family members were together, they consistently interacted in a high-energy mode, shouting and gesturing, and often with several people talking at one time. Both my observations and informants' comments indicated that there was an inverse relationship between the emotionality of the conversation and the significance of the content. In particular, anger was most often expressed on issues in which family members had little enduring emotional involvement. One man described the pattern precisely: 'I always vote for the Christian Democrats, and my mother knows it, but I love to tell her that I am going to vote for the Communists, because it makes her so mad. She knows I'm kidding, but we both love to fight about it.' The noisy-avoidance arguments, in short, are conducted for the sheer pleasure of emotional expression, release of tension, and to heighten the drama of everyday life. For people with deep feelings, argumentation may become a kind of recreation, and they are invigorated and refreshed by it. But this is only the case as long as the emotion is focused on neutral or nonthreatening issues and therefore does not affect the ongoing business of family life. Real tension may exist in these families, but it is defused by the emotional activity of the noisy-avoidance style. And because such emotional expression is culturally approved, it does not threaten the identity of the family as a close and affectionate group.

---

[6]The study involved both qualitative research and a more extensive survey of families in the village. For about six months, I concentrated on an intensive study of five farming families, using participant-observation methods, studies of cases of family conflict and decision-making, and interviewing about particular events in family life. Later, in collaboration with the other members of the 'Culture and Goals in the Nuclear Family Project', I administered a questionnaire on family life to three members each of thirty Valbellan families (90 respondents in all). In this latter task, I was assisted by the director of the primary school, Mr. Bernardino Desderi, whose help is gratefully acknowledged.

In families that use the noisy-avoidance style, serious issues are more often worked out behind the scenes, using intermediaries, or else they are not worked out at all, the participants settling into a grim silence on the matter. In the family of the man mentioned above, there are enduring tensions of various sorts. The family includes three generations, and there are longstanding points of irritation between the mother-in-law and daughter-in-law, between the husband and wife (of the younger generation—but the elderly woman indicated that the same kinds of tensions existed in her marriage while her husband was alive), and between the father and his teen-age sons. This is, nonetheless, also a very tight and affectionate family, one in which family loyalty and unity are striking. Good relations are maintained in part by the venting of emotions in noisy-avoidance arguments, and partly by putting some distance between family members for a part of the year. This family still engages in a traditional alpine farming transhumance, in which the family splits into two sections for the summer. The grandmother, her son, and one or two of her grandchildren remain on the farm in the valley to work the hay and grain, while the mother and a couple of her children take the cows into the high alpine pastures to graze. There are clearly economic motivations for this division of the family, but the family members also consciously recognize that the 'vacation' during the summer allows them a respite from the heat of family relationships.

This is not to imply that either the noisy-avoidance style or intermittent separation are always successful in the management of emotions in Valbellan families. Certainly it does occur that arguments move from neutral topics to very significant ones, and conflicts of this sort may have enduring consequences for family relations. Indeed, the noisy-avoidance strategy is probably only possible where the real tensions in the family are not exceptionally serious. When serious disputes do occur, they are often followed by a period of silence in family relations.

As the anxiety of family members about the expression of emotion increases, the likelihood of adopting the silent interactive style also increases. The greater the tension, both psychological and social, engendered by family conflict, the more likely family members are to retreat into the silent style. (Again, this is not to imply that quiet families have more objective basis for serious conflict, but simply that they are more concerned about the potential consequences of conflict.) Here again there is cultural approval, or at least respect, for the silence of others. Though most people enjoy talking, they respect the right of others to maintain silence. In arguments, when one of the participants ceases to respond, observers are quick to urge the others to drop the matter. Perhaps this is implicit recognition of the seriousness of matters when people become silent.

The culturally patterned use of silence to avoid confrontation involves situations in which the affective tension is so great that people fear that any expression of emotion, on any issue, might provoke a serious conflict with lasting effects. In other words, the silent style indicates a greater need for emotional control than does the noisy-avoidance style; the dangers are perceived as more immediate and more serious, and the anxiety levels of family members are higher. The distinct interactive styles can also be related to variations in personality as well as to the structure of family relations. At times, the anxiety about speaking is probably directly derived from the general anxiety about dependency and attachment. The fear of separation or estrangement from family members compels people to 'tacere' (to hold their tongues) on the issue at hand, and the potentially overwhelming strength of the emotion (anger) means that they are close to losing control. In this case, it is better not to talk at all.

Some people are more likely than others to experience these difficulties. Depressive personalities, with relatively high hostility and anxiety levels, are likely to prefer silence; these are more often men than women, and are fairly common in Valbella (see also Pancheri 1975:560). In addition, the particular style adopted by an individual may be influenced by his or her structural position in the family. Here it is important to recognize another significant function of silence—as a form of passive aggression. Children who are still dependent on their parents, for example, may use the silent style as a way of submitting to authority without affirming its legitimacy. By not challenging their parents directly and yet refusing to converse with them, they effectively show their unhappiness and—in this society where conversation is ordinarily so enjoyable—they also deprive their parents of one source of joy and satisfaction.

GRIM SILENCE AT HOME: AN EXAMPLE

An example of the 'silent type' of family relations may help illustrate these points. Mr. Taccino is an elderly farmer who lives with his wife and two children. He married late in life, and in 1974 was 70 years old. His wife is about 15 years younger, and his two children are teen-agers. Mr. Taccino rarely speaks unless spoken to and then responds with a single word or a short phrase. His family says that he has always been very quiet. He is nonetheless friendly and congenial, and has an easy smile despite his serious manner. He is a frankly anxious person with many fears and worries, and his worrying often brings the family into quiet conflict. For example, his son badly wanted to buy a car, but Mr. Taccino refused on the grounds that the highways are too dangerous. His daughter's school class was to take a chaperoned trip to Rome, but Mr. Taccino refused to allow her to go. When she presented the idea, he immediately objected to the trip as 'too dangerous', but did not make a firm decision until two weeks before the departure, when a bomb exploded in the Rome train station. Mr. Taccino said that he was not at all worried about his daughter's conduct on the trip, but that he was afraid something would happen to her while traveling. He said that he would be unable to sleep for the entire time that she was gone, and despite the mediation of Mrs. Taccino in favor of the trip, he held fast to his refusal. He also said that he was unable to sleep when either of the children were out at night, and Mrs. Taccino confirmed that this was so. This angered his children, as did many of his other passive interferences in their lives, and they often attempted to engage him in discussion of it. His approach was to state his opinion quietly and then refuse to discuss the matter further. He never used an angry, authoritative manner and often ended by saying that they could do what they wanted, but his feelings were clear.

In the Taccino family, these scenes were worked out with few words, and a general silence permeated interactions in the family. During the several weeks of silent negotiation about the trip to Rome, father and daughter rarely spoke to each other at all. Mrs. Taccino attempted quietly to negotiate for her daughter, but to no avail. She specifically instructed her daughter not to bring it up, because that would only make things worse. At first, then, the daughter's silence was strategic, and was an attempt to avoid an angry outburst against her father's authority. Later, it was a sullen, passive-aggressive silence, designed to deny him the pleasure of congeniality. Even as a form of passive-aggression, however, a major aspect of the silence was to control emotion in a situation where its expression would have severe consequences for family relations. On one occasion, I asked Mr. Taccino directly whether he thought it was better to air disputes in the family or to keep silent and avoid conflict, and he responded without hesitation that it was better to say nothing at all, because one was likely to get angry and say things that would lead to irreparable damage in family relations. This is the essence of my point about the silent style.

This silent style was also evident in a number of the other families with which I worked. In some cases, it was characteristic of only particular relationships in the family. Mothers-in-law and daughters-in-law, for example, often had a silent relationship. One elderly woman told me of the difficulties of life in an extended family household, and when I asked how they managed to get along (given the tensions she had been describing), she replied without hesitation, 'We don't talk.'

CONCLUSION: THE USES OF SILENCE

The silent pattern is probably very common in the cross-cultural record, and the silent man is certainly a typical figure in southern Europe.

Brandes cites a Spanish saying that reflects this theme: '*De las aguas mansas nos libre Dios; que de las otras me libraré yo*' ('May God free us from calm waters; from the rest, I'll free myself' 1980:115). Brandes goes on to note that 'Calm water in this proverb represents individuals who appear to be good and well-meaning, who never fight, argue, or contradict others. It is, in fact, these people, and not the open, demonstrative, combative types, who have to be guarded against'. Silence may thus mask intensity, and may also hide evil intentions. At any rate, the clear implication is that it is when people are silent that something is going on. Silence as a strategy in managing difficult situations is also noted by Witherspoon in consideration of Navajo speaking styles. 'Silence is . . . used in dealing with strangers', he says. 'As the ambivalence and distrust on one's relationship to a stranger are gradually broken down, verbal communication gradually increases from silence to open discussion. As the relationship becomes more intense and familiar, the use of language decreases again, at least with regard to intense emotional matters or matters of serious consequence. Feelings and emotions on these matters are seldom discussed on the verbal level' (1975:99). Finally, Bock has suggested that Shakespeare recognized the pattern as well. 'Clearly', Bock says, 'in Shakespeare's plays silence may express diametrically opposed relationships or emotional states (intimacy *or* alienation, joy *or* grief); and it may be more closely linked to the *intensity* of emotions than to their exact contents' (1976:292).

Silence, in sum, is a common strategy for the management of tense situations. It is especially appropriate when people are highly emotional (as Valbellans often are), particularly when fully satisfactory solutions to the issue are unlikely. Silence helps the individual to control the emotion, and may at times also allow the passive expression of discontentment without the dangers of a direct challenge. In Valbella, it appears that silence is called into play in more serious cases. People generally prefer to use the 'noisy-avoidance' style, which has the more satisfying, cathartic effect of allowing the expression of real affect, but focuses the emotion on inconsequential issues so that basic family harmony can be maintained. In a society where estrangement in family relations is considered the greatest tragedy conceivable, both of these strategies are of considerable importance.

REFERENCES

Bailey, F. G. 1983. The tactical uses of passion. Ithaca: Cornell University Press.
Barzini, Luigi. 1964. The Italians. New York: Bantam.
Basso, Keith. 1972. 'To give up on words': Silence in Western Apache culture. Language and social context, ed. by Pier Paolo Giglioli, 67–86. New York: Penguin.
Bateson, Gregory and Margaret Mead. 1942. Balinese character: A photographic analysis. New York: New York Academy of Sciences.

Bock, Philip K. 1976. 'I think but dare not speak': Silence in Elizabethan culture. Journal of Anthropological Research 32. 285–294.

Boucher, Jerry D. 1979. Culture and emotion. Perspectives on cross-cultural psychology, ed. by Anthony J. Marsella, Roland G. Tharp, & Thomas J. Ciborowski, 159–178. New York: Academic Press.

Bowlby, John. 1971. Attachment. Middlesex, England: Penguin.

Brandes, Stanley. 1980. Metaphors of masculinity: Sex and status in Andalusian folklore. Philadelphia: University of Pennsylvania Press.

Bruner, Jerome S. 1966. On cognitive growth. Studies on cognitive growth, ed. by Jerome S. Bruner, Rose R. Olver, Patricia M. Greenfield, 1–29. New York: Wiley.

Campbell, J. K. 1964. Honour, family, and patronage. Oxford: Oxford University Press.

Geertz, Clifford. 1973. The interpretation of cultures. New York: Basic.

Geertz, Clifford. 1980. Negara: The theatre state in nineteenth-century Bali. Princeton: Princeton University Press.

Geertz, Hildred. 1974. The vocabulary of emotion: A study of Javanese socialization processes. Culture and personality: Contemporary readings, ed. by Robert A. LeVine, 249–264. Chicago: Aldine.

Gilmore, Margaret M. and David D. Gilmore. 1979. 'Machismo': A Psychodynamic approach (Spain). The Journal of Psychological Anthropology 2. 281–300.

Goldschmidt, Walter. 1976. Absent eyes and idle hands: Socialization for low affect among the Sebei. Socialization as cultural communication, ed. by Theodore Schwartz, 65–72. Berkeley: University of California Press.

Heider, Karl. 1976. Dani sexuality: A low-energy system. Man II. 188–201.

Heider, Karl. 1979. Grand Valley Dani: Peaceful warriors. New York: Holt, Rinehart, & Winston.

Izard, Carroll E. 1980. Cross-cultural perspectives on emotion and emotion communication. Handbook of cross-cultural psychology. Vol. 3. Basic Processes, ed. by Harry C. Triandis & Walter Lonner, 185–222. Boston: Allyn and Bacon, Inc.

Kaufman, I. Charles. 1975. Learning what comes naturally: The role of life experience in the establishment of species typical behavior. Socialization as cultural communication, ed. by Theodore Schwartz, 37–50. Berkeley: University of California Press.

Kleinman, Arthur. 1980. Patients and healers in the context of culture: An exploration of the borderland between anthropology, medicine, and psychiatry. Berkeley: University of California.

Kochman, Thomas. 1981. Black and white styles in conflict. Chicago: University of Chicago Press.

Levy, Robert I. 1973. Tahitians: Mind and experience in the society islands. Chicago: University of Chicago Press.

Lutz, Catherine. 1982. The domain of emotion words on Ifaluk. American Ethnologist 9. 113–128.

Mead, Margaret. 1949. Coming of age in samoa. New York: Mentor. Originally published in 1928.

Munroe, Robert L. and Ruth H. Munroe. 1975. Cross-cultural human development. Belmont, CA: Wadsworth.

Pancheri, Paolo. 1975. Measurement of emotion: Transcultural aspects. Emotions: Their parameters and measurement, ed. by Lennart Levi, 547–560. New York: Raven Press.

Parsons, Anne. 1969. Belief, magic, and anomie. New York: The Free Press.

Peacock, James L. 1968. Rites of modernization. Chicago: University of Chicago Press.

Pitt-Rivers, Julian. 1966. Honour and social status. Honour and shame: The values of Mediterranean society, ed. by J. G. Peristiany, 19–78. Chicago: University of Chicago Press.

Radcliffe-Brown, A. R. 1952. On joking relationships. Structure and function in primitive societies, 90–104. New York: The Free Press.

Rohner, Ronald P. 1975. They love me, they love me not. New Haven: Human Relations Area Files (HRAF) Press.

Saunders, George R. 1979. Social change and psychocultural continuity in an Alpine Italian village. Ethos 7. 206–231.

Saunders, George R. 1981. Men and women in Southern Europe: A review of some aspects of cultural complexity. The Journal of Psychoanalytic Anthropology 4. 435–466.

Spitz, Rene A. 1945. Hospitalism. The psychoanalytic study of the child, Vol. 1. 53–74.

Spitz, Rene A. 1946. Hospitalism: A Follow-up report. The psychoanalytic study of the child, Vol. II. 113–117.

Super, Charles M. and Sara Harkness. 1982. The development of affect in infancy and early childhood. Cultural perspectives on child development, ed. by Daniel A. Wagner & Harold W. Stevenson, 1–19. San Francisco: W. H. Freeman.

White, Geoffrey. 1981. 'Person' and 'Emotion' in A'ara ethnopsychology. Paper presented at the Annual Meeting of the Association for Social Anthropology in Oceania, February 1981, San Diego.

Witherspoon, Gary. 1975. Navajo kinship and marriage. Chicago: University of Chicago Press.

Young, Harben Bouterline and Lucy Rau Ferguson. 1981. Puberty to manhood in Italy and America. New York: Academic Press.

Chapter 10

Eloquent Silence Among the Igbo of Nigeria

Gregory O. Nwoye
University of Benin, Nigeria

Traditional Igbo society was marked by the major importance of face-to-face relationships. With a total absence of writing, and only a rudimentary form of mechanical communication, oral communication held a central place in the transactions and values of the society. Igbo people are still reputed for their cultivation of the art of speaking, and much has been written about their use of proverbs to embellish speech (Achebe 1958; Isichei 1973, 1976). Oratory is a highly cultivated art form and orators are held in very high esteem.

The Igbo are typically very extroverted in their personal interactions. Greetings—verbal as well as nonverbal—are very elaborate in form, and grace in their execution is highly valued. Such greetings, which are normally expected between even total strangers, are exchanged at all times and under all circumstances, with significant exceptions to be noted below. Handshaking is the prevalent form of greeting, accompanied by protracted solicitations about the health and welfare of the person being greeted, and of his or her parents, children, and relatives, whether known or unknown to the speaker. It is against this background of ebullient loquacity and vivacity that the ominous meaning of silence among the Igbo can be interpreted. For a people with this type of disposition, silence is a highly marked form of behavior. It is not regarded merely as the absence of speech, but in almost all instances, silence is interpreted as having significant communicative functions. In short, silence can be very eloquent.

In this chapter I will examine the use of silence in several contexts in which it is mandatory and others in which the choice of silence would signal a socially understood message. These occur at all levels in the structuring of communication within Igbo society. For convenience in discussing silence in these contexts, I will follow the sequence set forth by Saville-Troike (Chapter 1).

INSTITUTIONALLY DETERMINED SILENCE

The Igbo view death as a part of the normal human life cycle. People die when they have completed one life cycle on earth, which ordinarily should happen at a ripe age. Since the Igbo reckoning of longevity is not necessarily mathematical, any person who dies before his or her parents, or before raising offspring to adulthood, is considered to have died young. The Igbo live in deeds, not in years. If someone dies 'prematurely', the grief caused by his or her death is so overpowering that the bereaved are almost physically weighed down by it. People who come to sympathize or mourn with the bereaved are not supposed to increase or sharpen the grief of the bereaved by any verbal reference to what happened.

Customarily, bereaved persons are avoided for some days following the death of a family member. About four days after the death it is deemed appropriate to visit them. Sympathizers walk in, go straight to the bereaved, stand before them for a short time, then find a seat somewhere among some other mourners and join them awhile in mutual silence. When they feel they have stayed long enough, they again approach the bereaved, repeat the process of showing themselves to them, and take their leave as silently as they came in. Although no word has been spoken, quite a bit has been communicated. They have shown by their physical presence that they sympathize with the bereaved and share in the loss of their beloved.

This is all the more physically demonstrated by standing before the bereaved. Apart from registering physical presence, the sympathizers have further shown that they had no hand in the death of the person. Since to die young is unnatural and can only be caused by malevolent forces, it is necessary to absolve oneself from any suspicion of being instrumental in an individual's death by showing up in person. It is believed that someone with magical powers that can cause death cannot stand before the spirit of the deceased (which is supposed to be hovering around his or her home until the final burial rites are performed) without receiving immediate retaliation. Additionally, it is assumed that since everyone knows what has happened, it would be superfluous to talk about it. Furthermore, such discussion would intensify the grief of the bereaved, which no genuine sympathizer intends.

Silence is also mandatory in many ritual contexts. For instance, the Igbo make sacrifices for many purposes. Sacrifices can be offered to appease, thank, or solicit the aid of the numerous spirits and elements that control, guard and guide people in their perpetual struggle against the malevolent influences of evil spirits and their fellow beings. When the sacrifice has been made, it is carried by the person for whom it is made to a place specified by the officiating priest. On the way to this place, the carrier neither greets nor is greeted by the people he or she meets. People not only refrain from speaking to anyone carrying a sacrifice, but show deference by giving the right of way, stepping aside until the carrier has passed. Thus body contact is also avoided.

Silence in this context, apart from marking the solemnity of the situation, further shows that the carrier of a sacrifice is engaged in a serious spiritual task and should not be disturbed by such mundane things as the exchange of greetings. Besides, the sacrifice might be for the purpose of diverting the attention of malevolent spirits from the carrier, in which circumstance it is to be expected that the malevolent force would be making all efforts not to be dislodged. Intervention of any form in this combat between the carrier of sacrifice and his or her adversaries might incur for whoever intervenes the wrath of the already offended malevolent spirit. Therefore, both in the interest of the carrier and any observers, it is better that he or she be left uninterrupted. Finally, and perhaps because of the above reasons, the officiating priest usually imposes the observance of strict silence as a prerequisite for the efficacy of the sacrifice. If and when this condition of silence is violated (a very rare occurrence), the sacrifice has not only to be repeated, but the offender has to make an additional sacrifice.

Other ritual contexts requiring silence include the annual *Ogbanigbe* festival among the Aniocha Igbo in the Bendel State of Nigeria. For two days certain male members of a village group are required to remain within the confines of their houses without ever coming out at all. Members of their families are expected not to utter any word during those two days. They are not even allowed to 'break firewood'. It is firmly believed that the men are in serious consultations with their ancestors and therefore should be neither disturbed nor distracted by any form of noise. The end of this period of mandatory silence is signalled by the firing of a dare gun at sundown on the final day.

Another ritual in which silence is mandatory is in the *Ichu iyi nwa* (literally 'going to the stream for a baby') ritual, which is the concluding part of the naming ceremony that takes place on the 28th day after a child is born. In this ritual, the mother of the new baby, accompanied by a young girl acting as a maid, takes a ritual trip to a stream, carrying a clay bowl. On her way to the stream and back to perform the ritual cleansing after childbirth, she is forbidden to speak to anyone. People who meet her tease her profusely, but she must not speak.

A final example of ritual silence is related to the belief in reincarnation which is widely held by the Igbo. Some evil children, called *Ogbanje,* are believed to come into the world simply to torment their mothers. This they do by dying shortly after birth, and then coming into their mothers' wombs to be born again in an endless cycle of birth and death. These children are believed to have made a pact with their kindred spirit in the 'other world', and this pact can be severed only by medicine men well versed in the ways of these 'repeater' children. The pact is severed when the personal symbol (*iyi uwa*) of the child is discovered and dug out of the ground, where it is believed the child buried it prior to the onset of its birth-death cycle. The child is asked threateningly by the medicine man to show where it buried the symbol and to identify and claim it as its own when dug out of the ground.

Since noise in any form is believed to interfere with the discovery of the *iyi uwa*, silence is demanded by the medicine man of all the observers. If ever this is violated, it is almost always by the mother of the *Ogbanje,* who adds her own motherly entreaties to the menacing demands of the medicine man. As the prinicipal victim of her tormentor (her child), her failure to comply with the requirements of total silence is ignored on the grounds that she is only attempting to end her torment. She is, in a sense, another ritual speaker, rather than a forcibly silent observer.

GROUP-DETERMINED SILENCE

Collective or group silence is a very effective means of social control in traditional Igbo society, where silence can be used as a sanction against the deviations of members of a village community. This is done by passing a law which makes it punishable by some stipulated penalties for any member of the village to greet, accept greetings, and/or be aided by the deviant. This extreme measure is resorted to when all other measures adopted to bring the offender to repentance and submission to the will of the people have failed. When this happens, the entire village—men, women, and children—are forbidden to talk to the offender and members of his or her immediate family. This ostracism is so complete that nobody trades with them or their family in the village market. Since it is almost impossible to survive for very long under such conditions, because of the mutual dependence upon which life in the village is based, offenders are quickly brought to their knees, and seek means of reestablishing themselves and their family in the good graces of the community. When this is done the embargo on speech is lifted and once more everyone may speak to them. They become full members of the society again.

Another group-determined context in which silence is expected is in the acceptance by a girl of a proposal for marriage. In traditional Igbo culture, the marriage proposal precedes courtship. Courtship is a group affair. After a young man has the consent of a girl he wishes to marry, courtship begins. In this, the young man is joined by his parents, his relatives, and friends who start treating and behaving toward the girl as his 'wife'. This involves, among other things, being generally nice to her, meeting her legitimate demands (which for a girl eager to please are bound to be few), and showering her with gifts. Marriage is a serious affair that needs some form of societal approval and witnessing. When the actual proposal is made, whether by the young man himself or through a middleman, it is always made in the presence of other people, usually the girl's parents and relatives. The witnesses at this scene watch the girl's nonverbal behavior and interpret her actions. If the girl accepts the proposal, she simply turns shyly and runs away to rejoice in the protective seclusion of her room. She is neither supposed nor expected to say yes or no. If she turns down the offer, she just stands there for as long as the suitor considers it decent to stay before taking his leave. Either way she is supposed to be so overwhelmed by emotion to be bereft of speech. If she accepts she should be too happy to talk; otherwise she should be too sad to say anything. Moreover, she is not supposed to know the right answers to give in either case because an answer, particularly if it is appropriate, would indicate she is versed in the ways of the world—an obvious disqualification for a girl who hopes to be married.

Silence is interpreted as meaning consent in many other circumstances as well. This is reflected in an Igbo proverb: *O gbalu nkiti Kwelu ekwe* 'He consents, who keeps silent'. Thus one who keeps silent over, for example, a collective decision by a community, has given consent and therefore partakes in the collective responsibilities attached to the decision.

Another meaning of silence among the Igbo is respect. Silence symbolizes respect in hierarchical parent/child, elder/younger, husband/ wife, and male/female relationships. Children are expected, as a mark of respect and evidence of good upbringing, to keep silent while their parents speak to, admonish, rebuke, or advise them. The young should listen while the old speak, and females generally should defer to males by remaining silent, unless asked to speak.

INDIVIDUALLY NEGOTIATED SILENCE

Because greetings have such a central place in the life of the Igbo, avoidance of them becomes distinctively marked. Morning greetings in particular are supposed to be very important. Since the morning is the beginning of the day, and since it is believed that the sort of person you first encounter in the morning determines your fortune for that day, people are rather careful about whom they greet first. It is assumed that one did not meet a person if one did not speak to him or her. Therefore people consciously refrain from speaking to those who they know or suspect can bring ill luck to them and thereby ruin their entire day. Silence in this context is a pragmatic instrument for avoiding misfortune.

Before the advent of western medicine, certain diseases were held in very great awe. One such disease was smallpox, an outbreak of which was a great disaster. Dread of its destructive capacity (not many people ever survived its attack) and belief that the disease can take human form and walk about, combine to impose a moratorium on greetings whenever the disease is known to be around. At such times, when one meets a person on the road, the greetings that are usual even with complete strangers are not exchanged. Since no one knows in whom the dread disease has been incarnated, discretion dictates that one speak only to those with whom one is familiar or much better still, in daily contact. These do not normally extend beyond the immediate nuclear family. It would not be strange to observe a mother passing a daughter who is married into another village on the road without even showing a sign of recognition, if it were known that someone in her marital village was stricken with smallpox. Anyone known to be even remotely related to a smallpox victim is not only not spoken to, but is totally avoided. Thus silence is a powerful tool for ritual protection in an extremely threatening situation.

Given the importance of greetings in all face-to-face encounters, silence becomes a recognized means of showing that two people or two groups of people are so unfriendly that they do not even exchange greetings. The Igbo expression of the English equivalent of 'not to be on speaking terms' is much more sinister than its English equivalent. While it is neither strange nor peculiar to the Igbo, they carry out this state of affairs with such elaboration that silence becomes an art. When one encounters someone to whom 'you do not speak', one is required not only to keep silent, but to make it known to whoever is around that you are not on speaking terms with the other person. This is achieved by stopping, if one is walking, turning one's back while at the same time covering one's mouth or at least making some such symbolic gesture. Meanwhile the other party does the same with an equal if not greater display. Thus by a combination of silence and kinesics, the Igbo tell anyone who may chance to witness it that the person coming in the opposite direction is an enemy who should be avoided.

Finally, although I have reported that silence means assent in most circumstances, in some situations it can imply deferred action. It is generally believed that if one hurts a person and that person keeps quiet, he or she is contemplating an action to take in the future, while a person who vociferates immediately would be unlikely to do much more. An Igbo folk tale about the kite (a predatory bird) and the duck illustrates this belief:

Once upon a time, the kite sent her son to hunt for food. He soon saw a duck with her brood. The young kite swooped down on them and carried off one of the ducklings. The duck stared at him, but said nothing. Meanwhile the kite came back to his waiting mother with his prey. The mother asked him what the reaction of the duck was. He answered that she merely stared at him and said nothing. The mother kite ordered her son to return the duckling to its mother, because her silence forbodes some future action. The son complied. On his way back, he saw a hen with her brood and once more swooped down and carried off one of the chicks. The mother fretted, shouted and cursed. On his return the kite asked once again what the reaction of the hen was. The son replied that she made a lot of fuss. Mother kite ordered her son to prepare the chick for dinner because there is nothing more its mother can do.

The story supports the belief that there is a potential and unfathomable decision or action in silence, whereas immediate verbal response to a vexing situation either reveals immediately one's intended line of action, or symbolizes the sum total of all expected action.

As in all cultures, silence in Igbo communication is a figure which reveals its meaning against the ground of speech. Given the values attached to loquacity in Igbo culture, silence becomes all the more marked in its expressiveness. As seen in a variety of situations, silence serves as a means of managing highly-charged situations and relationships. It serves both as a medium of communication in itself and as a context for communication through nonverbal channels. Importantly, it may provide social and psychic protection for one or both communicants in an interaction. The potential power of silence among the Igbo thus achieves a significance not always found—or not found to the same degree—in other societies. For, just as elaborate speech plays such a prominent part in both public and private life, so it is possible for silence in such a setting to become truly eloquent.

REFERENCES

Achebe, Chinua. 1958. Things fall apart. London: Heinemann's Educational Books.
Isichei, Elizabeth. 1973. The Ibo people and the Europeans. New York: St. Martin's Press.
Isichei, Elizabeth. 1976. A history of the Igbo people. New York: St. Martin's Press.

Chapter 11

The Silent Finn

Jaakko Lehtonen
Kari Sajavaara
University of Jyväskylä, Finland

An episode in an old Finnish movie:

SCENE: The common room in a traditional Finnish farmhouse. The farmer and his wife are carrying out their daily tasks in the room.

A middle-aged man enters, takes off his hat and shakes the snow from the top of it, walks slowly across the room, and sits down on the bench that runs along the wall. The man takes his pipe from his pocket, fills it very slowly, sticks it into his mouth, and smokes the pipeful in silence. The farmer and his wife go on doing their duties. Finally -

FARMER: Is it very far you come from?. . .

Each culture maintains its own norms concerning acceptable as well as unacceptable or aberrant speech behavior in social interactions. Values regarding appropriate behavior are often reflected in proverbs, popular sayings, and jokes. In Finland, the following proverbs and sayings illustrate such values:

> Listen a lot, speak little.
> One word is enough to make a lot of trouble.
> One mouth, two ears.
> A barking dog does not catch a hare.
> A fool speaks a lot, a wise man thinks instead.
> Brevity makes a good psalm.
> One word is as good as nine.

(Kuusi 1953)

It is evident that popular opinion as reflected in these proverbs and sayings is positive toward people who do not speak much. People are expected to ponder their words carefully because words are powerful. A word once said cannot be recalled, and a careless word may cause a fire which is difficult to extinguish. A common opinion is that wise persons keep silent: speaking a great deal is not desirable.

The same attitudes were reflected in a humorous pseudoscholarly paper published a few years ago by two Finnish linguists, Auli Hakulinen and Fred Karlsson, on 'Finnish Silence' (1977). The authors caricature some of the stereotypical characteristics of communication among Finns. Parodying Grice (1975), they provide a list of Finnish 'conversational maxims' which purport to 'guarantee' success in various interactional situations in Finland. The first general principle they give is: 'Do not speak'. If speaking cannot be avoided, however, they offer a number of alternative strategies, such as 'drink as much alcohol as possible', 'avoid direct address', 'never mention the addressee's name', and 'try to avoid unnecessary small words like *thanks, excuse me,* and *sorry*'.

Their second general principle is: 'Remain uncommunicative'. This injunction applies to nonverbal as well as verbal behavior, such as not smiling, and not looking an interlocutor in the eyes lest comprehension be revealed. Instructions given for specific situations include: 'Never ask anything in the classroom, because if you do, you are lost for good; if the teacher asks you a question, look out the window or scratch behind your ear looking thoughtful.'

Although these 'maxims' were intended as a humorous exaggeration, they are not without basis in fact. 'The silent Finn' is a popular image both within Finland and without. Even at international meetings and conferences, Finnish participants are frequently labeled with this characteristic, either because they avoid taking part in discussion due to a lack of communicative competence in other languages, or because they transfer communicative patterns from Finnish. We shall consider here some of the sources for the existence of the stereotype, both in folklore and in linguistic research. That the use and tolerance of silence by Finns is different from that of other national groups, at least within the Western European culture area, is attested to not only by the experiences of Finns in contact with other nationalities, but by the intuitive impressions of other Europeans visiting Finland as well.

INTERPRETATION OF SILENCE

We have little empirical data from any society regarding the limits of silence which will be tolerated by participants in conversation before they feel compelled to speak. It is obvious, however, that the threshold of tolerance varies from culture to culture and from language to language. Comparison of the intuitive data about the situation in Finland with similar data about America or Central Europe clearly indicates that the duration of silences tolerated by Finns in conversation is much longer.

Finns who live in Sweden report that they have to be particularly alert to be able to participate in conversation carried out in Swedish, because the tempo of the exchange moves much faster than in Finnish discourse. However, Allwood (n.d.) claims that the response time (the extent of time allowed between speaker turns) seems to be longer in a Swedish conversation than in an American one. Allwood hypothesizes that response time is shorter in cultures in which the speakers are more tolerant of being interrupted. This seems to be the case in Southern European cultures, where the norm that only one person speaks at a time does not hold to the extent that it does in Sweden. (See, for example, Tannen, Chapter 6.)

A Finn's tolerance of silence is not unlimited however. There are certain implicit norms in Finnish conversational behavior which set the limits in terms of the social constraints characterizing the situation. The duration of silence causing no embarrassment is shortest in informal situations between strangers while longer pauses between turns are tolerated in intimate, relaxed discussion, on the one hand, and in conversations dealing with abstract topics involving reflection and contemplation. This is what Baker (1955) terms 'positive' silence.

One of the basic principles in dyadic interaction is the exchange of speaking turns: while one of the participants is speaking, the other is supposed to take the role of the listener. Listeners are not, however, totally silent and passive. While listening, they are engaged in various types of backchannel behavior. They may nod or shake their heads, purse their lips, raise their eyebrows, or they may make use of vocal backchannel signals accompanying the speaker's verbal message, such as (in English) *uh-mhm, yeah, right, I see.* They may also finish off sentences begun by the other party, interrupt the other person's speech, or make brief independent statements. This activity of the listener is not meaningless to the speaker. It is not possible for the speaker to accomplish a successful speech act without first attracting the attention of those to whom the speech act is addressed. One of the things of which the speaker wants to be sure is that the listener understands what he or she is saying, which normally requires cooperation from the listener. As part of the process of communication, the speaker regularly examines and interprets the backchannel behavior of the interlocutor.

The social and cognitive organization of speaking and listening and, accordingly, the cues in the speech which give information to the interactant of the other's attitudes vary in different cultures and languages, and it is obvious that cross-cultural differences in feedback cues can lead to erroneous pragmatic interpretation of the interlocutor's intentions as a result of intercultural interference (cf. Erickson 1979).

The use of vocalizations and verbal backchannel signals is less frequent in Finnish than in Central European languages or in English as spoken in Britain and America. Verbal backchannel signals do exist in Finnish (e.g., *joo, niin, aivan, kyllä*), and they are used especially in informal and enthusiastic discourse, but too frequent use of them is considered intrusive; that this is negatively regarded is seen in the fact that such behavior is considered as typical of drunken people. Finns 'backchannel' primarily by nonverbal means: head nods, mimics, on and off eye contact with the speaker (with the gaze typically directed towards the distance), and occasionally wordless murmurs. Interruptions are not normally tolerated. The typical Finn is a 'silent' listener.

In cross-cultural communication, any of the three interaction strategies typically employed by Finns in discussion can lead to problems and misunderstandings:

1. *'Active' participation,* which for a Finn may mean delayed attempts at turn-taking, clumsy gambits, disfluency, slow speech, and silent observation of ongoing discourse.
2. *Silent participation,* which may result in a low level of attraction towards the Finn, because a person who does not speak remains invisible.
3. *Entire withdrawal from the discussion,* which can easily be misinterpreted cross-culturally as hostility towards the group, and the group may react accordingly, creating a vicious circle.

A Finnish listener's silence or the absence of verbal signals for active listening may result in a foreign interactant's inferring that the Finnish interlocutor is not paying attention, or that the Finn is indifferent, sullen, or even hostile. The long silences that tend to occur in interactional situations with Finns are sometimes interpreted by foreign participants as indicating that the Finn is feeling anxiety and wishes to conclude the interaction, or that the Finn considers the topic as annoying. In contrastive linguistic terms, this suggests that the Finnish interactant has transferred behavioral conventions and pragmatics from the native language/culture in ways that did not meet the expectations of the other participant. The result is a breakdown in communication in which the interactants are mutually unaware of the nature of the conflict.

THE RATE OF SPEECH

Does an average Finn speak slower than speakers of other languages? The results of speech rate measurements do not support such a perception. The percentage of pauses in Finnish out of total speaking time is about the same as it is in other languages. In a test, for instance, in which speakers of different languages gave verbal descriptions of cartoons, the average percentage of pause time of Finns was 39 percent, that of Swedish-speaking Finns 41 percent, of Swedes 34 percent, of native speakers of British English 39 percent, and of native speakers of American English 40 percent (Lehtonen 1979).

The actual rate of speaking varied drastically in the test when measured in words or in syllables. The figures for different languages cannot be compared, however, because of the differences in word and syllable structures in different languages. These differences are the reason for the seemingly paradoxical result that Finnish was spoken slightly faster than English when measured in syllables, the articulation rate being 305 syllables per minute for Finnish and 291 syllables per minute for English, but it was spoken much slower than English when the rate was measured in words, the rate being 146 words per minute for Finnish and 202 words per minute for English (obviously Finnish words are longer than English words). Moreover, differences between individual speakers were great, especially with regard to the amount of pausing and the overall rate of speaking.

Physical measures of speech rate and pauses do not necessarily serve as 'objective' parameters of time and tempo. There are no ideal values which could be used as norms to label speech as relatively fast or slow. The interrelationship between objective and subjective temporality is complicated by a multitude of intervening factors such as personality, contextual configurations, and register and style expectations.

The impression of an interactant being slow may also be a function of the interaction itself, when the personal style of one member of a dyad is more active than that of the other (cf. Bruneau 1980:104). Baker (1955) reports some experiments with interactions between psychiatrists and their patients. When the interviewer (psychiatrist) exercised a passive role, the subject's vocabulary expansion rate remained normal, but when the interviewer adopted a more active stand, the subject was forced to adopt a defensive role and there was less variety in speech.

Within a certain culture, members of a subcultural group, or even the inhabitants of a particular geographical area, may be considered slower or faster in speech than their fellow countrymen. In some cases, the speakers of an entire nation have gained the reputation of being slower in speech (and sometimes, pejoratively, in other cognitive tasks!). In Germany the slow speakers are the East Frisians; for the Frenchmen the slow speakers are found in Belgium; and in Switzerland the people who are alleged to speak slowly are those who live in the area of Berne or Zurich.

In Finland, the positive stereotype of fast and vivid speech rests with the inhabitants of Carelia in the southeastern parts of the country, while the speakers of the dialect of Häme in the southwestern areas of Central

Finland are negatively stereotyped as slow in speech, taciturn, clumsy, and often somewhat simple-minded. In some languages such people are even characterized by specific names; in Germany they are called *Schildbürger,* and in Finland they are *hölmöläiset,* who in many people's imagination live in Häme.

The reputed slowness of the Häme people is reflected folklorically in well-known jokes about them, such as the following taken from the Folklore Archives of the Finnish Literary Society:

> A Häme man enters a neighbor's house, sits for quite a while before the neighbor asks why he has come, and then says that he came to tell him that his house is burning.

> A popular Saturday night TV show was discontinued. What was the reason?—The Häme inhabitants had such a great time on Sunday morning in church.

> Two Häme brothers were on their way to work in the morning. One says, 'It is here that I lost my knife'. Coming back home in the evening, the other asks, 'Your knife, did you say?'

There are two possible reasons for this reputation of the Häme inhabitants: either they are really slower than other Finns or the impression of slowness in their speech results from certain linguistic features of their dialect, such as the relatively conservative morphophonology which lacks the consonant and vowel elision typical of other dialects.

As part of a research program examining the impact of the English language and Anglo-American culture on Finnish, the Finnish-English Cross-Language Project carried out experiments with a student population, which was differentiated in terms of the domiciles of the informants and their parents (Sajavaara and Lehtonen 1980a). Informants who had lived all their lives in Häme, and of whose parents at least one had done the same, were found to be statistically significantly slower then the others. The total amount of silence during pauses in their speech was longer, the number of hesitations was higher, and the number of repairs in the case of errors in reading tests was smaller (see Lehtonen and Heikkinen 1981). Thus at least part of the impressionistic stereotype appears to have a foundation in fact.

THE FINNISH CHARACTER

One of the recurring popular explanations of Finnish silence is the national character of the people. At the beginning of the twentieth century, Hugo Bergroth, a lecturer at the University of Helsinki, described the character of Swedish-speaking Finns as phlegmatic, introverted, reticent, and unimaginative (Bergroth 1916:31). The Finnish linguist Lauri Haku-linen accepted this characterization and stated that it was even more fitting for the description of Finnish-speaking Finns (Hakulinen 1979:32–34). While 'national character' is no longer a generally accepted social science construct, cross-cultural differences in the uses of talk and si-lence clearly exist. Americans ask questions and force others to talk to fill up interactional silence, because silence is not tolerated socially. In many cases, the function of talk among Americans is not in the transference of information or messages, but in the avoidance of silence. In Finland, silence is socially acceptable to a different degree. Differences of this kind may arise from differences in educational backgrounds. The American experiences the interactional situation differently because of differences in education and socialization.

Communicatively meaningful silence may result from a speaker's in-tentional switch from the verbal to the nonverbal communication chan-nel: silence can make up a silent speech act and thus becomes the mes-sage itself or part of it. In many cases, it can be the silence that contains the most important cues for the meaning of the message. Much can be said by keeping quiet. Silences of this type are often clearly culture-specific in their use and meaning, but even within one and the same culture such silences may function differently between different types of interactants and in different types of situations: meaningful silence be-tween friends is not the same as meaningful silence between strangers (cf. Baker 1955).

Samarin (1964) observes that 'in normal social intercourse between friends and between members of the same in-group, there seems to be a tendency to "translate" messages into informal, redundant, even poorly structured idiom—even when one knows clearly what one wants to say'. In such situations too much information content in speech can easily throw the interlocutor off balance. Silence may substitute for such idiom in certain cultures or subcultures. Samarin (1964:119) notes that the Gbeya of the Central African Republic do not seem to feel under any obligation to talk in social situations, that for them 'speech, not silence, is what gets a person into trouble'.

Samarin, in comparing the use of silence between Americans and the Gbeya, concludes that the American expects 'straight talk' from his in-terlocutors and does not understand silence at all. Casual conversation between an American and a speaker of a 'silent language' is liable to result in misunderstanding and disharmony (cf. Crocker 1980).

In Finland, children are traditionally not supposed to be engaged in conversation with adults unless the adults clearly indicate their wish to enter a conversation with them. Children may only talk under the conditions set by adults in the speech situation. At meals, silence rather than talk is the rule; it is not considered necessary to be engaged in social small talk while eating. This may have very important implications for socialization because for the important in-group of the family, meals are one of the few social situations where all the members are present.

The reasons for Finnish silence may also be at least partly historical. In Finland, the rural population, which until the 1960s meant a majority of the population, used to live in separate houses instead of villages. The forms of social interaction which developed in this situation were quite different from what develops in communities which offer more possibilities for interpersonal contacts. The scarcity of social contacts is reflected also in international relationships and cross-cultural contacts. The impact of international contacts is being felt in Finland today, and we predict that as a result the number of 'silent Finns' will be reduced considerably in the future. Many people see foreign influences as a threat to Finnish culture (see Sajavaara and Lehtonen 1980a), but if the result is a more communicative Finn, the development is not certainly for the worse.

REFERENCES

Allwood, Jens. 1981. Finns det svenska kommunikationsmönster? (Are there any Swedish communications models?) In Vad är svensk kultur (What is Swedish culture). Papers in anthropological linguistics 9. Göteborg: Institutionen för lingvistik.
Allwood, Jens. n.d. Ickeverbal kommunikation. En översikt. (Nonverbal communication. A survey) Papers in anthropological linguistics 2. Gothenburg (Göteborg): University of Gothenburg.
Baker, Sidney J. 1955. The theory of silences. The Journal of General Psychology 53. 145–167.
Bergroth, Hugo. 1916. Finlandssvenska. Handledning till undvikande av provinsialismer i tal och skrift. (Introduction to the avoidance of provincialism in speech and writing) Borgå: Holger Schildt.
Bruneau, Thomas J. 1980. Chronemics and the verbal-nonverbal interface. The relationship of verbal and nonverbal communication, ed. by Mary Ritchie Key. The Hague: Mouton.
Condon, John C., Jr. 1978. Intercultural communication from a speech communication perspective. Intercultural and international communication, ed. by Fred L. Casimir, Washington, DC: University Press of America.
Crocker, Jim. 1980. Nine instructional exercises to teach silence. Communication Education 29 (1). 72–77.
Erickson, Frederick. 1979. Talking down: Some cultural sources of miscommunication in interracial interviews. Nonverbal behavior applications and cultural implications, ed. by Aaron Wolfgang. New York: Academic Press.
Grice, H. Paul. 1975. Logic and conversation. Syntax and semantics: Speech acts, Vol. 3, ed. by Peter Cole & Jerry L. Morgan, 41–58. New York: Academic Press.
Hakulinen, Auli and Fred Karlsson. 1977. Den finländska tystnaden. Några teoretiska, deskriptiva och kontrastiva bidrag (The Finnish silence. Some theoretical, descriptive, and contrastive comments). Vardagsskrifter till Jan och Jens (Working-day papers to

Jan and Jens), ed. by Tove Skutnabb-Kangas & Olang Rekdal. Uppsala: Inst. för nordiska sprak.

Hakulinen, Lauri. 1979. (1941). Suomen kielen rakenne ja kehitys (The structure and development of the Finnish language) 4th ed. Helsinki: Otava.

Harper, Robert G., Arthur N. Wiens, and Joseph D. Matarazzo. 1978. Nonverbal communication. The state of the art. New York: John Wiley & Sons.

Kuusi, M., ed. 1953. Vanhan kansan sananlaskuviisaus (Old folks proverb wisdom). Helsinki: Werner Söderström.

Lehtonen, Jaakko. 1979. Speech rate and pauses in the English of Finns, Swedish-speaking Finns, and Swedes. Perception and production of English: Papers on interlanguage, ed. by Rolf Palmberg. AFTIL 6. Turku: Abo Akademi, Department of English.

Lehtonen, Jaakko and Hannele Heikkinen. 1981. Anglismit ja tekstin luettavuus (Anglicisms and text readability). Virittäjä 1981 (4). 327–339.

Murray, D.C. 1971. Talk, silence and anxiety. Psychological Bulletin 4. 244–260.

Samarin, William J. 1964. The language of silence. Practical Anthropology 11. 115–119.

Sajavaara, Kari and Jaakko Lehtonen. 1980a. English influence on modern Finnish: Sociolinguistic aspects. Congressus Quintus Internationalis Fennougristarum VIII: Pars III, Turku.

Sajavaara, Kari and Jaakko Lehtonen. 1980b. The analysis of cross-language communication: Prolegomena to the theory and methodology. Towards a cross-linguistic assessment of speech production, ed. by H. W. Dechert & M. Raupach. Kasseler Arbeiten für Sprache und Literatur 7. Frankfurt/M.: Peter Lang.

PART V

SILENCE AND NONVERBAL COMMUNICATION

Chapter 12

Interaction Structured Through Talk and Interaction Structured Through 'Silence'

Susan U. Philips
University of Arizona

The purpose of this chapter is to discuss the view that both talk and silence have very different structures and functions, depending on whether interaction is structured through talk or through silence. This view entails the assumption that wherever and whenever people have visual access to one another, they acquire information from one another's nonverbal behavior. Thus whenever there is silence in such circumstances, there will still always be nonverbal behavior that constitutes the organization of face-to-face interaction.

Interaction structured primarily through talk then refers to activity in which the attention of participants is focused primarily on the verbal utterances produced by those who are party to the interaction. A situation where a group of people sit around a table in relatively fixed positions, and do little physically with their bodies other than moving their mouths exemplifies the phenomenon of interaction structured through talk.

At the other end of a continuum is interaction structured through silence, or rather interaction in which focus of participants' attention and production and reception of messages is overwhelmingly through nonverbal physical activity in the visual channel. Dance, mime, coordinated physical labor, and athletic activity are all examples of interaction structured through physical activity.

Most interaction can best be conceived of as falling within the range between two ends of a continuum for which the two extreme ends are interaction structured exclusively through talk and interaction structured exclusively through silence or physical activity. Thus people often talk and eat or talk and walk at the same time, and much coordinated physical labor involves regular giving and receiving of verbal instructions. Nevertheless, for any given phase of interaction either talk or physical activity predominates, and it will be useful to consider the structure of interaction in terms of the consequences of the predominance of verbal activity versus physical activity.

INTERACTION STRUCTURED THROUGH TALK

Interaction structured through talk is different from interaction structured through silence in both the nature of the talk and the nature of the silence.

First, interaction of this sort entails relatively long chunks of talk, so that continuous flows of speech with little gap or overlap between speakers is characteristic (Sacks, Schegloff and Jefferson 1974). In our own society, the gaps in speech typically do not last more than a few seconds. In my own transcripts of interaction structured largely through talk, in classrooms and courtrooms, gaps of greater length usually involve recourse to visual stimuli in the form of written materials.

Interaction structured through talk can for the most part be comprehended without reference to the nonverbal environment. Nonverbal behavior in the form of facial expressions, gaze direction, and gestural patterns do provide relevant information. But when this information is missing, as when a tape-recording of a situated conversation is made, most of the conversation is comprehensible. One does not have to see what is going on to make sense of it.

There are several features of interaction structured through talk that contribute to this comprehensibility. First, there is considerable interdependence of utterances. A given utterance is understood through reference to the utterances around it. Those other utterances provide a context of interpretability for the utterance in question. Consider the utterance, 'that's right', as it fits into the following dialogue:

A. Marge will have to leave next week.
B. But she won't like it.
C. That's right.

The interpretability of 'that's right' depends on 'having heard' (Sacks 1967) what went before. One important aspect of such discourse coherence in interaction structured through talk is the phenomenon of anaphora. The term 'anaphora' is most often used to refer to the substitution of pronouns for full nouns in discourse where the referent is initially referred to by a full noun, and then by a pronoun (e.g. Halliday and Hasan 1976). Anaphoric pronoun use is evident in the discourse example above, where 'Marge' is replaced by 'she'. One feature of interaction structured through talk is that the full nouns must be returned to intermittently or else clarity of reference is lost. Thus one cannot as a rule use anaphoric pronouns indefinitely in interaction structured through talk.

Like anaphora, ellipsis also contributes to the interdependence of utterances in interaction structured through talk (Gunter 1963). Question-answer pairs regularly exhibit ellipsis:

> Q: Where did he go?
> A: To the store.

Here ellipsis refers to the deletion of part of the sentence in the answer, where the sentence can be made complete. For example 'He went to the store', is inferred from 'To the store' by retrieving the rest of it from the form of the question. Such deletion, where the rest of a sentence's structure can be inferred from preceding sentential material, is widespread in interaction structured through talk.

Thus far I have discussed two basic features of interaction structured through talk. First, talk itself provides the central structuring of interaction, which means that one can comprehend most of what is said without recourse to the nonverbal context. Second, discrete utterances and turns at talk are highly interdependent, largely through anaphora and ellipsis, so that one cannot understand a given utterance, without having heard what went before.

A third characteristic of interaction structured through talk is that utterances in such interaction are often quite complex, in that they have multiple embeddings or subordinate constructions. Examples of complex utterances from courtroom discourse are:

> 1. Judge: Mr. Identmen, if you would have your client at least at this point, sign the uh, conditions of release order that has the new trial date in it then he will be aware of that to that extent and then I will complete the balance of it once I've made my decision.
> 2. Judge: Okay [3 sec.] Has your attorney explained to you that before one can be found guilty of this offense they have to know or have good reason to know that the items were stolen?

Ochs (1979) has argued that there are more relative clauses in more planned speech, which suggests planning may be a factor in predicting within what contexts interaction structured through talk may be more or less complex. And Hill (1973) has argued that embedding is associated with the transmission of new information, and is less common in ritual language. Thus the locus of new information too may affect where, in interaction structured through talk, one will find greater or lesser complexity. My own legal data suggests complexity is often a feature of role differentiation as well. Thus in proceedings consisting primarily of talk between judges and defendants, the defendants' speech regularly exhibited less complexity than the judges'. But the main point here is that interaction structured through talk exhibits complexity, which is patterned in its distribution.

There are several major functions or meanings to silences or breaks in talk in interaction structured through talk. Silences can indicate a temporary shift to interaction structured through physical activity, or visual stimuli, as when talk is interspersed with pauses to eat, to pass food, to light another's cigarette, or to silently read a legal document in the midst of a legal proceeding. Here the nonverbal context takes over.

Silences may also be interpreted as junctures between turns at talk, or larger segments of interaction. Junctures are clearly associated with particular types of nonverbal behavior. Kendon (1967) and Duncan (1972) have both described body movements and gaze patterns associated with changes of speaker. And Erickson (1975), McDermott (1978), and Philips (1977) have all described movement patterns that constitute boundary markers for verbal units within the stream of interaction.

The behavioral marking of junctures in speech and their recognition or interpretation as present or absent are at the same time subject to cultural variation. Reisman (1974) and Tannen (Chapter 6) describe a society and a subculture respectively where there is more overlap of speakers than in 'our own' society, while Philips (1972) has described a situation where pauses are longer.

But the main point here to be noted is that silences can function as junctures or boundary markers of speech units in the flow of interaction structured through talk.

Finally, silences can be interpreted as gaps, where nothing is said to be happening, as Scollon (Chapter 2) observes. Such gaps can come to be seen as indication of a breakdown in interaction, if they go on long enough. We know little of how these silences differ nonverbally from the other two types of silences in interaction structured through talk. Clearly it is not really the case that literally 'nothing' goes on in silences perceived as gaps, for information continues to be sent and received in the visual channel through positioning and movement of various parts of the body. But the patterned facial expressions and hand movements associated with speech are stopped. There may be some sense in which patterns of physical behavior become disorganized as well, for there to be said to be a gap in talk.

Gaps, like junctures, are cultural constructs, and what may be perceived as a gap in one context or culture, may be perceived as a juncture in another.

These, then, are some features of interaction structured through talk.

We know as much about it as we do because recent studies of face-to-face interaction have focused almost exclusively on interaction structured through talk. Conversation (Sacks, Schegloff, and Jefferson 1974), therapeutic interviews (Labov and Fanshel 1977), classroom interaction (Mehan 1979), and legal defense (Philips 1979) and depositions (Walker, Chapter 4) are all examples of interaction structured through talk. As we will see, considerably less attention has been given to interaction structured through silence.

INTERACTION STRUCTURED THROUGH 'SILENCE'

By interaction structured through silence, I refer to those activities for which the focus of attention is in the visual rather than the auditory channel. More specifically, I have in mind interaction in which individuals focus their attention on the physical behavior of other persons, rather than on primarily solitary activity like reading or sewing, or repairing a car, where the focus of attention is also visual.

In practice, activity for which the focus of attention is visual and physical involves a diversity of arrangements of such a focus. Thus the relation of mutual monitoring of two dancers, who are coordinating their actions, is quite different from the relation between the dancers and the audience, where the monitoring is not mutual, or is quite differentiated in its nature. Similarly, the mutual monitoring of two people moving the same piece of furniture may be greater than and different from that of two factory workers operating identical but independent machines side by side.

My efforts here to begin characterization of the nature of talk and silence in interaction structured through silence are intended to apply to the full range of types of arrangements of focus of attention on human physical activity. But because relatively little is known about the organization of behavior in such interaction, the characterization may apply more successfully to some types of interaction structured through silence than to others.

Activities in which interaction is structured through silence vary in the extent to which talk occurs, and in the nature of that talk. There can be interludes or segments of interaction structured through talk in the midst of interaction structured through silence, as when two viewers of a football game are diverted from the game itself and chat briefly about past games they have seen. But the talk I wish to characterize here is the talk that *accompanies* a focus on physical activity, rather than that which turns away from it.

The first and most fundamental feature of talk in interaction structured through silence is that its comprehensibility depends on visual access to the nonverbal context, rather than on access to prior discourse, as in interaction structured through talk. In other words, one cannot understand what is being said without seeing what is going on, and utterances lack the interdependence one finds in interaction structured through talk.

Instead, the utterances are dependent on nonverbal context. Interestingly enough, however, the same devices used in interaction structured through talk to accomplish interutterance interdependence, are used to tie utterances to their nonverbal context in interaction structured through silence.

Just as pronouns are used anaphorically in interaction structured through talk, they are used deictically in interaction structured through silence. Thus in 'Give it to me', both 'it' and 'me' can be understood either through anaphora or deixis, depending on the larger organization of interaction at the time. It is likely, however, that the patterning of such proforms is different for interaction structured through silence than it is for interaction structured through talk. Most notably, in interaction structured through silence, pronouns and the proverb 'do', as in 'Don't do that', can be used repeatedly in sequence without the revival of full noun forms that is sometimes necessary in interaction structured through talk.

Ellipsis which involves the deletion of words in the production of utterances that are complete, but not full sentences in surface structure is also common in interaction structured through silence, as it is in those aspects of interaction structured through talk. Consider expressions like 'Got it', or 'The ball, the ball', and 'There'. But once again it appears that the elements retrievable from nonverbal context are different from the elements retrievable from past verbal context. Thus deletion due to retrievability from context will differ for the two kinds of talk.

A second feature of interaction structured through silence, which is evident in what has already been said, is that the syntactic forms of utterances are different from those in interaction structured through talk in frequency of occurrence. My overall impression is that the utterances in interaction structured through silence are more often nonsentence forms involving more deletion of words and less complexity of the sort created through embedding of one sentence within another. This lesser amount of embedding may be due to the lesser amount of planning of utterances and/or the lesser amount of transfer of new information in interaction structured through silence, but such interaction has been little enough studied that it is difficult to assess the factors involved.

In interaction structured through silence, silence fulfills obviously different functions than in interaction structured through talk. Quite simply, silence is not a gap in structure, but structure itself in the organization of interaction.

As I have already suggested, we know relatively little about either speech or silence in interaction structured through silence, when compared with our knowledge of interaction structured through talk. Almost all of the research on talk has focused on situations where the participants are doing nothing but sitting and talking.

There are reasons why this is the case. Interaction structured through talk is easier to gather data on. It is easier to tape record or videotape. And it is easier to analyze because one need not consider the nonverbal in the analysis. Academic researchers who make a living by talking may, along with other white-collar workers in industrialized societies, also overemphasize the importance of interaction structured through talk in the general scheme of life.

DISCUSSION

If we are concerned with the contributions of both verbal and nonverbal communication to the ordering of social life, and human endeavor in general, then it may be useful to inquire into the cross-cultural similarities and differences in the occurrence and functions of interaction structured through talk and interaction structured through silence.

Minimally, societies appear to differ in the amount of interaction structured through talk that their members engage in. In my own field work on the Warm Springs Indian Reservation (Philips 1980), I was struck by the extent to which Warm Springs Indians engaged in a proportion of interaction structured through silence that was much greater than that of people from a white middle-class background. Most noticeably, they spent more time in physical labor—procuring and processing foods, building and repairing households and household items. On the job working for a living, they worked as lumberjacks, maids, cooks, and road workers. More people in the community spent more time in recreation that was physical, particularly athletic competition and horseback riding. And more of Indian ritual involved physical action and activity.

It seems reasonable to hypothesize that in nonindustrialized nonliterate societies, people devote a larger proportion of time to interaction structured through a focus of attention on others' physical activity than in industrialized and/or literate societies. And there are probably other factors that similarly affect the relative occurrence of these two ideal types of interaction.

The relative functions of interaction structured through talk and interaction structured through silence also differ cross-culturally, as is evident in the greater use of talk than physical activity to structure white middle-class religious ritual when it is compared with Warm Springs Indian ritual, or with Quaker worship (Maltz, Chapter 7).

But there may also be commonalities cross-culturally in the allocation of the two types of interaction. Basso's (1972) Kalapalo data analysis, for example, suggests that where groups speaking different languages have intergroup encounters, joint ritual is largely nonverbal. This suggests that nonverbal modes of communication are more shared, more universal in the form-meaning relation. This may account in part for the very rapid cross-cultural transmission of sporting events, so that the same Western physical game sports are played today in radically different cultural settings.

The point of all this is that both talk and silence have been viewed largely in the context of interaction structured through talk. There is a need, then, to pay more attention to interaction structured through silence in our efforts to describe both the discourse structure of speech and the larger organization of communication in interaction as a whole.

REFERENCES

Basso, Ellen. 1972. The use of Portuguese relationship terms in Kalapalo (Xingu Carib) encounters: Changes in a central Brazilian communications network. Language in Society. 2. 1–21.
Duncan, Starkey. 1972. Some signals and rules for taking speaking turns in conversation. Journal of Personality and Social Psychology 23. 283–92.
Erickson, Frederick. 1975. One function of proxemic shifts in face-to-face interaction. Organization of behavior in face-to-face interaction, ed. by Adam Kendon, R. M. Harris & Mary Ritchie Key. 175–188. The Hague: Mouton.
Gunter, R. 1963. Elliptical sentences in American English. Lingua 12. 137–50.
Halliday, M. A. K. and Ruqaiya Hasan. 1976. Cohesion in English. London: Longman.
Hill, Jane. 1973. Subordinate clause density and language function. You take the high node and I'll take the low node, ed. by Corum, C., T. C. Smith-Stark, & A. Weisen, 33–52, Papers from the Comparative Syntax Festival. Chicago: Chicago Linguistic Society.
Kendon, Adam. 1967. Some functions of gaze-direction in social interaction. Acta Psychologica 26. 22–63.
Labov, William and David Fanshel. 1977. Therapeutic discourse. New York: Academic Press.
McDermott, Ray P., Kenneth Gospodinoff and Jeffrey Aron. 1978. Criteria for an ethnographically adequate description of concerted activities and their contexts. Semiotica 24. 1–31.
Mehan, Hugh. 1979. Learning lessons. Cambridge: Harvard University Press.
Ochs, Elinor. 1979. Planned and unplanned discourse. Discourse and syntax, ed. by T. Givon, 51–80. New York: Academic Press.
Philips, Susan U. 1972. Participant structures and communicative competence. The functions of language in the classroom, ed. by Courtney Cazden, Vera John & Dell Hymes. 370–94. New York: Teachers College Press.
Philips, Susan U. 1977. The role of spatial positioning and alignment in defining interactional units: The American courtroom as a case in point. Paper presented at the 1977 American Anthropological Association Meetings, Houston, Texas.
Philips, Susan U. 1982. The language socialization of lawyers: Acquiring the cant. Doing the ethnography of schooling: Educational anthropology in action, ed. by George Spindler. New York: Holt, Rinehart & Winston.

Philips, Susan U. 1983. The invisible culture: Communication in classroom and community on the Warm Springs Indian reservation. New York: Longman.
Reisman, Karl. 1974. Contrapuntal conversations in an Antiguan village. Explorations in the ethnography of speaking, ed. by Richard Bauman and Joel Sherzer, 110–124. Cambridge University Press.
Sacks, Harvey, Emanuel Schegloff, and Gail Jefferson. 1974. A simplest systematics for the organization of turn-taking for conversation. Language 50. 696–735.
Sacks, Harvey. 1967. Lecture Notes.

Chapter 13

Some Uses of Gesture*

Adam Kendon
Connecticut College

In this chapter I shall review some of the ways in which people use gesture in face-to-face interaction. I shall suggest that a careful consideration of these uses will have implications for theories about how ideas are stored in our heads; for theories about how utterances are planned and produced; and for any model we might wish to construct for the skills and implicit knowledge a competent interactor must be supposed to possess. Although the recent literature on gestural usage will be considered, the main argument will be developed with the use of examples collected in the course of ordinary participation in interaction in daily life. These observations will serve to illustrate the various ways in which gesture may be employed. It is the purpose of this chapter to draw attention to the variety of gestural usage and to point out some of the implications of this usage for theories of human communication.

The term 'gesture' will be used to mean any distinct bodily action that is regarded by participants as being directly involved in the process of deliberate utterance. Gesture, in my use of the term, comprises visible bodily action that is regarded by participants having 'given' (Goffman 1963) or intended communication as its primary function. Although I share the widely held assumption that all actions, insofar as they provide information for others, participate in the communication process, I wish

*Earlier versions of this paper were presented at the Second Congress of the International Association for Semiotic Studies in Vienna in 1979 and at the meetings of the Northeastern Anthropological Association in Amherst, Massachusetts in March 1980. A version similar to the one given here was presented to the New England Child Language Association in New London, Connecticut in April 1980 and to the University of South Carolina, also in April 1980. I should like to acknowledge the generosity of the Henry R. Luce Foundation and also help received from the Faculty Travel and Research Fund at Connecticut College.

to distinguish—as ordinary participants in practice also distinguish (Kendon 1978)—those actions that are taken in the course of deliberately conveying something to another from those that are not. Bodily actions that are deemed to be produced in the service of such deliberate or intended communication—whether or not they they are produced in association with spoken utterance—will be referred to here as 'gesture'.

Included here are such actions as beckoning, waving, or thumbing the nose which do not depend upon a context of speech for their comprehension. Also included, of course, are the various pantomimic actions that a person may improvise during the course of speech. We also include as gesture *gesticulation*—the actions of wagging the head or waving the arms in vigorous talk. What are not included, besides patterns of behavior deemed to be reactive or emotionally expressive, are those numerous small actions, such as self-touching or 'nervous' movements which, however revealing of a person's mood or character they may be for others, are yet not regarded as part of what that person can be held to be fully responsible for and are not included in what Goffman (1974) has referred to as the 'story line' track of the interaction. It will be clear that the boundary between what is to be regarded as deliberate and what is to be regarded as unintentional, inadvertent, subconscious, or unconscious cannot be sharply drawn. In our daily dealings with one another, however, we all, in effect, attempt to draw such a boundary (Kendon 1978). It is with visible bodily actions that are regarded as falling within the range of conscious or deliberate action that I am concerned. It is these that I shall refer to as 'gesture'.

Gesture, in the sense in which I am using the term here, can carry in varying amounts the functional burdens of spoken utterance, depending upon circumstance. Where speech is impossible, whether because of sensory incapacity, as in deafness (Stokoe 1980), because of environmental circumstances, as in sawmills (Meissner and Philpott 1975), or because of speech taboos, as among Australian aborigines (Meggitt 1954, Kendon 1980a), gesture can become elaborated to the point where it can take over all of the functions of spoken utterance. However, gesturing is also widely employed by people who have speech fully available to them, and it is to this everyday use of gesture that I wish to attend here. I am especially interested in the nature of the circumstances in which we find gesture to be employed by speaking individuals in speech situations. A study of these circumstances may enable us to see how the two different media that utterance employs, the gestural and the aural, are suited to somewhat different communication tasks and are used accordingly.

Gesture and speech, considered as media of expression, have very different properties. First, since gesture requires sight for its transmission where speech requires hearing, the conditions that are suitable for the reception of the one do not necessarily coincide with the conditions required for the reception of the other. However, we may also note that the two modes of expression can occur simultaneously, and when they do they need not interfere with one another. It is possible, in fact, for participants to receive information from gesture at the same time as they are receiving information from speech, and this, as we shall see, has important consequences for how gesture may be employed.

Second, the way in which information is preserved in the two media tends to be very different. In spoken utterance the elements by which meaning is conveyed are concatenated in temporal sequence, and the way in which such sequences are organized depends not so much upon what meaning is being conveyed as it does upon rules of syntax. Whether one is describing action, referring to the visible appearances of things, or giving an account of spatial relationships, in spoken language the lexical elements by which meaning is conveyed have to be related to one another by rules that govern either their form or their sequential order, or both, and these rules impose a structure on spoken utterance which conforms it to the rules of the language system, in the first instance, and only indirectly to any aspect of the structure of what is being referred to. In contrast, in gesture, motions can be employed which have a direct relationship to action sequences; pictorial diagrams may be produced; spatial relationships can be directly portrayed; and parts of the body, and even the whole body, can be moved around as if they were actual objects. This means that there are possibilities available for expression in gesture of a different order from those which are available for spoken utterance.[1]

We shall note that, despite such radical differences, these two modes of expression are employed together in a highly integrated fashion, participants often freely choosing between the two modes, or employing a combination of them, to meet the requirements of the communication task at hand. We shall see that, in the organization of the utterance, the employment of speech and gesture are planned for together, at the outset. The encoding of the substance of the utterance into a spoken language form is only part of the process. Aspects of the substance may also be encoded simultaneously into gesture (cf. Kendon 1972a, 1975, 1983). We may ask, however, which aspects these are. Here I suggest that we may seek the answer to this question by examining the occasions of gestural usage. Given that gesture, as a mode of expression, has very different

---

[1]For a discussion of the expressive possibilities of gesture, as compared to those of speech, see Hockett's comments on 'syntactic dimensionality' in Hockett (1978), and discussion in Stokoe (1974, 1979). Huttenlocher's (1975) paper is also extremely useful. All of these discussions, it should be added, are done in reference to sign language, but they have full relevance for the use of gesture generally.

properties from those of speech, we may expect that it may be suitable for a rather different range of communication tasks. What are the communication tasks for which it is employed, and to what extent is the use of gesture fitted appropriately to the changing demands of the interaction situation?

RESEARCH ON GESTURE

Previous work on gesture has rarely attended to how it is employed. There are very few investigations indeed, it would seem, which have attempted to examine in detail, within the context of speech situations, just what information is encoded in gesture, how it is encoded, and what function any of this information may have for cointeractants. There are a number of studies of highly coded (or emblematic) gestures, but these have rarely done more than list such items and provide verbal glosses for them. Examples of such gestural listings include Saitz and Cervenka (1972), Green (1968), Munari (1963), Wylie (1977), Sparhawk (1978), and Barakat (1973). Although several workers have explored the origins and history of such gestures (Taylor 1956; Morris, Collett, Marsh, and O'Shaughnessy 1979), there is no study that I know of that has looked into their interactional uses. Studies of gesturing in association with speech have mainly been concerned with it as a symptom of a general psychological state, of cognitive style, or, in a few cases, from the point of view of such evidence as it may provide about the processes by which thoughts are encoded into speech. Some writers (for example, McNeill [1979] and also Kendon [1972a]) seem to take the view that such gesturing is significant only from the point of view of the light it may throw on such inner processes. As McNeill has put it: 'gesticulation can be viewed as an external dynamic trace of the internal speech program' (1979:12).

Efron (1941), in his well-known comparative study of the gesturing styles of Southern Italians and East European Jews, did offer a number of observations on how speech-concurrent gesture could relate to what was being said. He suggested that some gestures seem to serve as batons, marking out the rhythmical organization of the speech. Some gestures seem to have what he called an ideographic relationship to the speech, providing a dynamic diagram of the logical structure of what is being said. Yet other gestures may provide depictions of actions or objects serving, he suggested, rather as if they were slides illustrating what is said in words. Ekman and his colleagues have lately revived Efron's observations (Ekman and Friesen 1969; Ekman 1977). They have provided a list of eight different ways in which speech-concurrent gesturing may relate to the speech content. These are referred to as 'types of illustrators' (Ekman 1977). As yet, however, Ekman's observations remain in summary form, and he has provided no detailed analyses. Furthermore, he has published no studies of the ways in which these may be employed by interactors, and how they may benefit the interaction when they are employed.

Graham and Argyle (1975) have published an experimental study which does show that recipients may, under some circumstances, make direct use of information that speech-concurrent gestures may provide. Furthermore, their results show that people of some cultural backgrounds may be inclined to make more use of the gestures offered by a speaker than others do. In their study, subjects were confronted with the task of drawing a geometrical figure of greater or lesser complexity that was described to them by a sender. Under some conditions the senders were permitted to use gestures; under other conditions they were not. It was found for all recipients that accuracy in understanding the drawing that was described was greater in the conditions in which gestures were employed than in the condition where they were not employed. However, in a comparison of Italian with English speaker-recipient pairs, it was found that the Italians showed a much greater improvement when they had gestures available, suggesting that they are more inclined to make use of the information available in concurrent gesticulation in these circumstances than are the English. This finding agrees with Efron's (1941) observation that the Italians in his sample had a very strong tendency to employ pictorial gestures when talking, as well as having an extensive repertoire of emblems.

Birdwhistell (1970) has presented several detailed studies of how movement concurrent with speech is patterned in relation to it. He describes how contrastive movement patterns differentially mark stress in speech, and also how they mark pronominals and deictic particles. He provides a highly interesting summary of these observations in which he suggests that the *direction* of movement of a moving body part marking a pronominal or deictic particle is systematically related to the meaning of the particle. Thus in association with *this, here, now, I,* and *we,* the body part moves towards the speaker. In association with *that, there, then, you,* and *they,* the body part moves away from the speaker. He also says that the form of the movement differs according to whether the word being kinesically marked is plural or singular (Birdwhistell 1966).

Birdwhistell, however, offers little in the way of concrete evidence for the part such patterning in speech-associated body movement may play in the communication process, though he does make several suggestions. He suggests, for example, that it is of communicative value in virtue of the fact that, in paralleling speech in this manner, it contributes to the redundancy of the uttered message. The availability of the same message in more than one channel allows for communication to take place in a wider range of circumstances and among people more variously equipped with capacities to send and receive than would otherwise be the case (Bird-whistell 1970:107–108). He also suggests, however, that certain kinesic actions may be functionally *equivalent* to linguistic items. Thus he says, 'both the kinesic and the linguistic markers may be alloforms, that is, structural variants of each other' (1970:127).

Sherzer (1973) has illustrated this last point in some detail in his study of the use of lip pointing among the Cuna Indians of Panama. He shows how lip pointing can be used in conjunction with spoken utterance in a variety of ways. Sherzer argues, however, that analysis of the functions of lip pointing must be done in conjunction with an analysis of the discourse structure of Cuna speech events. Thus he shows how a gestural element must be considered as fully integrated with spoken linguistic elements in the Cuna linguistic system.

The view that gestural elements may serve at the same level of functioning as spoken elements with a discourse has also been urged by Slama-Cazacu (1976), who has pointed out how kinesic elements, whether of the face or of the hands, can be inserted into utterances in such a way that they can replace elements that might otherwise have been spoken. She refers to this phenomenon as 'mixed syntax', and offers a series of examples—for instance, a film director who calls to the lights man 'Five balcony' and makes a motion of moving a light switch as he does so; or a foreman instructing a worker in an electrical plant how to roll a coil who says 'I've told you, like this' as he rolls one hand around the other.

Slama-Cazacu concludes:

> As far as expression is concerned, the entire message is achieved, from a peripheral viewpoint, simultaneously or with slight contrapuntal over-lapping, both verbally and kinesically, and its reception is equally bivalent. Yet the mental elaboration of the message, as far as the emitter is concerned, as well as the synthesis of the elements at the moment of decoding, is achieved at a single level. (1976:225)

Kinesic elements thus achieve, with words, a synthesis into a single code, 'structured *sui generis* and comprising verbal and (kinesic) elements mutually modified and fused in *linguistically* analyzeable units' (Slama-Cazacu 1976:225, author's emphasis).

The observations of Sherzer and Slama-Cazacu are of particular interest, because they show how gesture may function on the same level as speech. They show that gesture does more than 'illustrate' what is being said. Rather, the gestural elements are an integral part of what is being said. However, neither Sherzer nor Slama-Cazacu nor Birdwhistell nor anyone else, as far as I can find out, has sought to investigate to which aspects of an utterance gesture may be selected to contribute, nor has anyone attempted to examine whether this selection is related in any systematic way to the requirements of the interaction situation.

EXAMPLES OF GESTURAL USAGE

In order to pursue these questions, I have begun to collect examples of gestural usage. These examples are collected from occasions of interaction in which I myself have been a participant, and in many cases the communicative effectiveness of the gestures observed was directly appreciated by me. Notes were made on each occurrence as soon after as was convenient.[2] All of the occurrences collected are spontaneous, and I have tried to analyze them from the point of view of how the circumstances of the interaction made the employment of gesture especially appropriate.

I shall now review some of these examples, and on the basis of this review I shall argue that participants in interaction are often highly skilled in their use of gesture. I shall maintain that any model that we might wish to develop of the interacting person will have to include a *practical* knowledge of the different properties of the two media of expression and we shall also have to agree that interactants have a capacity to engage in a continuous assessment of the interaction situation, from the point of view of how suited it is to the differential employment of these two modes of expression.

First of all, we may note that gesture is often made use of when the communication circumstances make it difficult or impossible for speech to be received. Distance is one such circumstance and too high a level of ambient noise is another.

Within occasions of conversation it sometimes happens that a momentary increase in ambient noise makes hearing impossible. It seems that interactants may be quite sensitive to this and that they may, in conjunction with such noise increases, bring in the use of gesture to overcome the momentary blocking of the speech channel. Thus, my son was explaining to me something about fencing, as we were driving into town one day. He said 'You know, how they do in fencing.' Just as he said the word 'fencing' a large truck went by, making the word inaudible. He

---

[2]Schiffrin (1977), in her useful study of greeting encounters, employed a very similar method in gathering her examples. Obviously, such a method cannot provide us with representative samples of gestural usage free from observer bias. The examples accumulated in this way are the result of chance, luck, and of the observer happening to be in a particular mood. On the other hand, the method does provide a wide range of examples which can serve to illustrate the kinds of uses people make of gesture, and for this purpose, I would argue, it is perfectly adequate.

immediately continued 'you know/GESTURE/fencing'. For the gesture he used a movement of the hand that enacted a bit of the hand movement one might employ if one were using a sword in a duel. Here he brought in a gestural representation of part of the action of fencing just as he began his restatement. What is notable here is that the recourse to gesture was directly in response to the increased ambient noise. He appreciated exactly what it was I had not heard in the sentence he had just uttered and, without hesitation, he was able to deploy an alternate mode of expressing it that overcame the transmission difficulties that the sudden increase in ambient noise had created. In other words, he had a clear appreciation of the communication conditions prevailing and he brought in gesture, as appropriate, to meet them.

The speech channel may be momentarily blocked by noise, but it may also be blocked because it is already occupied. In multiparty conversations one may occasionally observe the employment of gesture by participants who are not, for the moment, engaged directly in a current spoken utterance exchange, so that some additional exchange may be accomplished. Thus, seven people were at dinner in a country cottage in the mountains. One person, a guest and also a notorious monologuist, is holding forth at length. A strange noise is heard outside in the valley. One member looks across the table to another with raised eyebrows. The other replies by raising two fisted hands, palms facing downwards, and then lowering them sharply, as if pushing down a blaster's plunger, thereby suggesting that the strange noise was due to blasting. Later, when the hostess must tell her husband to go and make the coffee, she can do so without interrupting the monologuist, again by means of gesture. Gesture, evidently, need not intrude upon the sustained forms of talk. It can be both enacted, at least briefly, and received concurrently, with the sustainment of the main focus of involvement in talk.

Some exchanges may, of course, involve the talker himself. A professor giving a talk to a seminar of about 30 people found himself at a loss for a particular expression. A member of the audience held up her hands in an arrangement that suggested to the speaker the word 'brackets', which exactly fitted the sense of what it was that he was trying to say. In this case the listener, by employing gesture, made her suggestion to the speaker without interrupting his flow of speech and without altering the attention structure of the seminar situation. By making this suggestion gesturally the listener did not establish a turn for herself in the audience-speaker system and, thereby, she did not force the speaker to specifically acknowledge her suggestion as she would have done if she had made her suggestion verbally. Her gesture thus served to make her suggestion merely available to the speaker, which he was free to take up or to ignore as he chose.

This example draws our attention to one feature of gesture which is that, for its employment, people do not seem to have to enter into the same kind of relationship of mutual obligation with regard to one another that they do when they engage in a spoken utterance exchange. It would appear that gestural exchanges can take place between people who have not otherwise established themselves in a 'state of talk' together and who have not, thus, entered into the complex of ritual obligations that are thereby implied, such as the turn-taking system. Clearly, it takes time for people to negotiate such a state of talk and accordingly, if, in the employment of gesture, such negotiations may be bypassed, gestural exchanges may under some circumstances be much faster than speech exchanges. Furthermore, because gestural exchanges do not require the ritual arrangements of talk, to address someone in gesture may sometimes be undertaken as a way of addressing them without demanding that they relinquish their current involvement, whatever that may be, and without implying that one is oneself expecting to establish a sustained encounter with them.

For example, a travel agent is talking on the phone, sitting behind a desk which faces toward the glass door of the agency which opens on to the street. A man opens the door, leans in toward the travel agent while still holding the door with his left hand. He extends his right hand toward the agent, jerks his extended thumb upwards, and then rotates his forearm to point his thumb downwards. The travel agent responds with an upwardly jerked thumb, cups his hand over the phone, and calls out a date to him. In this instance, the customer—by addressing the travel agent in gesture—not only employed a mode of address to which the recipient could have replied without relinquishing his current involvement, but by employing that mode of address he at the same time indicated that he intended to ask his question in passing, and that he did not intend to enter with the travel agent into any sort of sustained focused interaction.

That gestural exchanges can be undertaken without the full establishment of the ritual obligations of focused interaction that spoken utterance exchanges seem to require derives, we suggest, from its character as a silent, visual medium of expressing. In consequence, we find not only that gestural exchanges can be employed in such 'in passing' interactions as we have just described, but also that gesture is often adopted as a medium of utterance where the utterer seeks to be less fully bound or officially committed to what he or she has to say. Thus it is that we find gesture being adopted as a substitute for speech, where speech might be regarded as too explicit or indelicate.

For example K, a dinner guest of D, was sitting with D in D's living room after dinner, drinking coffee. D himself had not taken a cup of coffee and this fact became a topic of conversation when D offered K a second cup. D, in fact, wanted K to go home, although it was still early and not long since D and K had finished eating. D explained why he was not having any coffee. He said: 'Last night I had more coffee than usual at the restaurant and I didn't sleep well, so maybe we oughta/GESTURE/.' In this gesture he placed his two extended index fingers side by side and then extended both arms away from himself and upwards in the direction of the door. He thereby clearly indicated that he and K should leave (D had to drive K home). In this example, thus, for just that part of the utterance which was socially awkward for D, a gestural expression was chosen.

It will also be seen, in this example, how D's gesture was fully integrated with the *spoken* part of the utterance. A complete analysis of his utterance would not be possible except by considering his gestural expression fully on a par with what he had said in words. This is an excellent example of the phenomenon of 'mixed syntax' described by Slama-Cazacu to which we have already referred.

So far, all of the examples I have given are examples in which the gestural element alternates with a spoken element, either serving as a complete utterance in itself or, as in the last example, as an element in an utterance in which spoken elements and gestured elements are mixed. However, gestured elements may co-occur with spoken utterances where the spoken utterance, taken by itself, is grammatically complete. In many of these cases, however, we find that if the gestural element is ignored the utterance remains informationally incomplete and its function within the discourse in which it occurs cannot be accounted for.

A common form of such concurrent use of gesture can be observed in the employment of directional or pointing movements by speakers. These directional or pointing movements often serve to point to referents which are referred to, in speech, only by determiners or pronominals and the pointing movements may thus disambiguate the referents of such particles.

Sherzer (1973), as I have already mentioned, has provided quite a detailed study of the different ways in which the Cuna Indians may use lip pointing. He fails to mention, however, whether the Cuna use other methods of pointing as well. American and British English speakers do not use lip pointing, as far as I know, but they readily employ any other body part that happens to be available for a directional movement, as well as pointing with the index finger. The head, the eyes, and elbows, even the whole body, may be employed in producing a directional movement with a deictic function. Birdwhistell (1966, 1970), as I have also already mentioned, drew attention to this some years ago in his analysis of what he called kinesic pronominal markers. Such directional movements in

association with pronominals and other deictic words are often important, for they provide a necessary disambiguation. Thus, at a recent
meeting of anthropologists, a colleague—on seeing the chairman of a
symposium in which he was to participate approaching him—said:
'Where are we gonna be?' The chairman replied, as he hurried forward
with his arms fully loaded with books and slide boxes, 'Oh/GESTURE/in
here'. Between 'oh' and 'in here' he jerked his head backwards in a rapid
movement, directing the back of it towards the door of the room from
which he had just emerged. The deictic word 'here', without the clarification the head jerk provided, would not have sufficed.

Such pointing movements do not only occur in association with pronominals and determiners, however. A husband, at the end of the day,
was sitting in the living room talking in a casual way with his wife about
what the children had done during the day. At one point he said: 'They
made a cake, didn't they'. The word 'cake' in this phrase received primary stress. It was also marked by a movement of the head. In this case, the
head moved in a rightward tilt over 'cake' in the direction of the window
which overlooked the garden. Here the speaker was pointing with his
head to the garden in which, so he had been told by the children, a mud
cake had been made. By pointing to the garden as he said 'cake' he
referred the cake to its location, thereby specifying that it was indeed the
mud cake to which he was referring, and not some other cake. (This
example was reported earlier in Kendon 1972b.)

The uses of pointing are many, and the two examples I have given here
will serve only as reminders of some of them. In the last example it will be
noted how what was referred to in the head point could have been accommodated in a phrase, such as 'in the garden'. Had the speaker said this,
however, it would have taken more time, and it is possible that on occasion concurrent gesture is employed as a means of 'telescoping' what one
wants to say where the turn-space that one has available is smaller than
one would really like it to be. The following example, involving this time a
characterizing gesture rather than a pointing gesture, may be an instance
of this. It also shows how a characterizing gesture may be used for disambiguation.

I have a Minolta SLR camera, and whenever I refer to this in my family
I always refer to it as 'my Minolta'. Recently, I acquired a Minolta super-8
movie camera. Consequently the word 'Minolta' became ambiguous, for it
could refer either to my SLR camera or to the super-8 movie camera. In
the course of a conversation with my son—soon after this new camera
had been acquired—he said to me: 'you could do it with yours, your
Minolta'. As he said 'Minolta' he lifted his hands up, thumb and forefinger
of each hand extended at right angles to one another and held on either
side of his face, thereby modeling the action of holding a camera in front

of his eyes, as one would when snapping a photograph with it. By doing this he disambiguated 'Minolta', clearly indicating that it was the SLR he was referring to and not the movie camera. In this instance it would appear that the speaker had anticipated his recipient's possible misunderstanding and he added a gestural characterization as he said 'Minolta' as a way of making sure that it was clear what it was he meant. One can also see that he succeeded in specifying the particular camera he meant within the time it takes to utter the word 'Minolta'. Had he been less urgent about his talk, or had the turn slot he had available to him at that time been longer, he might have employed a verbal expression instead. It would seem that gesture can be employed in this way as a means of telescoping into a currently available time segment, more than could otherwise be provided if only words were being used.

OTHER USES OF GESTURE: BEYOND WORDS

Gesture, of course, does not only come in handy as an alternative or substitute for what otherwise might be said in words. It also comes in handy because, being the kind of expressive medium that it is, it allows for the possibility of representing aspects of experience that can be represented in words at best only indirectly and in some respects not at all. It is impossible to display the *appearance* of action except by some form of action, for example. The representation of spatial arrangements cannot be accomplished directly in words, but by moving the hands or the body about in space it is possible to demonstrate them.

Accordingly, it is not uncommon to observe speakers incorporating gesture into their utterance where the gesture is employed, not as a substitute or alternative to speech, but as an additional component of the utterance in which aspects of what they are referring to are represented, which are not represented in the words that are being used.

Three examples will be given here. When an Englishman first arrives in the Eastern United States and encounters the Sunday edition of the *New York Times* he is always amazed at its enormous bulk. It is almost always a matter for remark. An Englishman who has lived for many years in the United States encountered one Monday morning a compatriot who had only arrived the week before, and he fell into conversation with him at a railroad station while waiting for the arrival of a train. In the course of exploring his reactions to things American, the resident Englishman said: 'Have you made your acquaintance with the/GESTURE/*New York Times*'. The gesture he here employed was one in which he first placed his two hands forward, palms facing each other, and he then placed them one above the other, palms facing downwards, thereby depicting a thick oblong object. The newly-arrived Englishman laughed in response, and comments on the size of the Sunday *New York Times* were duly exchanged. The gesture in this example, it will be noted, provided a visual representation of just the feature of the Sunday *New York Times* that always surprises an Englishman. What the speaker was attempting to do here was to recreate the surprising appearance of the Sunday *New York Times* for his recipient, for in doing so he thereby can make a direct reference to that moment when the Sunday *New York Times* is first encountered and he thereby can recreate that first encounter in something like the form in which it actually occurs. A verbal description of the size and weight of the Sunday *New York Times* could not achieve this. In his effort to get his compatriot to relive that surprising moment, he provides him, in his gesture, with a depiction that will call up again the reaction that he had upon first seeing and handling the Sunday *New York Times*.

It will be noted, of course, that although 'Have you made your acquaintance with the *New York Times*' is a perfectly good sentence in itself, unless we had the gestural component, we could not give a proper account of how it functioned within the particular context in which it occurred. Although, in this example, the gesture does not substitute for any element within the spoken part of the utterance as we had seen it can do in other instances, it is, nevertheless, an integral part of what the utterer had said. We cannot here say, any more than we can in our previous examples, that the gestural component can be left out of any analysis of the utterance as a linguistic event. The gesture, it will further be noted, occurred precisely as the speaker said 'with the', the first part of it over 'with', the second part over 'the'. This makes it clear that the gesture was not added in as an afterthought, but was incorporated from the very first as an integral part of the entire utterance plan. The utterance, in its construction, thus had both verbal and gestural components. The gestural component was designed to take care of an aspect of the utterance that the verbal component was not appropriate for. There was, thus, differentiation of function incorporated into the utterance plan.

The second example further illustrates this point. A lecturer was discussing the behavioral forms of baboons. He was describing how a certain behavioral form was to be seen as having an evolutionary history and how a current behavioral form was to be seen as being the outcome of a long process of natural selection. He said: 'under the influence of/GESTURE/in the end natural selection'. The gesture here was inserted in a pause between 'of' and 'in' and the gesture consisted in moving the hand, with index finger extended, from a position where the hand was extended well above the lecturer's head to close to the lecturer, in a series of arc-like movements. In this gesture the lecturer appeared to be diagramming a series of steps or stages, thereby indicating that the influence of natural selection he was here referring to was an indirect one, working through a long and complex chain of influences. The gesture, thus, augmented the verbal form at just the point where the verbal formulation did not incorporate the notion the lecturer clearly had of an extended succession of stages of influence. However, what we may further note is that the lecturer's pause here was just long enough for him to accomplish the gesture. The *preparation* for the gesture (cf. Kendon 1980b), which involved lifting the hand on an extended arm to the raised position from which the series of downward arc-like movements could be performed, was accomplished during the portion of the utterance in which he said 'under the influence of'. This means that the gestural form, here dealing with an aspect of what was to be expressed that was not included in the verbal formulation, was conceived of as an integral part of the whole utterance, well in advance of the point at which it would be needed. The program for carrying out the utterance was thus both verbal and gestural when it was initiated, yet the gestural form served to take care of an aspect of what was to be expressed that was not included in the verbal formulation adopted.

A third example: A fourteen year old boy had just returned from an excursion, and he was recounting his experience to his father, who had remained at home. The excursion had been to an open air museum located close to a large interstate highway. The boy described the very long queue of cars off the highway into the museum, and he described how he had visited a blacksmith's shop there and how they had had lunch at the cafeteria. He then described how he had seen a lady taking photographs of her children, but there were features of the woman's actions, her expression, and the behavior of the children that he found very amusing. When he reached this part of his narration he suddenly moved away from his father to the center of the room and acted out the actions of someone standing back, holding up a camera as if preparing to take a photograph. He then took up another position and acted out the actions of the children who the woman was trying to pose for the photograph. Throughout, he was talking, explaining what the woman and then the children did. It appeared that, in this instance, those parts of the boy's narrative that referred to events, such as the queue of cars, or settings, such as cafeterias and blacksmith shops which were familiar to both father and son, the son could narrate without using gesture. However, the incident involving the woman taking photographs was a unique event; it was an event which had, for the son, specific features unlike others he might have witnessed. In his recounting he wanted to represent those unique features which had struck him as interesting or amusing. Thus he sought to represent the event more completely in a form that came closer to the form in which he had actually witnessed it. A spoken account, no matter how well-wrought, would not approach a re-presentation of the event in a form that was similar to the event as it had been witnessed. In his effort to get his father to appreciate the event in the way he had when he had witnessed it, the boy had no other means but to act parts of it out.

In these examples, it will be seen, it is the character of gesture as a form of graphic representation that is being exploited. This character is being exploited to meet not transmission conditions of the interactional event, but the requirements of representational adequacy. In the last two of these examples, especially, the utterer decides where gestural action is required in the light of his understanding of the relationship between the verbal formulation he has available and the image that he wishes to convey.

These examples, it may be noted, appear to have implications for theories about how ideas are stored. It will be seen that, since the gestural expressions are fully integrated with the spoken aspects, they must be planned for together at the outset. This means that, however ideas are stored, they must be stored in a way that allows them to be at least as readily encoded in gestural form as in verbal form.

The issue of the mental representation of ideas has been the subject of much debate recently. There are those who maintain that ideas are represented in an abstract propositional format and that this is the same format that is used to encode verbal information (e.g. Pylyshyn 1973). On the other hand, there are those who believe that the representation of ideas is modality-specific, and that visual ideas are encoded in terms of structures that are spatial and that are transforms of the things they represent (e.g., Metzler and Shepard 1974, Shepard 1978). Anderson (1978) has reviewed these positions and argued that at the present time it will not be possible, using the techniques available in experimental psychology, to decide whether all ideas are encoded propositionally or whether they may be encoded pictorially as well. Either hypothesis, he argues, accounts equally well for experimental findings.

Here it is suggested that the observations offered on the deployment of gesture as an integral part of an utterance show that any theory of representation that gives primacy to a representational format modeled on spoken language structures will not do. There is some evidence that the expression of ideas in words takes longer to produce and is a more elaborate and demanding task than the expression of ideas in gestural form. Thus people may employ gestures to express something during pauses in their speech when they are searching for the correct form of words (Kendon 1975, Butterworth and Beattie 1978). Persons speaking a language foreign to them have also been observed to use more gestures than when they are speaking their own language (Elzinga 1978). It has also been observed that even in fluent speech, gestural expression may precede the speech with which it is associated (Kendon 1972a, 1975, Schegloff 1983). If the format in which all ideas are stored, whether visual or not, is the same as that used for storing verbal information, we would not expect this to be so. Indeed, we might expect gestural expression to follow verbal expression, and this it does not do.

The examples we have cited also have implications for our understanding of the processes of utterance production. It appears that utterers select different aspects of what they intend to convey for encoding in one expressive medium or the other. In formulating utterances it is as if they undertake a process of apportionment, assigning some aspects of what they have to say to gesture, other aspects to speech. Evidently in the formulation of an utterance, the utterer is able to match as yet unenacted utterance forms against the pre-encoded image of what it is they wish to say, and they are able to deploy available utterance forms, both spoken and gestural, in the light of this comparison. This implies that utterers' utterance formulations are available for inspection, as it were, before they have actually produced them, and they are able to compare their representation of meaning with the pre-encoded form in relation to which the current utterance has been formulated.

GESTURE AS A VISUAL EXPERIENCE

In this chapter I have given emphasis to the way in which an utterer will select a mode of formulation, not only in the light of a comparison between its adequacy of representation and the image that it is intended to convey, but also in the light of what the current communication conditions are. These include transmission conditions, as we have seen, but they also include an appreciation of the kind of impact a gestural formulation may have on a recipient as compared to a verbal formulation. I take it that gestural forms are often resorted to for insults and for urgent commands because a gestural action can be reminiscent of actual physical action, and it may derive some of its added forcefulness from this. Here, however, I wish to point out how gesture may also be selected because it is able to remind the recipient of the visual features of what is being referred to. As we saw in the *New York Times* example, this may be done to induce a particular mood or reaction in the recipient. By employing gesture, the visual experience itself may be more directly recalled for the recipient, and the recipient's response to this experience may thus also be recalled.

The use of gesture to recall the visual appearance of something may also be done, which the last example I shall now offer will suggest, as a way of showing that one particularly appreciates the visual appearance of something.

In this example a *recipient* of a spoken utterance engages in a gestural utterance, simultaneously with the spoken utterance, and in doing so displays understanding and appreciation of the event the speaker is describing. As Jefferson (1973) has described in her study of precison timing of spoken utterances, recipients in conversation will sometimes make a remark that overlaps precisely with a stretch of speech of a current speaker and which has the same form as the speech that it overlaps, and in doing this the recipient's appreciation or understanding of the current speaker's utterance may be displayed. In the example to be given this overlap was accomplished gesturally. Here the choice of gesture was especially apt because it was an impressive visual event that the speaker was describing.

In this example, A was in conversation with T, and he was listening as T described how he had watched a kestrel hover and then fold its wings and plunge to earth. T said: 'I saw a kestrel—ooh he must have been five hundred feet up. He hovered there and then he suddenly folded his wings and plummeted to earth.'

Precisely over 'folded his wings', A lifted his extended arm to shoulder height, folded the fingers of his hand together, and then dropped his hand rapidly. A was here in anticipation of T's description and, by producing this gesture, which depicts the sight that T was describing, he shares this description, displaying his appreciation of what it was that T was saying he had seen. Notice how appropriate a gestural utterance was here. T was describing something very impressive to see. What A did, in this gesture, was to depict the event in visual terms. Thus it is not only current speakers that will bring in gesture where their current verbal formulations are not adequate to the image they wish to convey. Recipients also may display their grasp of what another is saying by gestural utterance, which is chosen because it is a medium of graphic representation, capable of showing that it is the visual aspect of the event being described that is understood and appreciated.

CONCLUSIONS

Before concluding, I would like to point out that in this chapter I have been primarily concerned with the functions of gesture in respect to the referential meanings of utterance. In producing utterances, however, conversationalists not only make statements. They also try to persuade or seduce, to urge or command, to question or to obey. Gesture is deployed in the service of these aims also. When in a conversation a speaker said, 'But all the fires in the Bronx are arson', extending his slightly flexed arm laterally and pronating his forearm as he did so to expose his palm, he is not, with this gesture, thereby contributing to the proposition he has just asserted. He is, rather, displaying the attitude that informs his utterance at that moment, marking it as a move of a certain sort within the immediate conversational context. Likewise, when a daughter said to her mother, 'You don't know anything about it' and, as she did so, moved her arm laterally away from her in the direction of her mother with the palm of her hand toward her mother as if pushing her mother away, the gesture here served to enact the daughter's wish to exclude her mother from the discussion at the moment. It did not bear upon the referential meaning of what she had said.

A discussion of these functions of gesture is beyond the scope of the present chapter. Here I have confined my attention to how gesture may be employed to convey some propositional message and to show how it may be variously deployed in doing so. In particular I have attempted to suggest that the variety of ways in which gesture may contribute to this aspect of utterance functioning is systematically related to the utterer's assessment of how his communicative aims within a given interaction situation may best be served by its use. We have seen how it may be employed as a substitute for what might be said in words, to take advantage of its properties as a silent, visual means of expression, where such a means is more useful than a means that depends upon the transmission of sound. We have also seen how the use of gesture appears to bypass the ritual arrangements of talk situations, and that this feature may be taken advantage of when speed of exchange is at a premium or where neither party wishes to become drawn into a more demanding kind of encounter. Gesture also is often accorded a kind of 'unofficial' status—perhaps because it may be used in circumstances which do not demand the ritual structure that speech requires—and in consequence it may be used to say things that are delicate or not quite socially acceptable. However, because gesture makes possible the depiction of action, visible form, and spatial relationship, it is often employed in conjunction with speech, not so much to 'illustrate' what is being said, but to add to what is being said, to convey aspects of meaning that cannot readily be conveyed in words. Utterers, thus, often call upon gesture because words alone are not adequate to the task of representation that they have set for themselves.

We must see, thus, that gesture is not to be accounted for in terms of any simple idea. It is not adequate to account for it as a kind of motoric trace or by-product of the processes of speech production. Nor can we dismiss it as a mere paralinguistic decoration surrounding the verbal core of the utterance, illustrating it, perhaps, or marking out the rhythm of the speech, but not participating centrally in the task of the utterance, whatever this may be. On the contrary, it would appear that utterers frequently plan their utterances and execute them in a way that takes full account of the expressive possibilities of gesture. As our examples show, gesture frequently participates directly and systematically in the realization of the communicative aims of the utterer. We can best account for whether it is employed or not, and for how it is employed, I suggest, if we look upon it as an available resource, and try to see how participants deploy it in the light of how they understand how its properties may best meet the current communicational requirements of the interactional situation in which they are taking part.

REFERENCES

Anderson, J. R. 1978. Arguments concerning representations for mental imagery. Psychological Review 85. 249–277.

Barakat, Robert A. 1973. Arabic gestures. Journal of Popular Culture 6 (4). 749–787.

Birdwhistell, Ray L. 1966. Some relationships between American kinesics and spoken American English. Communication and culture, ed. by A. G. Smith. New York: Holt, Rinehart & Winston.

Birdwhistell, Ray L. 1970. Kinesics and context. Philadelphia: University of Pennsylvania Press.

Butterworth, Brian and Geoffrey Beattie. 1978. Gesture and silence as indicators of planning in speech. Recent Advances in the Psychology of Language: Formal and Experimental Approaches, ed. by R. N. Campbell and P. T. Smith. New York: Plenum Press.

DeLaguna, G. 1927. Speech: Its function and development. New Haven: Yale University Press.

Efron, David. 1941. Gesture and environment. New York: Kings Crown Press. (Republished in 1972: Gesture, Race and Culture. The Hague: Mouton.)

Ekman, Paul. 1977. Biological and cultural contributions to body and facial movement. The Anthropology of the Body, ed. by John Blacking. New York: Academic Press.

Ekman, Paul and Wallace V. Friesen. 1969. The repertoire of nonverbal behavior: Categories, origins, usage and coding. Semiotica 1. 49–98.

Elzinga, R. 1978. Temporal aspects of Japanese and Australian conversations. Unpublished PhD. dissertation, Australian National University, Canberra.

Goffman, Erving. 1963. Behavior in public places. New York: The Free Press of Glencoe.

Goffman, Erving. 1974. Frame analysis. New York: Harper and Row.

Graham, Jean Ann and Michael Argyle. 1975. A cross-cultural study of the communication of extra-verbal meaning by gestures. International Journal of Psychology 10. 57–67.

Green, Jerald R. 1968. Gesture inventory for the teaching of Spanish. Philadelphia: Chilton Books.

Hockett, Charles F. 1978. In search of Jove's brow. American Speech 53. 243–313.

Huttenlocher, Janellen. 1975. Encoding information in sign language. The role of speech in language, ed. by J. F. Kavanagh & J. E. Cutting. Cambridge, MA: MIT Press.

Jefferson, Gail. 1973. A case of precision timing in ordinary conversation: Overlapped tag-positioned address terms in closing sequences. Semiotica 9. 47–96.

Kendon, Adam. 1972a. Some relationships between body motion and speech. Studies in dyadic communication, ed. by A. W. Seigman & B. Pope. Elmsford, NY: Pergamon Press.

Kendon, Adam. 1972b. Review of Kinesics and context by R. L. Birdwhistell. American Journal of Psychology 85. 441–455.

Kendon, Adam. 1975. Gesticulation, speech and the gesture theory of language origins. Sign Language Studies 9. 349–373.

Kendon, Adam. 1978. Differential perception and attentional frame in face-to-face interaction. Semiotica 24. 305–315.
Kendon, Adam. 1980a. The sign language of the women of Yuendumu: A preliminary report on the structure of Warlpiri sign language. Sign Language Studies 27. 101–112.
Kendon, Adam. 1980b. Gesticulation and speech: Two aspects of the process of utterance. The relationship of verbal and nonverbal communication, ed. by M. R. Key. The Hague: Mouton.
Kendon, Adam. 1983. Gesture and speech: How they interact. Nonverbal interaction, ed. by J. R. Wiemann & Randall Harrison. Beverly Hills, CA: Sage Publications.
McNeill, David. 1979. The conceptual basis of language. Hillsdale, NJ: Lawrence Erlbaum.
Meggitt, Mervyn. 1954. Sign language among the Walbiri of Central Australia. Oceania 25. 2–16.
Meissner, M. and S. B. Philpott. 1975. The sign language of sawmill workers in British Columbia. Sign Language Studies 9. 291–347.
Metzler, S. and R. Shepard. 1974. Transformational studies of the internal representation of three-dimensional objects. Theories in cognitive psychology, ed. by R. Solso. New York: Lawrence Erlbaum.
Morris, Desmond, P. Collett, P. Marsh, and M. O'Shaughnessy. 1979. Gestures: Their origins and distributions. New York: Stein and Day.
Munari, B. 1963. Supplemento al Dizionario Italiano. Milan: Muggiani.
Pylyshyn, Z. W. 1973. What the mind's eye tells the mind's brain: A critique of mental imagery. Psychological Bulletin 80. 1–24.
Saitz, Robert L. and Edward C. Cervenka. 1972. Handbook of gestures: Colombia and the United States. The Hague: Mouton.
Schegloff, Emanuel A. In press. Iconic gestures, locational gestures and speech production. Structures of social action, ed. by M. Atkinson and J. Heritage. Cambridge: Cambridge University Press.
Schiffrin, Deborah. 1977. Opening encounters. American Sociological Review 42. 679–691.
Shepard, R. N. 1978. Externalization of mental images and the art of creation. Visual learning, thinking and communication, ed. by B. S. Randharva & W. E. Coffman. New York: Academic Press.
Sherzer, Joel. 1973. Verbal and nonverbal deixis: The pointed lip gesture among the San Blas Cuna. Language and Society 2. 117–131.
Slama-Cazacu, Tatiana. 1976. Nonverbal components in message sequence: 'Mixed syntax'. Language and man: Anthropological issues, ed. by W. C. McCormack & S. A. Wurm. The Hague: Mouton.
Sparhawk, C. M. 1978. Contrastive identificational features of Persian gesture. Semiotica 24. 49–86.
Stokoe, William C. 1974. Appearances, words and signs. Language origins, ed. by R. W. Wescott. Silver Spring, MD: Linstok Press.
Stokoe, William C. 1979. Syntactic dimensionality. Paper presented to the Linguistics Section, New York Academy of Sciences, November 12.
Stokoe, William C. 1980. Sign language structure. Annual Review of Anthropology 9. 365–390.
Taylor, Archer. 1956. The Shanghai gesture. Folklore Fellowship Communications No. 166. Helsinki: Suomalainen Tiedeakatemia, Academia Scientiarum Fennica.
Wylie, L. 1977. Beaux Gestes: A Guide to French Body Talk. New York: E. P. Dutton.

Appendix

A Sampling of Sources on Silence

Emma Muñoz-Duston
Georgetown University
Judith Kaplan
DePaul University

A very broad definition of silence was used as the criterion for inclusion in this annotated bibliography, which is representative of work being done in the areas of sociolinguistics, discourse analysis, anthropology, literature, religion, psychology, psychiatry, business, and law. Like the chapters in this volume, cited sources regard silence as ranging from hesitation phenomena (the largest percentage of sources cited, reflecting the greater number of studies done in this tradition) to nonverbal communication. Rather than dividing the topic into possibly overlapping areas, we have ordered all entries in a single alphabetical sequence.

Baker, Sidney J. 1955. The theory of silences. Journal of General Psychology 53. 145–67.
This article concludes that 'The underlying (i.e. unconscious and unpremeditated) aim of speech is not a continued flow of speech, but silence . . .' It posits two basic forms of interpersonal silence. The first, 'negative silence', results from the lack of reciprocal identification between interactants that leads to 'acute psychic disequilibrium'. The second, 'positive silence', is a pleasurable, nonthreatening silence that often occurs among intimates. The discussion is set within a description of the psychological mechanism of the interpersonal speech relationship.

Basso, Keith H. 1972. 'To give up on words': Silence in Western Apache culture. Language and social context, ed. by Pier Paolo Giglioli, 67–86. New York: Penguin.
An Apache's decision to speak or remain silent is based upon the nature of the social relationship in which s/he is a participant. Individual roles and status vary and are defined according to social context. Situations in which Basso notes 'it is right [for an Apache] to give up on words' includes meeting strangers, the initial stages of courting, the return of children from boarding school, receiving insults and criticisms, being with the bereaved, and being with someone 'for whom they sing'. Silence in each of these situations indicates that relationships are perceived as ambiguous and unpredictable, and therefore threatening.

236   MUÑOZ-DUSTON, KAPLAN

Bauman, Richard. 1974. Speaking in the light: The role of the Quaker minister. Explorations in the ethnography of speaking, ed. by Richard Bauman & Joel Sherzer, 144–60. London: Cambridge University Press.

In discussing the role of the minister within 17th century Quakerism, the author expands on the topic of plain speech and silence in that setting. Speaking was, to the 17th century Quakers, symbolic of all the outward values they rejected. Silence, in contrast, 'assumed high symbolic significance'. In addition, the author explains the dual functions of the minister: prayer and preaching. These presented a paradox to the individual acting as minister in that he had to refrain from his own silence in order to help achieve the silence of others. The author points out the importance of taking silence as well as speaking into account in the ethnographic study of language use.

Bock, Philip K. 1976. I think but dare not speak: Silence in Elizabethan culture. Journal of Anthropological Research 32. 285–94.

An analysis of scenes from 26 Shakespearean plays suggests the functions of silence in Elizabethan culture. The resulting typology is compared to Basso's description of silence in Western Apache. The types of silence noted are (1) the 'mere quiet' of nature and death, (2) the functional silences adopted for the maintenance of secrecy and order, and (3) the expressive silences indicating social relationships, situations, character traits, and emotional states.

Boomer, Donald S. and Allen T. Dittmann. 1962. Hesitation pauses and juncture pauses in speech. Language and Speech 5. 215–20.

Based on the attitude assessment of 25 adult native speakers of English, a distinction is drawn between hesitation and juncture pauses. Each subject listened to four spoken sentences selected from a radio broadcast and a series of sentences in which artificial silence was inserted. Juncture pauses were found to be more subject to cultural control and to have a definite syntactic function—i.e. to reinforce awareness of the preceding juncture and of the syntactic structure of the message. In contrast, hesitation pauses were found not to be syntactically restricted but rather to occur unexpectedly within, rather than between, phonemic clauses. These results stress the importance of analyzing pauses only within the context of their occurrence.

Boomer, Donald S. 1965. Hesitation and grammatical encoding. Language and Speech 8. 148–58.

The spontaneous speech of sixteen male native speakers of American English provides data for the determination of the size and nature of grammatical encoding units. Hesitations in the form of filled and unfilled pauses were found to occur most frequently following the first word in the phonemic clause. This finding challenges the theory that hesitations occur randomly throughout clauses. Because hesitations in spontaneous speech tend to occur in positions where decisions are being made, they identify the phonemic clause as the grammatical encoding unit of speech.

Bruneau, Thomas J. 1973. Communicative silences: Forms and functions. The Journal of Communication 23. 17–46.

Silence is discussed in terms of its relationship to sensation, perception, and metaphorical movement. It is also seen as an imposition of mind and in its relationship to mental time (as opposed to artificial time). Bruneau makes reference to three major forms of silence. First, psycholinguistic silences include fast-time silences, which are mental silences linked to the temporal-horizontal sequencing of speech, and slow-time silences, which are those related to the semantic processes of speech. Second, interactive silences are 'pausal interruptions in dialogue, conversation, discussion, debate, etc.' Third, sociocultural silences are defined as 'those related to the characteristic manner in which entire social and cultural orders refrain from speech and manipulate both psycholinguistic and interactive silences'. Bruneau provides new directions for future research by examining silence in light of other processes.

Cook, John J. 1964. Silence in psychotherapy. Journal of Counseling Psychology 11. 42–46.

Data gathered from psychotherapeutic counseling sessions point to the relationship between silence and movement in client-centered therapy. Forty two-minute segments from ten sessions were rated by two judges on the Rogers and Rablin Process Scale. The results indicate that less successful therapy cases were associated with segments of continuous speech (speech that consisted of zero to three percent silence) while more successful cases were associated with silence. In addition, the results confirm the optimum range of silence for a successful two-minute therapeutic segment as 40 to 20 percent of that segment.

Dechert, Hans W. and Manfred Raupach. 1980. Temporal variables in speech: Studies in honour of Frieda Goldman-Eisler. The Hague: Mouton.

These papers are from a conference entitled 'Pausological Implications of Speech Production' held at Kassel, Germany, June 1978. Sections include 'General Aspects', 'Syntactic and Structural Aspects', 'Conversational Aspects', 'Prosodic Aspects', and 'Crosslinguistic Aspects'.

Farr, James N. 1962. How to communicate with silence. Nation's Business 50. 96–7.

Focusing on the communicative effects of silence, this article reviews ways in which silence may aid or disrupt successful business transactions. While silence can serve to invite others to talk, it can also, when unexpected or obvious, be the cause of anxiety or tension. It is suggested that managers invoke silence when they wish to (1) encourage subordinates to reason out arguments before presenting them, (2) encourage subordinates to present their arguments, and (3) increase the chance of uncovering emotionally weighted information.

Ganguly, S. N. 1968. Culture, communication and silence. Philosophy and Phenomenological Research 29. 182–200.

After a philosophical discussion of culture, civilization, communication, and the individual, the author approaches the subject of silence. Considering the Sanskrit word *shantam* ('quiet, peace, silence, restful'), Ganguly suggests that 'silencers' in a given culture are 'steps or points or statements through which we request others to be silent'. The discussion ends with the axiomatic statement: 'Silence is silence and completely different from any kind of language'.

Goldhaber, Gerald M. 1973. PAUSAL: A computer program to identify and measure pauses. Western Speech 37. 23–26.

The report describes a two-part program designed (1) to identify pauses in speech according to two parameters and (2) to compute the ratios for expressing pauses. Included is the circuitry design for the analog computer and the program, written in Fortran IV, for the digital computer. This design and program enables the computer to analyze speech samples and generate as output (1) total pause time, (2) number of pauses, (3) total speech time, (4) number of nonpauses, (5) ratio of pause time to total time, and (6) ratio of pause time to speech time.

Goldman-Eisler, Frieda. 1958. The predictability of words in context and the length of pauses in speech. Language and Speech 1. 226–31.

The study investigates the influence of a given degree of information on a speaker's ability to complete sentences containing deletions. Four spontaneously occurring sentences were recorded and transcribed, and then presented to subjects in two different versions: first with high information content words deleted and second with low information words deleted. The subjects were asked to complete the sentences as they read them. When the sentence schema and associated cultural aspects permit the subjects' reconstruction of meaning to match the original speaker's intentions, there is a greater similarity between length and location of pauses than when the deletion of certain words disturbs meaningful reconstruction.

Goldman-Eisler, Frieda. 1961. A comparative study of two hesitation phenomena. Language and Speech 4. 18–26.

The study sought to determine the functions of filled and unfilled pauses in spontaneous speech. Data are subjects' descriptions and explanations of uncaptioned cartoons. Her findings show that the presence of filled pauses tends to reflect emotional factors whereas the presence of unfilled pauses is associated with cognitive activity. In describing the cartoons, those subjects who displayed a more concise style and less predictable linguistic formulations also displayed a greater tolerance of silence, as compared to those subjects whose descriptions were more predictable and more wordy.

Hall, Edward. 1959. The silent language. New York: Doubleday.

Hall defines the silent language as that nonverbal human behavior which is taken for granted rather than actively enforced. As the language of behavior, the silent language provides nonverbal clues to the cultural beliefs and activities of a given group. Hall suggests that culture is communication and communication is culture. Since culture controls behavior in ways removed from awareness and beyond the conscious control of the individual, any individual wishing to interact with members of a foreign cultural group must identify the nonlinguistic as well as linguistic patterns meaningful to both that group and her or his native group.

Hawkins, P. R. 1971. The syntactic location of hesitation pauses. Language and Speech 14. 277–88.

A grammatical analysis of the hesitation pauses present in the spontaneous speech of 48 children reveals that two-thirds of the pauses and three-quarters of the pause time occurred at clause boundaries. This high frequency of pausing at clause boundaries is the result of both the speech situation and the decisions that await a speaker at the end of a clause. It is at this point that the speaker needs to choose the units that will constitute the following clause and/or the overall content of the discourse. In addition to decisions involving the lexicon, choices also need to be made concerning syntactic structures and information distribution.

Jaksa, James A. and Ernest L. Stech. 1978. Communication to enhance silence: The trappist experience. Journal of Communication 28 (1). 14–18.

The passing from enforced solitude and silence to limited interpersonal communication among monks is investigated on the basis of interviews, observations, and questionnaires. The need for solitude and interaction is described as cyclical with each individual requiring different amounts, but a balance, of each. It was found that the presence of interpersonal contact produced greater self-awareness and increased feelings of security in relationships. When silence did occur it was then understood as part of the necessary human process of interaction and contemplation.

Jensen, J. Vernon. 1973. Communicative functions of silence. ETC. 30. 249–57.

Silence, often accompanied by other nonverbal cues, may occupy a variety of roles in the process of communication. Silence can help to bind or sever relationships. In its affective role, silence may communicate and, at times, shield a full range of emotions. In its revelational role, silence may impart some information while preventing the disclosure of other. Silence may also be used to express judgment. Finally, silence, as an activator, may be associated with thoughtfulness or the absence of thought. Each of these functions or roles is defined by the contexts of their occurrence, both linguistic and social.

Johannesen, Richard L. 1974. The functions of silence: A plea for communication research. Western Speech 38. 25–35.

This article explores the role of silence in terms of four cognitive and social perspectives. Considering the first, human thought processes and cultural development, the relationship between silence and speech as well as the cultural specificity of silence is reviewed. The second perspective examines the role of silence in everyday, interpersonal communication and reflects upon the meanings and values individuals may assign to silence in varying social contexts. The role of silence in civic and political life constitutes the third perspective—one which explores the individual's right to be silent and her or his ability to impose silence strategically. The final perspective examines the role of silence in counseling and psychotherapeutic contexts. The author calls for future research into silence to further address and clarify questions of definition, situation, and context.

Jones, Pauline A. 1974. Elaborated speech and hesitation phenomena. Language and Speech 17. 199–203.

Speech samples from 25 pairs of fifth-grade boys matched for general intelligence yielded data on the relationship between hesitation patterns and verbal ability. High verbal boys exhibited more communication units, longer communication units, a higher index of subordination, shorter mean pause duration, and fewer pauses overall than did the low-verbal boys. The greater frequency of pauses in the low-verbal boys is attributed to both cognition and emotional tension as well as to the inhibition that accompanies the difficulty in expressing oneself effectively.

Keenan, Elinor Ochs. 1974. The universality of conversational implicatures. Studies in language variation, ed. by Ralph W. Fasold and Roger W. Shuy, 255–68. Washington, D.C.: Georgetown University Press.

True conversational maxims which guide one's expectations of conversational behavior must be reinterpreted with each new cultural group one encounters. In this article Keenan notes the different manner in which American and Malagasy cultures view Grice's 'Be Informative' maxim. Keenan states that interlocutors in Malagasy society choose silence rather than divulge all the information they possess because of the status of new information and the fear of committing oneself to some particular claim or belief. It is, according to Keenan, the motivation for the use or abuse of any maxim that will reveal those values and orientations that separate societies and social groups within a society.

Lalljee, M. G. and M. Cook. 1969. An experimental investigation of the function of filled pauses in speech. Language and Speech 12. 24–28.

Testing the findings of Maclay and Osgood (1959), the authors question whether a turn contains more filled pauses when the speaker is subjected to increased pressure in conversation. Fourteen male university students participated in two conversations each. The authors found that interruptions and other manipulations of a subject's speech do not increase the number of filled pauses in conversation. Although this differs from Maclay and Osgood's conclusion, those data consisted of monologues, in which a prolonged pause can become an embarrassing silence. In a dialogue, the interlocutor is free to take a turn whenever the speaker's pause seems noticeably long and/or marks the completion of her or his turn.

Levin, H. and I. Silverman. 1965. Hesitation phenomena in children's speech. Language and Speech 8. 67–85.

In investigating the presence of hesitations in children's speech, this study concentrates on story-telling in two different situations. Forty-eight fifth graders were asked to tell two stories: one before four adults and one into a microphone with no audience present. Among the variables analyzed were (1) number of words, (2) number of hesitations, (3) rate of words per second, (4) unfilled pauses, (5) filled pauses, (6) repetitions, and (7) corrections. The degree of stressful hesitations was related to the absence or presence of an audience.

Levin, H., I. Silverman, and B. L. Ford. 1967. Hesitations in children's speech during explanations and descriptions. Journal of Verbal Learning and Verbal Behavior 6. 560–4.

Twenty-four elementary school-age children were asked to discuss three physical demonstrations they had witnessed. The purpose was to determine how the rate and length of hesitations compare in children's explanations and descriptions. Each discussion included a description of what had happened in the demonstration and the child's explanation of the occurrence. More hesitations and pauses occurred during explanations than during descriptions, suggesting that pause length corresponds to the degree of stress present and the type of cognitive task demanded.

Livant, William Paul. 1963. Antagonistic functions of verbal pauses: Filled and unfilled pauses in the solution of additions. Language and Speech 6. 1–4.

This study investigates the effects of filled pauses (e.g. ah, er, um) and unfilled pauses (silences) on the solving of addition problems. Five college students were asked to solve fifty problems. Each subject was to alternate her or his computations by solving one problem under a sound condition and the next under a silence condition. The results indicate that the length of time required to solve addition problems under conditions of filled pauses is greater than that required under conditions of silence. While filled pauses may impair performance in one sense, however, they may provide an important social function in allowing the speaker to maintain control of her or his turn at talk while considering future contributions.

Maclay, Howard and Charles E. Osgood. 1959. Hesitation phenomena in spontaneous English speech. Word 15. 19–44.

This investigation quantifies the filled pauses, unfilled pauses, repeats, and false starts in speech samples from 12 male conference participants. It illustrates differences among speakers in the frequency of hesitation. The overall distribution of hesitation types indicates that (1) false starts typically involve lexical items, (2) repeats typically involve function words and occur before lexical items, (3) filled pauses typically occur before function words and at phrase boundaries, and (4) unfilled pauses typically occur before lexical items and within syntactic phrases. The authors suggest that because hesitations occur nonrandomly and aid in the identification and circumscription of linguistic units, they should be included in any study of speech style.

Martin, James G. 1970. On judging pauses in spontaneous speech. Journal of Verbal Learning and Verbal Behavior 9. 75–78.

The author's stated goal is 'to identify some grammatical and acoustic correlates of unfilled pauses, to compare listener judgement against physical measures, and to suggest that for many purposes the latter are often superfluous'. Use of a spectrogram in a sample of spontaneous speech indicated that syllables preceding a judged-pause location were usually longer than those following. This was the case whether or not the actual silent interval was present. Most of the judged-pause locations were actually junctures. Independent of juncture cues, syllable length governed most of the pause judgments.

Murphy, Marjorie. 1970. Silence, the word, and Indian rhetoric. College Composition and Communication 21. 359–63.

Murphy traces contemporary American Indian rhetoric to various cultural factors. She includes anecdotes from Native Americans who stress both the sacredness of words and the respect due silence. The rhetoric is rooted in the system of tribal government, where public opinion outweighs coercion, and also in child rearing, where patience precludes aggressive persuasion. Silence reflects perfect equilibrium in the balanced ideal of mind, body, and spirit. Although this respect for words and silence remains today in American Indian culture, there is a new generation of native women who question the limits of the rhetoric. According to one, for example, 'I don't like being a clown or a militant, but sometimes you have to break this conspiracy of silence'.

Murray, David C. 1971. Talk, silence, and anxiety. Psychological Bulletin 75. 244–260.

Studies tracing the relationship between verbal productivity and anxiety are presented and discussed in three groupings. Situational anxiety studies are those in which subjects are exposed to stressful situations. Dispositional anxiety studies are those in which subjects are judged in terms of their stress vulnerability and tolerance. Concurrent anxiety studies measure degree of anxiety in relation to the occurrence of ongoing speech disturbances or physiological changes. Analysis of the results of these studies indicates that verbal quantity correlates positively with dispositional and concurrent anxiety, but negatively with situational anxiety. In contrast, silence correlates positively with situational and concurrent anxiety, but negatively with dispositional anxiety.

Myers, Charles Raymond. 1975. Silence and the unspoken: A study of the modes of not speaking. Doctoral dissertation (Philosophy). University of Texas at Austin.

Myers aims (1) to turn to the objects of silence and (2) to distinguish these objects by means of the relation of silence to speech. The object of an abstention from speech may be something about to be spoken, something left unsaid while other things are being said, or something which remains unspoken after all that can be said has been said. The study ends with a reflection on the modes of silence, and suggests that the bond between silence and speech is stronger than the distinction between them because silence and speech are originally one.

O'Barr, William M. 1982. Controlling the effects of presentational style. Linguistic evidence—language, power, and strategy in the courtroom, 93–111. New York: Academic Press.

Considering silence as a stylistic factor, O'Barr examines whether the effects of different speech styles in the courtroom can be controlled, managed, or eliminated. This investigation is part of a larger report from the Law and Language Project at Duke University. Some of the legal aspects of silence are discussed: the right to remain silent, refusing to remain silent, and silencing the record. At the interactional level, the author considers silence during the trial process and the numerous ways in which silence can be interpreted and manipulated.

Philips, Susan Urmston. 1976. Some sources of cultural variability in the regulation of talk. Language in Society 5. 81–95.

A comparison of verbal and nonverbal regulation of talk by Anglo-American and Warm Springs Indian conversational interactants is presented. Among the features reviewed within the areas of turn-taking and turn-selection strategies are body movement, gaze direction, and speaker identification of addressed recipients. One area in which the systems differ is in the use of silence in certain interchanges. Among Warm Springs Indians, there is a greater tolerance for silences and, therefore, pauses between turns are frequently longer than those between Anglo turns. Consequently, there tend to be fewer instances of overlapping in Warm Springs Indian conversations. Silence in response to questions and invitations is both meaningful and common.

Picard, Max. 1952. The world of silence. Chicago: Regnery. (translated from German by Stanley Godman)

Picard considers silence in relation to numerous aspects of the world, of humanity, and of knowledge, including: love and silence; animals and silence; childhood, old age, and silence; silence and the peasant; and the noise of words. Silence is also directly linked to speech and language.

Rice, George P. 1961. The right to be silent. Quarterly Journal of Speech 47. 349–54.

Rice argues that the first amendment, in guaranteeing freedom of speech, may also be understood to guarantee freedom of silence. Results of recent legal cases have preserved the right to silence by supporting (1) the right not to say what one does not believe, (2) the right not to say what one does believe, and (3) the right not to say what one has knowledge of. However, even with these rights, the full legal aspects of the rights to silence have yet to be explored. Rice suggests that a fully tested and supported theory of silence may establish a clear and unquestionable basis on which to form silence judgments in legal issues.

Samarin, William J. 1965. Language of silence. Practical Anthropology 12 (3). 115–119.

Once he establishes that silence during periods of linguistic interaction can have meaning, the author calls attention to cross-cultural differences. He reports his observations of the use of silence among the Gbeya in Central Africa, where he had been a missionary.

Author Index

Italic page numbers indicate bibliographic citations.

243

Subject Index